.

Wildcatters

Wildcatters

★ ★ ★

The True Story of How Conspiracy, Greed, and the IRS Almost Destroyed a Legendary Texas Oil Family

Charlie Moncrief

Since 1947
REGNERY
PUBLISHING, INC.
An Eagle Publishing Company • Washington, DC

Copyright © 2002 by Charles Moncrief

Library of Congress Cataloging-in-Publication Data
Moncrief, Charlie.
    Wildcatters: the true story of how conspiracy, greed, and the IRS almost destroyed a legendary Texas oil family/Charlie Moncrief.
        p. cm.
Includes index.
    ISBN 0-89526-142-1
    1. Tax evasion—Texas—Fort Worth—Case studies. 2. Moncrief Oil. I. Title.
    HV6344.U6 M663 2002
    364.1'33—dc21

                                                    2002008302

Published in the United States by
Regnery Publishing, Inc.
An Eagle Publishing Company
One Massachusetts Avenue, NW
Washington, DC 20001

Visit us at www.regnery.com

Distributed to the trade by
National Book Network
4720-A Boston Way
Lanham, MD 20706

Printed on acid-free paper
Manufactured in the United States of America

10 9 8 7 6 5 4 3 2 1

Books are available in quantity for promotional or premium use. Write to Director of Special Sales, Regnery Publishing, Inc., One Massachusetts Avenue, NW, Washington, DC 20001, for information on discounts and terms, or call (202) 216-0600.

Contents

INTRODUCTION ★ vii

CHAPTER ONE
The Raid ★ 1

CHAPTER TWO
Family Tradition ★ 21

CHAPTER THREE
Roughneck's Revenge ★ 35

CHAPTER FOUR
The Snitch ★ 67

CHAPTER FIVE
Self-Examination ★ 87

CHAPTER SIX
Telling Tales ★ 115

CHAPTER SEVEN
The IRS Settlement ★ 151

CHAPTER EIGHT
The Truth at Last ★ 165

CHAPTER NINE
The Lady Sings ★ 179

CHAPTER TEN
Three Trials ★ 197

EPILOGUE
Law and Order 2000 ★ 223

APPENDIX ★ 243

INDEX ★ 247

Introduction

THIS IS A TRUE STORY.

It's an examination of how life can irreversibly change. One day, you're living in peace, and then you're at war. Sixty-four armed agents from the Criminal Investigation Division of the Internal Revenue Service are kicking down your door. The newspaper headlines scream accusations against you and your family. And your hometown is following the lurid spectacle that your life has become.

You don't know the reasons, much less the players, that have turned your life upside down. But if you don't find out quickly, you may be financially devastated and possibly even headed to jail.

This is the story of how my family and I had to fight to uncover a powerful conspiracy that had been launched against us. The IRS was the weapon used by the conspirators. Those who planned it included one of our own employees, a network of highly placed attorneys, and even an opposing faction of our own family—all of whom stood to get rich if they brought us down.

This is my story.

The reason I write this book is simply because it happened. And if my story can prevent events like this from ever happening again, then the book will have served some purpose.

—*Charlie Moncrief, April 2002, Fort Worth, Texas*

The Moncrief Family Tree

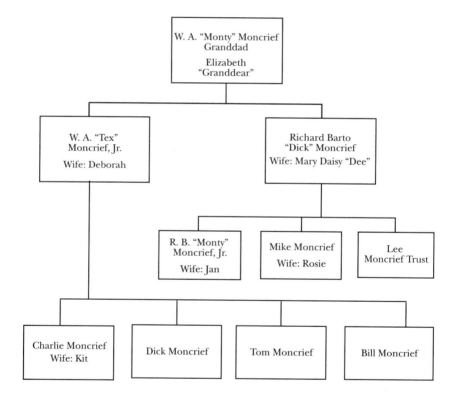

Chapter One

The Raid

I WASN'T THERE AT THE MOMENT when my life and the life of my family forever changed. But from the accounts I later heard from our employees, as well as exhaustive records and depositions, I can reconstruct the scene as if I had been there. On that morning, I was having blood drawn in a routine physical. "All right, Charlie. This is a good vein. All you'll feel is a little sting," the nurse said. Meanwhile, down the street at my office, a busload of sixty-four IRS agents was landing like an army on an enemy beach.

It began early on the morning of Thursday, September 1, 1994, the opening day of dove season. Opening day is nearly a holiday to our family and many others in Texas, but otherwise a typical business day. At 7:45 A.M., the thirty-three employees of Moncrief Oil began arriving for work. First to show up was our petroleum engineer—Scott Bouline, thirty-three, and our geologist Mark Cook, thirty-six. Mark began the day sprawled flat on the carpet, either resting his bad back or just goofing off, while Scott tried to fix Mark's broken-down computer.

Outside, in front of our building, called the Moncrief Building, in downtown Fort Worth, Texas, two men sat quietly in an unmarked car. They didn't give a damn about dove; they were hunting different game. Their windows were fogged with nervous breath. Maybe there was a song on the radio, and—this being Fort Worth—it would have to be a country song, a tune about too much cheating and too many broken hearts.

The Moncrief Building occupies a full city block at the corner of Ninth and Commerce streets. It's a white marble three-story building, headquarters of our third-generation independent oil family. The building was built by my grandfather, one of the pioneer wildcatters, the late W. A. "Monty" Moncrief. "We're 100 percent family owned and we intend to stay that way: unincorporated and independent!" he liked to brag, and we still follow his philosophy.

That the building sits squarely in the middle of downtown Fort Worth is also significant. Fort Worth is where the West begins and where the East peters out. It's a million mental miles away from that showboat city forty-five minutes to the east, Dallas. Some say that Dallas–Fort Worth is becoming one big homogenized metropolis. But the people saying that don't really know how different Fort Worth is, a laid-back town instead of an uptight city, where everybody knows everybody. The late local writer Jerry Flemmons wrote that, in Fort Worth, "High society is always one generation removed from flour sack underwear."

The two men got out of the unmarked car. Wearing pistols on their hips, they walked through our unlocked double glass doors and took the elevator to the second floor. They stood silently in the doorway at Mark Cook's office for a second or two before speaking.

"Get away from that computer!" the older agent barked.

Scott saw a gray haired man flashing a badge standing beside a younger, shorter man.

"IRS!" said the younger man.

The use of the word "IRS" shocked Scott Bouline. He threw up his hands and backed away from the desk, trying to remember the details of his last tax return. Finally, he asked, "Are you after me?"

Thinking this is surely an extravagant practical joke, the geologist Mark Cook didn't even rise from the floor. "Get up!" the men barked in unison. "What are you doing down there?"

Looking at the badges and pistols.

"Is it about back taxes?" Scott repeated.

"This is a criminal investigation of the Moncrief's family business," one of the agents said. "We have a search warrant. We're taking over the building and confiscating the files."

Scott's first reaction was relief, immediately followed by shock.

"Well, that's none of my business," he told the agents. "I'll have to call Mr. Moncrief." He meant my dad, W. A. "Tex" Moncrief.

"You're not calling anybody," instructed the older agent. "You're going downstairs."

"Do you have any weapons?" asked the other.

This being Fort Worth, a great many people carry guns. "There's a nine millimeter pistol in my briefcase," Mark said. He surrendered the handgun; then both he and Scott reached for their briefcases. "Leave those behind," said the agent. "Everything in the building is now evidence—and that includes briefcases."

"Where's your search warrant?" asked Mark.

"Yeah, let's see your warrant!" echoed Scott. "How do we know you're not just two guys off the street flashing badges?"

One of the agents yanked out a copy of a poorly copied search warrant and then pulled it away before the boys could read the fine type. Warrant enough. Flanked by the agents, Mark and Scott were led down the hallway and downstairs into the executive first-floor lunchroom, which we call "the dungeon." It's a cramped room equipped with two dining tables and twelve chairs.

Scott and Mark were ordered to take two chairs, and a third newly arrived agent was posted at the door to guard them. After a minute or two, they heard the sound of footsteps, first a few agents, then a dozen, then a dozen more—storming through the front door of the Moncrief Building. The agents, all plainclothes IRS and wearing U.S. Department of the Treasury badges on their belts, crawled out of unmarked cars, vans, and a school bus.

They fanned out to our building's three floors searching individual offices. At around 8 A.M. in the third-floor Xerox room, Capt. Walter Word, a seventy-two-year-old World War II navy veteran who has served as my family's chief pilot for forty years, was making copies of flight maintenance records for the FAA. Two agents rounded the corner and flashed their badges.

"Good morning," said Walter.

"Get away from that copying machine!" barked an agent. "We're with the Criminal Investigation Division of the IRS."

"The hell you are!" Walter exclaimed, thinking the men were playing a practical joke. Then, the agents opened their jackets to show Walter their pistols.

"Now you'll have to go down to the cafeteria," they ordered.

Walter asked to see a warrant; the agents refused. They questioned him about weapons and then hustled him toward the door. "I was a navy pilot," he told the agents. "I did two tours of duty in World War II to get rid of sons-a-bitches like you. You guys remind me of the Gestapo!"

By 8:20 A.M., agents had engulfed every inch of the Moncrief Building. Our security chief, George Watkins, arrived from the post office with the day's mail. A large black man who has worked for my family since three men in ski masks robbed my mother and father of $1.4 million in jewelry a few years ago, George knows how to handle himself in a fight.

But lately, strange happenings at the Moncrief Building had left him edgy. As he walked through the crowd of agents at the front door, he remembered a recent burglary. The complete haul: a single computer hard drive. What kind of crook would steal a single hard drive in an office filled with valuable oil field memorabilia? That was weird enough, but even weirder was that the window in the computer room, where the hard drive had been stolen, was broken from the *inside* out. George knew it had to be an inside job.

"Where do you think you're going?" one agent shouted at George at the front door. "This is a crime scene."

"Crime scene?" George asked. "You gotta have the wrong building."

The agent remained stone-faced. "We're conducting a criminal investigation," he repeated. "You'll have to stay out."

"I've got to go into that building!" George said. "I'm in *charge* of that building."

The agents let him enter but then led him into the dungeon, which was now a "holding pen" for all Moncrief employees.

Three-quarters of Moncrief Oil's employees are women. As they arrived for work, each was apprehended, questioned about weapons, and then escorted by two agents down to the lunchroom.

A few of the women made it to their offices before the agents arrived. Joan Barnhart, a.k.a. "Sarge," who once worked as a court reporter for the U.S. Marine Corps, is a stern, but crackerjack,

secretary and land analyst. "Off the floor and into the lunchroom," one of the few women IRS agents on the scene demanded, with three male agents at her side.

The agents moved next to the office of Kay Capps, our division
order analyst, who keeps track of working interests and royalties.
After nineteen years on the job, Kay knows Moncrief Oil inside
and out. She was startled at her computer by a hand in her face
flashing a badge, followed by the command, "Get your hands off
that computer NOW!"

Kay looked up.

"Do you have a gun or mace in your purse?" the agent
demanded.

"Who are *you*?" Kay countered.

"Don Smith, special agent, IRS," he replied.

We'd later learn that Smith was the chief agent in charge of the
investigation. He knew whom to apprehend personally and whom
to leave to his juniors. Kay was singled out as a big fish, someone
worthy of personal attention. She had no doubts whatsoever about
her tax return. She thought the agents had simply raided the wrong
building.

"Show me your warrant," she demanded.

"Just get your purse and come with me to the lunchroom," said
Agent Don Smith.

Downstairs in the dungeon, Kay found everyone crammed
together, sitting, standing or leaning against the edge of the two
tables. Through the big picture windows, they could watch agents
rolling file cabinets and an entire computer system toward the
front of the building. Occasionally, a crash from one of the upstairs
floors literally shook the walls. The agents kept dropping heavy
boxes full of files and whole filing cabinets.

Cramped into the small dining room, the employees' initial shock was turning to fear. Some began to cry quietly. Many were senior citizens; one was a cancer patient; another was extremely thin and frail, only weeks away from retirement. But even the young employees were visibly shaken. They asked the junior agents, *Why are you here? What are you doing? What do you want?* But they got no explanation. No additional chairs were provided so everyone could have a seat. There was no food. No water. No phone calls allowed.

In the coming weeks, all these employees would become part of a full-fledged criminal investigation, interrogated before a grand jury, even surprised by the IRS and interviewed in their homes. But for now, they were left to watch the passing parade of file cabinets and white boxes emblazoned with the letters *IRS*. The boxes were filled with Moncrief Oil files, passing on dollies in front of the tinted lunchroom windows. Agents with cameras had arrived to take pictures of every office and its contents. Sometimes, agents would come downstairs to the dungeon to escort key employees upstairs, ordering them to unlock doors or, they threatened, "We'll kick it down!"

In Dallas, IRS representatives arrived at the offices of Moncrief Oil's consulting accountants, confiscating records. Out at Meacham Field in Fort Worth, two more agents watched the Moncrief hangar, where the Lucky Liz, our private jet was parked. It's a Bac 111 (circa 1967) that's been in our family for thirty years and has flown Presidents Nixon and Johnson. We later learned that the airport surveillance was to make sure that we wouldn't attempt a quick getaway by air.

The Moncrief Building and its affiliate offices had been surrounded.

Finally, the lead agent, Don Smith, entered the dungeon.

"This is a criminal investigation of the Moncrief company," he said "And we are armed. If you want to leave the building, you can leave now. But if you leave, you will not be able to reenter for the rest of the day."

Many hands shot up. One of them was Captain Walter Word's. He had work to do at the Moncrief hangar. Two agents escorted him upstairs when he insisted on getting his briefcase from the copying room. They confiscated the records he was copying for the FAA and made him open his briefcase before letting him leave with it. Its contents: pages of jokes for his navy squadron reunions.

Walter handed the agents a sheet from the stack. "The definition of stress is when one's mind overcomes the body's basic desire to kick the shit out of some asshole who really needs it," it read.

★ ★ ★

After my morning at the doctor's office, I had been planning to stop back by the house for a minute to pick up my coat and tie for a morning at the office. Then, I'd head off with the family for the dove hunt that afternoon.

I'm a third-generation independent oilman. I spent six years working in the oil fields of Wyoming, two years working as a land man, and the rest of my adult life learning from my dad and granddad. I'm an ex-marine and a former U.S. marshal. I've got a great family: my wife Kit, two daughters from my first marriage and three from my second. I make time for the weekly golf game and an occasional Crown Royal. But like most wildcatters, we work twenty-four hours a day. Drilling rigs, gas plants, and oil and gas production don't quit at five o'clock.

I figured I would have plenty of time to stop by Dad's house for coffee as I did every morning. Half a cup with Dad, then ten minutes of talking after Mother's arrival, then off to the office. Never late, never different. Until today.

The minute I wheeled into my driveway, I knew something was wrong. Kit ran out of the back door, hit the car with both hands, and screamed before I could open the window. "You need to get to your dad's! Right away! Something's happened!" I didn't ask any questions. I just backed out and headed toward Dad's house, pronto.

Either a medical emergency or an oil well blowout, I thought. We had significant interests in a dozen or so drilling wells, so a blowout—or a screwup—wouldn't be out of the question. But as I raced through River Crest, the neighborhood of sculptured lawns and spectacular mansions of second- and third-generation oil families, I couldn't help but focus on Dad, a likely candidate for a medical meltdown. He'd been under stress from a couple of lawsuits and, at seventy-four, he was getting a little too old for wrestling lawyers. But as soon as I stepped out of my car in front of Dad's house, I knew something entirely different was happening.

Mother met me at the door.

"The IRS has taken over the offices!" she shouted. "They've got all of the employees holed up in a room on the first floor!"

I saw a wild look in her eyes. She led me to Dad, W. A. Moncrief Jr., "Tex" to everyone. If you'd seen him at breakfast in his bathrobe, surrounded by his four yapping pug dogs, you might want to sit down for a chat. His mind is still sharp. and like many old time wildcatters, he's tough as boot leather. Growing up in the shadow of his famous father, Dad continues to operate as he thinks

Granddad would have. Dad can be friendly as a pup, but if you try and butt heads with him, he'll bite back hard and fast. I speak from experience.

Today, he was slumped in his chair, surrounded by the silent pugs, staring through the broad plateglass window. His face was pale, and there was a lost expression in his eyes. He slowly turned his head towards me. The phone call, Mom said, had come from the office at nine that morning.

"Sixty-four agents," Dad said finally. "What do they want? Can you think of anything at all?"

Unfortunately, I couldn't. All I could think was that it all had to be a mistake.

Dad said he'd already talked to Dee Kelly, our longtime attorney and one of the most powerful lawyers in Texas. His team was on its way over to the Moncrief Building.

"I gotta go," I said.

"Where are you going?" asked Dad.

"To the office. I'm gonna find out what's going on."

"You sure that's okay?"

"You're damned right it's okay," I said. "I've got to talk to our employees."

He nodded, and then returned to gazing out his picture window. I knew what he was doing: talking to Granddad. He did it quite often.

"Give me a call when you get there," he said at last.

★ ★ ★

I walked into a crime scene. A bobtail trailer was backed up to our south door. I spotted only three well-marked government cars. Back in 1973, when I worked as a U.S. marshal, we raided the

Gooch meat packing plant in Abilene. There were dozens of us, and we came in buses. Obviously, that's what these guys had done.

The entrance to our building has two swinging glass doors. One of them was propped open and an IRS agent was leaning back in a metal chair. He wore a sports coat and white shirt with open collar and had a badge pinned on his belt loop. When he saw me, he didn't budge an inch.

"Good morning. I'm Charlie Moncrief," I said from about fifteen feet away.

The agent rocked forward in his chair and onto his feet. I'd already extended my hand and said, almost as a reflex, "How ya doin'?"

"Are you armed or do you have a weapon in the building?" he asked.

"No, I'm not armed," I said. "I do keep a Marine Corps knife in my desk drawer. But I don't imagine you're going to let me get to it, are you?"

"Nope."

I asked him his name. "Marty Shiel."

"Who's in charge here?"

He told me the lead agent was Don Smith.

"Let me see him,"

"You better go in and see your employees."

"Don't worry, that's exactly what I intend to do," I said. "You get Smith. I want to see him. Right now."

Before heading off to fetch his boss, he handed me one of his business cards. I found that sort of amusing. As a U.S. marshal in the middle of a raid, I didn't hand out my calling cards! I walked inside the building, where I felt the upstairs floors rumbling and shaking.

As I entered the dining room, I could hear a few muffled voices, but everybody stopped talking when they saw me. Most of the women were seated, with the men either standing or sitting on the edge of the tables. All were clearly shaken. A few of the women were sitting straight backed on the edge of their chairs, their hands tightly clasped in their laps, as if in church. They were obviously relieved to see me. A couple of them made a motion as if to move toward me to speak or maybe even to give me a hug. A few of them only stared at me, too frightened to speak.

"We don't have any idea what all of this is about," I said, "but I'm going to talk to the agent in charge and find out. I want all of you to go upstairs and get back to work."

"They won't let us," said Kay Capps. "They won't let us go back upstairs."

"Okay if that's the case, then there's no reason for all of you to stay here; you had just as well go home. I'll need a couple of you to stay here and man the phones."

At that point, another agent walked up behind me, a clean-cut, heavyset man sporting a mustache. He was constantly fidgeting, not standing square on his feet.

"Mr. Moncrief, I'm Don Smith," he said. "I'm in charge of this operation."

"Our people can't go back upstairs, is that correct?" I asked.

"That's correct," he said. "And they can't come and go. Once they leave, they're out of here."

"Well, I don't know what you're after, but what I'm going to do is get a couple of people to stay here and help with the phone," I said. "We've got a business to run. We've got rigs running, and we've got other offices. I'm going to come and go as I please, and that's all there is to it! Now, when are you going to be out of here?"

"We'll be here all day, maybe longer," Smith snapped.

"You gotta be kiddin' me!"

He assured me that he wasn't.

"All right, let me see your warrant," I said.

Smith handed me the search warrant. I scanned it quickly. The search warrant was labeled "criminal," not "civil." The warrant noted that the focus of the investigation was 1984 to the present. Exhibit B of the warrant, entitled "Evidence, Fruits, and Instrumentalities of Criminal Offenses," revealed what they wanted. The list was long. I could read only part of it: oil production documents and memoranda, contracts, agreements, diaries, journals, accounting books, storage facility keys, bank documentation for all checking, savings, and credit card accounts, yearly bank statements, canceled checks, foreign drafts, check registers, safe deposit box records and keys, wire transfer receipts, documentation of family ranches, residences and vehicles, trust documents, computers, computer data, computer hardware, instruction manuals. . . . It went on and on, before finally ending with a demand for "any other documents or items which constitute evidence of the crimes of tax evasion, the preparation of false tax returns, the attempt to interfere with administration of the Internal Revenue laws, and conspiracy to commit these offenses and defraud the United States. . . ."

I called Dad. He picked up the phone on the first ring.

"Pa, I'm here in the dining room," I said. "I talked to all of the employees as well as several of the IRS agents including the agent in charge, Don Smith, who gave me a copy of the search warrant. It's incredible, to put it mildly. They're going to be here all day, maybe tomorrow, too."

My father had rallied and was ready to roll. "All right, now, sit down and listen," he said. "Dee Kelly just got back to me. Two of his associates are on the way—Marshall Searcy and Clive Bode. They'll find out what's going on."

The lawyers arrived before I could even sit back down with the remaining employees. By the time I got to the front door, the two of them were talking to Marty Shiel. Marshall Searcy—a compact, fireplug of a lawyer—shook my hand without breaking his rather heated conversation with the agent. He was forceful with Shiel, asking him questions and demanding a copy of the warrant.

When the conversation ended, I walked out to the curb with Clive and Marshall. "Charlie, this is total bullshit!" Marshall began. "You'd think this was a drug raid! Don't you talk to these guys, and don't answer *any* questions. I'm going to send Hugh Connor down here. He's a young lawyer with the firm, and he'll stay here all day in case anything comes up. If they've got any questions, Hugh can answer them or get in touch with me. Clive and I are heading back to the office to get to work on this full-time. We'll see what we can find out. We'll get back in touch this afternoon."

My brothers arrived soon after the lawyers. First was Tom, getting to work as usual, at 10:30 A.M. Tom Oil Moncrief. That's right, Oil is literally his middle name.

"Who are you?" asked Agent Shiel when Tom ambled toward the front door.

Tom is mild-mannered, but he can become unglued in an instant.

He leaned in close to the agent's face. "I work here," Tom snapped. "Who are you?"

After assuring the agent he wasn't armed, Tom was finally admitted inside.

My older brother, Dickie, flew back immediately from a visit to Santa Fe when he heard news of the raid. Now, Dickie *is* an oilman but not in the old-school vein. He's always been the "handsome

Moncrief": dark hair, tan, suave, a real ladies man. On the day of the raid, he had just signed a deal for a megamillion-dollar exploration deal in Russia and was expecting important faxes about it that very morning.

Dickie cornered an agent; he had to get to his office and switch his fax from office to home mode to intercept those faxes. Two agents escorted him upstairs, and he got off the elevator on the third floor where he saw a dozen agents eating barbecue sandwiches at my desk. One agent reached out with his boot heel and slammed the door shut in Dickie's face.

Downstairs, lead agent Don Smith entered the lunchroom.

"There's a safe in your office," he said to me. "You can either come open it, or I'll get someone down here to open it for me."

I told him I'd open the safe. He led me to the elevator, and we went up to the third floor. The offices were swarming with agents. Each office door had been numbered with yellow Post-It notes. Post-Its also labeled drawers in each desk and file cabinet. Boxes lined every hallway and file cabinets were being dollied out one after the other.

I opened the safe and couldn't get out of the way fast enough. Two agents began jerking open various drawers and rifling through files. I felt a rush of anxiety. The noise of the file cabinets rolling by downstairs and the cacophony of agents on the floors above was making my head spin.

"You can go back downstairs, Mr. Moncrief," Don Smith told me. Another agent motioned for me to come with him in the elevator. When the elevator doors closed, the agent said, "Charlie, do you remember me?"

I looked him up and down. "Yes, I certainly remember your face," I said. "But I can't place you."

"Mike Sanders, TCU Kappa Sig," he said.

"Well, I'll be damned. What the hell's going on here, Mike? Where'd all these agents come from?"

He shook his head. "I don't know. I've never seen half of 'em. Must be from all over the state."

He escorted me to the dungeon's door. "Thanks for your help, Charlie," he said.

I went outside to get a breath of air. At the building's entrance, I spotted Royal Hogan, eighty-nine, ambling up the street. Dressed as always in his dark brown suit and snap-brimmed straw hat, Hogan—brother of the late golfing legend Ben Hogan and an old friend of Granddad's—ate lunch with us with such regularity we'd have to phone him if we wanted to take a day off.

"This building is secure," the agent told Hogan as he reached for the door.

Hogan turned and, without a word, ambled back down the street. No free lunch today.

Dad showed up around three o'clock, just in time for our appointment at Dee Kelly's office. Before we left, a female agent arrived with a thirty-five millimeter camera. She'd been in once before that morning, taking snapshots throughout the raid. Dad just sat in a chair watching everything until it was time for the meeting. He looked tired and slump shouldered.

Dad, my brother Dickie, and I headed over to Dee Kelly's law office seven blocks up the street. Kelly has close and long-standing ties to my family. Granddad was his first major client. Now he represents every major power in Fort Worth: the Bass family, American Airlines, the western boot baron John Justin, and the big ranching and oil family, the Marions.

Kelly had discovered that a twenty-one-page affidavit had been filed with the U.S. attorney's office. Clearly the whole process had moved through a huge loop—stretching as far as Washington, D.C. The search warrant had been signed by a magistrate in Dallas, which spoke volumes, Kelly told us. A raid in Fort Worth would have been handled by the Fort Worth office of the IRS and Fort Worth–based U.S. attorneys, but it was obvious that the Fort Worth magistrate had refused to sign the warrant, Kelly said. Therefore, the agents had to go begging forty-five miles east in Dallas. Kelly thought that the whole process had been pushed and pushed hard by someone with influence. Kelly already had hatched plans to file a motion to quash the search warrant as too vague and all-encompassing. We would ask for all of our records to be returned immediately and to unseal the affidavit, so that we could at least know the reasons for the raid.

But first we had to do some soul searching.

"What could have possibly gone on in your business to prompt this whole episode?" Kelly asked.

The short-statured, cherubic Kelly is sixty-five years old, but he looks at least ten years younger. He's always nervous, but when he gets upset he begins jabbering, actually stuttering and stammering. Kelly's right leg will bounce up and down, seemingly out of control. Today, both legs were bouncing wildly.

"Something has to be there," he said. "Begin combing your minds for anything that might be questioned by the IRS. You literally need to start making a list of anything and everything that could possibly be questioned, no matter how minuscule."

Kelly's primary concern seemed to be the so-called "late wells," where you'd know for sure that a well is going to be a producer, and you slip your kids or your best friend in for a 5 or 10 percent interest.

"All oil families have done it in the past," said Dad. But he couldn't remember when it last occurred in our family. He said it would have been a long time ago, well before Granddad's death. The only thing that concerned me at the time was Dad's trust fund. Dad loaned the trust some money to invest in oil wells, and our accountants, Bright & Bright, wanted us to be sure to have a legally binding signed note since it was a close family relationship. We had never gotten that done; however, all of the transactions were on the books and clearly spelled out in our accounting records. The trust would go to us kids tax free, so Dad had always wanted to build up its assets.

This scenario and a few others were buzzing around in my head—and this was only the beginning. Kelly pointed out that the most important thing to consider about a criminal warrant is that it basically alleges a conspiracy, which takes at least two people. The search warrant included all of our names, as well as our corporation and our two estates. Kelly said we'd need criminal attorneys.

"Tex, you and Charlie are the primary targets of this investigation," he said. "You'll need attorneys immediately." He turned to Dickie. "You won't need one, yet."

His firm could handle the local legwork, he said, but he couldn't administer the entire case. We needed the best lawyers money could buy. "You'd better get somebody big time," Kelly advised. "Because this thing is going to get worse."

We checked back with the office. The IRS had finished loading up practically the entire contents of the Moncrief Building and had just rolled away in a fleet of unmarked cars, with two big trucks trailing behind. It was coming up on 5 P.M. Our security chief, George Watkins, had remained on the scene to secure the building for the night.

On my way home, I thought about the opening day of dove season, how we never failed to be at the ranch to hunt together. Now

I had a challenge before me. It was something that would have seemed inconceivable only a few hours before: I had literally to fight for our family and our reputation. It was almost 7 P.M. I was exhausted. I wanted to get home and spend the evening with my family. I knew that they would be anxious to hear what had happened and that the kids would certainly need some preparation for tomorrow, when the raid would be splashed across the front pages, and the gossip would be running rampant in Fort Worth.

I got in my car and pulled out of Kelly's office driveway. But before driving home, I looked down the street at the Moncrief Building—at least what was left of it. In a single day, it had been reduced to an empty hull, not one shred of paper left inside. But I knew that its most important part still remained: the ghost of my granddad. I could see him just as he'd been on the morning of the day he died eight years before. At ninety, he arrived at the office dressed in his customary suit and tie. He was so weak that he had to be steadied by his assistant as he walked from his Cadillac into the office. But as soon as Granddad got into the elevator, he ordered his helper to turn him loose. Power roared back into his creaky old bones. His back straightened. His chest puffed out proud. And when those elevator doors opened, he stood transformed: big and strong, with thick white hair and a movie star's profile. Walking out of the elevator, he had a grin for the ladies and a backslap for the boys. He was once again W. A. Moncrief, grand old man of the oil patch. "What are you fellahs talkin' about?" he asked my dad and me when he found us in my office on the day of his death. "I want in on the deal."

He was heading down to the lunchroom when the pain hit him. He gritted his teeth and had to be helped down onto the carpet. We didn't even have time for an ambulance. By the time the paramedics arrived and shocked him with the defibrillators, he was gone. My dad swore he heard his father's voice telling him, "Tex, I'm in heaven."

I didn't understand it then. I wanted to agree with our minister who told Dad he was merely grieving. After all, he had lost not only his father, but also his best friend. But now I could hear my grandfather's voice, too. Not in my ears, but in my heart. It wasn't just a message. It was a command: *"Go after whoever did this, Charlie. Go after those sons-a-bitches and clear our family's name."*

Chapter Two

Family Tradition

THE NEXT MORNING, WE MADE THE HEADLINES. "IRS Raids Moncrief Building," read the front page of the *Fort Worth Star-Telegram* with a quote from my brother Tom Oil Moncrief below: "They were just like burglars ransacking your home." "Texas Oil Family in U.S. Tax Inquiry" was the headline in the *New York Times,* alongside a photograph of the agents loading the truck. The news had been released to UP and AP. Even the *Gunnison Country Times* splashed the news on its front page.

But the headlines were already old news to most of Fort Worth, where gossip is as much a spectator sport as Dallas Cowboys football. Because it's the biggest small town in Texas, Fort Worth gossip spreads *fast.* From the card players at the Men's Tavern at the River Crest Country Club to the blondes at Salvador's beauty salon to the cowboys on the northside and the socialites on the west— everybody was talking about our encounter with the IRS.

This wasn't mere gossip: it was scandal. Gossip was filled with characters that were expected to mess up: stewardesses-turned-oil-queens hiring hit men to torch their mansions for the insurance money; oil secretaries who marry their bosses and pull off drunken public acts wilder than any rodeo clown's; second generation oil-men going crazy before the whole town on too much cash, cocaine, and cowgirls. You expect antics from these people. Scandal blows in from out of the blue, with characters and scenarios you'd never expect.

It wasn't the first scandal to explode at the corner of Ninth and Commerce. Before the Moncrief Building was built, the Metropolitan Hotel had been on that site, and old timers still talk about "the shooting." On the night of January 13, 1919, Beal Sneed, thirty-six-year-old son of a wealthy cattle baron, blew away the grand old man of the cattle business, Capt. A. G. Boyce, seventy, while Boyce read a newspaper in the hotel's lobby. Seems Capt. Boyce's son ran off with Beal Sneed's young wife.

That's a scandal.

In the immediate aftermath of the raid, we felt like Capt. A. G. Boyce: blinded by bullets without knowing who fired them—much less the reasons why.

Of course, the entire Moncrief family could be viewed as one long history of scandal: people you'd never imagine doing things you wouldn't believe.

My family is a product of the combination of cattle and oil, the twin forces that built Fort Worth. The city's nickname is Cowtown. Cattle barons erected "town house" mansions along Summit Avenue, which became locally famed as "Cattlemen's Row." From their mansions, the old cattle kings could literally look down upon the oil-field "trash" who arrived in the thirties and forties like some greasy army. The oil crowd, from the field hands to the wildcatters, whooped it up in the old Westbrook Hotel, where they wiped their oil leases for good luck on the bronze butt of the Golden Goddess, a naked-lady sculpture ostensibly smuggled in from Italy.

My mother, Deborah Beggs Moncrief, was a genuine cattle baroness, one of two beautiful Beggs sisters born into a Summit Avenue cattle fortune. The Beggs were cattlemen, and, at least in the beginning, cattlemen didn't mess with oil-field trash. Even today, recalling my dad in his youth, my mother remembers him as being in "that oil crowd. And, oh, golly, that was a really fast crowd."

But the oil crowd was only the latest bunch of roustabouts to roll into Fort Worth. Right where our office now sits was the site of the notorious Hell's Half Acre, a gambling, whoring, street-dueling boomtown centered south of the stockyards where cattle were fattened for the kill. Outlaw gangs hid out. Cattle rustlers wreaked havoc. Butch Cassidy and the Sundance Kid had their picture taken there for posterity.

In Fort Worth, headquarters of massive ranches sprawling westward, the term "cattle baron" was no exaggeration. Early on, the barons saw oil derricks as a gross desecration of good grazing land. But that soon changed. The feedlots moved to the plains of West Texas, where raising cattle was cheaper, and the railroads and packing houses followed. Almost overnight, the cattle industry—and the characters that worked in it—moved on or just died, leaving Fort Worth destined to die like so many boomtowns. It was ironic that the force that the cattle barons despised most—oil—would become their economic salvation. "The oil business saved many of the ranching families," my mother would later say.

Of course, she was partial. While she was married to Harry Johnson, a perfectly respectable Fort Worth lawyer, she had been carrying on with a Fort Worth oilman, W. A. "Tex" Moncrief. She'd known Tex all her life. She'd seen him at the horse races or the cocktail parties where the Texans gathered together. Tex was married, with three young sons to boot. But then they bumped into each other in a hallway at a dinner party and the slightly tipsy cattle baroness kissed the oilman square on the lips.

Not long afterwards, they sneaked off together for a weekend in Los Angeles. An earthquake struck while they were in each other's arms, they liked to joke. Roughly nine months later, an earthquake hit Fort Worth when Deborah Beggs Johnson gave birth to me: a blond-haired boy who didn't look at all like her husband.

With their love child in a crib, and every prying eye upon them, they held hands under the hymnals in church until they could divorce their respective spouses and give their baby a name—Charles Beggs Moncrief.

In our family, Granddad ruled. To his children and grandchildren, he was a god. He had such a nose for oil his friends liked to say he could sit at his desk in Fort Worth and *smell* good leases as far away as Wyoming and Florida.

If you saw him, you'd immediately think "Texas oilman." Tall and broad shouldered with a full head of wavy white hair, Granddad was the personification of rags to riches. Born dirt-poor in Sulphur Springs, Texas, he was the son of Lafayette Barto "L. B." Moncrief, a distant descendant of the Moncreiffe clan of the Scottish Highlands, whose sole contribution to his family's later wealth was picking up and moving to Checotah, Oklahoma, to sell hardware to the Indian braves. Those same braves would soon be rich enough to drive Packards. Because of the blessings of oil.

★ ★ ★

Oil was our family's present, past, and future, and we knew its history as well as most kids knew the folklore of cowboys and Indians.

The first "theme" paper I ever wrote was in grade school, and my subject was Venezuela's Maracaibo Basin. The paper was prompted by Dad's discussion of oil discoveries in other parts of the world, which he and Granddad got around to telling after they'd exhausted the stories of oil discoveries in America by the men who risked everything to find it: the wildcatters. "We're wildcatters," Granddad would say repeatedly. "We're 100 percent family owned and we intend to stay that way: unincorporated and independent!"

A wildcatter is to the oil business what the cowboy was to the increasingly urban frontier—independent, self-reliant, and dedicated to a single passion: the sniffing out of increasingly elusive oil and gas deposits. A wildcatter pursues oil and gas as doggedly as the cowboy rides herd on cattle, on a range increasingly filled with realtors and Range Rovers.

In many ways the wildcatter is as much of an endangered species as the cowboy, possibly even more so. In the fifties, ten thousand independent oilmen scoured America for oil. Twenty years later, the number had dwindled to five thousand. Now you can count the number of wildcatters in the hundreds. We Moncriefs remain true to the best wildcatter traditions. Every minute of our waking lives is spent in pursuit of oil, nothing but oil.

In 1857, forty years before Granddad's birth, the first wildcatter would set the standard for those to follow. He was long on confidence and short on just about everything else. His name was Edwin L. Drake. His mission: to find a way to extract oil from the springs, pools, and seepages that dotted the ground in an area outside of Titusville, Pennsylvania, called "Oil Creek."

In his top hat and black coat, Drake first skimmed the oil from the ground with boards. No luck in gathering sufficient quantities. Then, he soaked it up with blankets, which he later wrung out into tubs. This method also failed. Drake dug ditches to divert oil into pools. Still, nothing but such minuscule amounts that it brought gales of laughter from the skeptical Titusville townsfolk.

Finally, after repeated failures, Drake hit upon a new idea. "I made up my mind that oil could be obtained in large quantities by boring as for salt water," he later said.

Now, *everyone* thought Drake was crazy. Determined to prove everyone wrong, he set up headquarters on a farm that had a sizable oil spring, where locals had been collecting three to six gallons of oil daily—by hand. Drake hired "Uncle Billy" Smith, a "salt borer," who drilled for salt deposits with a wooden derrick with a clapboard siding. With two sons for muscle, and with Drake overseeing his every move, Uncle Billy built a wooden derrick in Oil Creek and began the slow and expensive process of boring for oil.

As Drake's demands grew, his backers began backing out one by one. But on August 27, 1859, his salt drill bit hit sixty-nine feet, dropped into a crevice, lowered another six inches, and stopped. The bit hit an apparent fissure in the rock. Thinking they were in trouble, and preferring to deal with it the next day, the oilmen stopped work and went home.

The next day, Colonel Drake came to his well and peered into the pipe to find it brimming full of oil.

Attaching a hand pump to the borehole, Drake began pumping up the oil by the gallon, then by the barrel, until every whiskey barrel in Titusville and all of the surrounding towns was filled with it.

Crazy Edwin Drake had struck the world's first oil well.

But where there's oil, there are scoundrels. Titusville became infamous as a boomtown populated by frauds, fakers, and oil swindlers who would stop at nothing to get in on the action. "The oil business is a waste of time without ownership," said Granddad. Colonel Edwin Drake was the father of the oil business, but his partners not only got back into the action, they shut him off from all profits. Drake died penniless in an unmarked grave.

★ ★ ★

Granddad wasn't born an oilman. His first job was nailing satin into coffins in his father's hardware store. Later he worked as a soda jerk in Oklahoma. He wanted to become a lawyer and eventually saved up enough money to put himself through two years at Oklahoma University. But with WWI, "Monty," as he was nicknamed by his OU fraternity brothers, signed up for the cavalry. While at officer's training school in Little Rock, he met and married Elizabeth Bright, a pretty local girl who played the piano and sang for the soldiers.

He served only a few months in the 334th Machine Gun Battalion in France when the Armistice came. One of his best friends, Captain Jack Cleary of Ponca City, Oklahoma, was going to work for his uncle at a newly formed oil company back home. "Why don't you do the same?" he asked Monty.

Oil was being discovered all over Oklahoma. Horse traders, poker players, and hustlers were becoming independent oilmen. By giving landowners the right to minerals beneath their land, the U.S. government gave the independent oilman an opportunity to get rich. Wildcatters were soon barnstorming across the plains, leasing land and sinking primitive wells, guided by little more geology than what they felt in their gut.

After his discharge, Monty and his bride moved to Ponca City, and Monty took a $150-a-month job in the accounting department of the Marland Oil Company. It didn't take Monty long to realize the real action wasn't in the office but out in the field. So Monty became a land man, the oil patch equivalent of a real estate agent: sweet-talking small-time ranchers and poor farmers into granting a lease, the right to drill an oil well on the land for a number of years. If the well hits, the landowner is paid a royalty, usually one-eighth of gross profits.

In his western-cut shirt and jacket, Granddad would knock on the landowner's door. "Hello, I'm Monty Moncrief," he'd say. "I'm the land man representing the Marland Oil Company." His hand would extend for a shake; the door would open a little wider. "There's an oil play heating up in this area, and I'd like to take a lease from you."

The door would swing open even wider as the landowner pondered the deal. Granddad would offer the standard commission. Sometimes, there would be cash, too. Thirty or forty dollars an acre for land that might not be worth half that. "And there's more where that came from if we hit," Granddad would say. Then, he'd mention the magic word: *Oil*! Pens would be pulled from pockets and with a signature—or, in some cases, a crudely drawn X—the landowner would enter the oil business. His acreage, once a poor dirt farm or scrub oak ranch, was now part of a patchwork quilt of sometimes hundreds of individual leases in every oilman's quest for the "Big One," an oil field bigger, wider, and deeper than the imagination could conjur.

Monty Moncrief was one hell of a land man. Nine times out of ten, he left with the landowner's signature on a lease. Along the way, he picked up two important qualities. First, a good name. Secondly, an equally crucial quality, luck. Good luck seemed to follow Monty Moncrief. "I'd rather be lucky than smart," he liked to say.

When E. W. Marland expanded his company into Texas, he sent Granddad, his best land man, to run it as executive vice president. With his wife and two young sons—my dad, W. A. "Tex" Moncrief, and his younger brother, Richard Barto Moncrief— Monty moved first to Dallas, then Houston, then, finally, Fort Worth. He moved to Fort Worth not because of any oil strike— none had been discovered even close to the city limits—but "because of the persuasiveness of Amon Carter."

When the cattle companies left Fort Worth's stock yards in a stampede, the good Lord gave our town Amon "Gaw-damned" Carter, the Wise County blacksmith's son who became the king of Cowtown. As publisher of the *Fort Worth Star-Telegram,* Carter became the city's chief booster and, ultimately, the creator of modern-day Fort Worth. He was a showman, riding a palomino with a $5,000 silver saddle. He dressed in boots, spurs, bandanna, a knee-length vicuña coat, and a ten-gallon hat. He traveled across America firing pearl-handled pistols and bellowing, "Come to Fort Worth, where the West begins!" And people came, all because of Amon Carter.

Amon Carter was sympathetic to the independent oilman's struggle. He knew that the dreams of the oilman could serve his own dreams and that, together, they could turn Fort Worth into a world-class city, the oil capital of the new Southwest. Like all the rest, Granddad came to Fort Worth because of Amon Carter. Carter's Shady Oaks Ranch was an amusement park designed to promote Fort Worth. One year the American Association of Independent Petroleum Producers, the wildcatter's unofficial Elks Club, accepted Amon Carter's enthusiastic invitation to hold its annual meeting at Shady Oaks. The country was in the grips of Prohibition, but you'd never have known it at Shady Oaks. Carter had the foresight to buy up the entire Casey-Swasey Liquor Franchise before temperance closed it down. He stashed the booze on his ranch in an underground bank vault with a burglar alarm.

Granddad joined the trail drive of wildcatters in Cowtown. He and his wife Elizabeth rented a modest home with a backyard full of chickens and their own Jersey cow, which Granddad would milk twice a day. Sometimes, wearing black tie and tails, he'd serve his guests fresh milk in cocktail glasses, everybody toasting to good luck in finding "the Big One."

Dreams of the Big One kept the wildcatter afloat. When the stock market crashed in 1929, E. W. Marland, who had diversified from oil into stocks and bonds, was headed towards bankruptcy. Granddad decided to go out on his own. When he reminded his wife that salary or security would not follow him out the door, she told him that he hadn't had his salary long, and she could always fire the help and go back to washing, ironing, and cooking. Promising never to overextend himself financially or take his company public, which he saw as E. W. Marland's downfall, Granddad rented a one-room office in the W. T. Waggoner Building in Fort Worth. In 1927, he became an independent oilman, a wildcatter. His first twenty-nine wells were dry holes.

But he wasn't known as "Dry Hole Monty" for long. He'd heard of prospecting in East Texas, which was broken up into little dirt-poor hog farms, cotton fields, and squatters' shanties. Because the land was tangled up in cloudy titles, it was tricky to lease. But Granddad felt East Texas had potential. His opinion was pushed along by the amateur geologist "Doc" Lloyd. Lloyd was a big, fat, usually unwashed country boy who wore sombrero hats. He had been married six times and had been involved in dog and horse doctoring, drug merchandising, and gold prospecting before falling into the oil business.

Geologists from the major oil companies had declared East Texas barren. So Lloyd was considered a crackpot. He had drawn a map of the major oil fields in the U.S. with lines stretching out from each to the point where all the lines intersected. He called this point "the apex of the apex," and promised that beneath this apex waited an "ocean of oil." The apex fell precisely on top of the little East Texas town of Rusk.

Granddad listened to Lloyd. But he didn't rush into business with him. Lloyd eventually partnered with "Dad" Joiner, a Shakespeare-quoting frontier Okie scholar, womanizer, and con artist. On Lloyd's assurance about the ocean of oil, Dad Joiner leased one hundred acres in East Texas. After drilling two dry holes, Doc Lloyd sweet-talked the widow Daisy Bradford into letting him sink a well on her land seven miles outside of Henderson, Texas. He built a derrick of cast-off yellow pine and sold $25 interests in the "Daisy Bradford #3" three times over. On September 5, 1930, with Joiner's investors ready to lynch him, the Daisy Bradford #3 exploded in a gusher of black rain. The boom was on, but it turned out to be a bust for Dad Joiner, who didn't know the size of his find until it was too late. The Arkansas gambler, H. L. Hunt, kept the debt-ridden Joiner holed up in a room in Dallas's Baker Hotel until he sold out his holdings for $1.3 million.

In his one-room office in the Waggoner Building, Monty Moncrief was far removed from East Texas—until luck found him once again. A promoter named B. A. "Barney" Skipper, who held leases on four thousand acres just northeast of Dad Joiner's well, wanted to sell his leases cheap to pay off debts he owed on them. He'd written letters to 750 major and independent oil concerns offering them free leases if only they'd drill a well. Convinced that the East Texas field stopped short of Longview, the majors decided to pass. Granddad snapped up those cheap leases in partnership with an associate. Selling off pieces of their holdings to finance their drilling operation, Granddad began scoping out the best place to drill. He decided that it lay in a "window," an unleased section right in the middle of a forty-acre hog farm belonging to a country doctor named Falvey, who had a booming medical practice among the black farmers in the area. Granddad made an appointment with the doctor.

In the doctor's waiting room, Granddad waited...and waited...and waited. Finally the doctor emerged, listened to the lease proposal, and showed Granddad the door. "I don't want no oil well messin' up my hog farm," Dr. Falvey said at last.

Granddad was dejected, but not for long. On the very night after Falvey's rebuff, he was eating dinner alone in the Gregg Hotel when a hog farmer blew into the dining room.

"Mr. Moncrief, my name is Frank Lathrop. I work for the Kelly Plow Company, and I own four hundred acres in the block leased by B. A. Skipper, on which you now own the oil and gas lease," he said breathlessly.

Granddad invited the stranger to sit down. Then Frank Lathrop said something that, Granddad would later say, convinced him that 99 percent of the oil business is being in the right place at the right time.

"Mr. Moncrief, I would like to make you a proposition," he said. "If you drill your first well on my land, I will give you one-fourth of my royalty."

Granddad stood up, extended his hand, and said, "Mr. Lathrop, you done gone and made yourself a deal!"

They drilled the well with rotary tools beneath a wooden derrick. On the night of January 25, 1931, at 3,500 feet, the rotary bit hit a soft formation, and the crew took a core. When they laid the core sample out on the floor of the Gregg Hotel, everyone gasped. The sample looked like brown sugar coated in oil. The Frank Lathrop Number One was going to be a producer. The news spread so fast that schools were let out the next day so the kids could watch an oil well blow in.

A crowd of fifteen thousand gathered around Granddad's well that morning. When they opened it up, oil shot from the pipe extending from the wellhead into a sludge pit. First five feet, then ten feet, then twenty, then one hundred feet, the oil shot across the pit, spraying the crowd with black gold. Granddad and his partners were dancing in the spray, throwing their hats into the air.

My dad, Tex Moncrief, age ten, stood in the crowd of kids and watched his daddy strike the Big One and toss his Stetson toward heaven. Before the hat landed, my father stared up at his mother and said, "Mama, when I grow up I wanna be an oilman."

The well came in at 18,000 barrels a day. Doc Lloyd's vision of a sea of oil was dead-on. Soon, twenty-five thousand oil wells poked the oil-rich, thirty-mile sandbar known as the East Texas Field. But Granddad's Lathrop Number One would be known as the "Daddy of Them All." Later, a well was sunk on Dr. Falvey's property. The well was as dry as a bone.

The market was soon flooded with oil. Without funds to fully develop the adjoining acres, Granddad was forced to sell his holdings. His first prospect was oil company giant Harry Sinclair, who traveled to Texas from New York in his private Pullman car to meet Granddad. When Sinclair expressed a few doubts about the discovery, Granddad took him out to the well and opened her up for thirty minutes. The oil shot through the two-inch tubing, shaking pinecones off adjacent trees. Sinclair made an offer, but the partners decided to sell out instead for $2.5 million to the Yont-Lee Oil Company of Beaumont, which later sold the same acreage to Standard Oil for $37 million. "In the oil business, there's no 'what if,' " Granddad liked to say. "There's only 'what happened.'" He knew there was more oil where the Frank Lathrop #1 came from.

So in 1931, Monty Moncrief returned to Fort Worth and built a house beside the fifth hole of the River Crest Country Club. It was the depths of the Depression, but you wouldn't have known it in Fort Worth. Cattle heiresses drove Dusenbergs along the long serpentine driveways leading to their mansions, and oil-field hands became overnight millionaires. Fort Worth had become an oil Mecca, and Monty Moncrief became a legend in a town full of oilmen. Hollywood celebrities like Bob Hope and Bing Crosby sought him out to invest in his oil wells. He helped them earn millions and made oil and gas investments a fashionable Hollywood hobby.

But first, with his wife Elizabeth at his side, Monty Moncrief settled in to raise his family.

Chapter Three

Roughneck's Revenge

ONE ROUGHNECK ON THE FRANK LATHROP #1 well would figure large in our family saga, although nobody knew it at the time. F. F. "Ferrell" Trapp, a roughneck on the crew on Granddad's East Texas discovery well, became the pumper on the well. A pumper's job is to turn the wells on and off and monitor production.

But Ferrell was pumping something other than Granddad's oil well. He married Granddad's big sister, Jewell.

The couple had set up house in the East Texas oil field, accompanied by their young son, Jack Trapp. Things stayed the same for fourteen years. But then Ferrell Trapp just up and left. Nobody really remembers why. But Jewell didn't let it bring her down. She went on to run things. Boy, could she run things! She ran the lodge at Granddad's Gunnison River Ranch, where they began taking in boarders. Aunt Jewell was as tough as any marine sergeant. It didn't pay to cross her. When her son, Jack, went to the University of Texas, Jewell was dispatched by Granddad to cook and maintain a house for Jack Trapp, my dad, and O. L. Chenoweth, a family friend we call Uncle Rattlesnake.

Jack took after the Trapp side of the family. He'd rather goof off than study and promptly flunked out of UT. Before leaving UT, he married his college sweetheart, Mary Daisy Wiley, a sweet girl from Houston whom everybody called "Dee." On September 27, 1944, somewhere between the time Jack left college and joined the air force, Jack Trapp and Dee gave birth to a son: Michael Joseph Trapp.

The marriage didn't last. Dee must have been close to divorcing Jack Trapp when she brought her baby to visit Aunt Jewell at the Moncrief River Ranch in Gunnison, Colorado, in the mid-1940s. During this visit, Dee bonded with Dick Moncrief, the twenty-four-year-old younger son of Monty Moncrief. Not long after leaving the ranch, Dee and Jack divorced. Not long after that, Dick married Dee Trapp and adopted her son, Mike Trapp, giving him the Moncrief name.

Everyone scratched their heads to comprehend fully what Dick had done. *He'd married his Aunt Jewell's son's ex-wife!* And one more wild card was thrown into the family deck: Michael Joseph Trapp Moncrief.

Granddad's two sons were polar opposites. Both attended Culver Military Academy, both earned college degrees, both returned home to join the oil business with their father. But that's where their roads diverged. W. A. "Tex" Moncrief was a natural-born, second generation wildcatter, ever since he watched his father's oil-stained Stetson fly into the air on the day of the East Texas gusher. He married while still a student at the University of Texas, graduated with a degree in petroleum engineering, and had three sons by his first marriage by the time he returned home to join the family business. He idolized his father and became his constant companion, learning from the master until he was confident enough to make oil deals on his own.

Tex and Monty were inseparable, operating on a handshake arrangement on every well they drilled together. Their discoveries included major strikes in Oklahoma, Florida, Wyoming, New Mexico, Utah, Michigan, Colorado, Canada, and Texas. As they prospered, they used their oil fortunes for philanthropy, donating millions of dollars to charities including the Culver Military Academy, TCU, the University of Texas, and what would become the University of Texas Southwestern Moncrief Cancer Center in Fort Worth.

Richard Barto Moncrief didn't want anything to do with oil. Heavy-set and bespectacled, good-natured and bighearted, he had been plagued by asthma and food allergies since childhood. When he got out of the air force, he ran the family's oil operations in Wichita Falls for a while, but Dick didn't join Tex and Granddad when they relocated their offices to a new building they'd purchased. He kept his own office in the W. T. Waggoner Building with a secretary and bookkeeper, calling his operation W. A. Moncrief and Sons.

From that point on, Dick's real office became his home, while his office became mostly just a place to collect royalty checks and handle accounting. His real business was his hobbies. In his basement, he'd build remote-controlled model airplanes, dozens of them, their enormous wingspans stretching across the room. He also loved to race motorized toy slot cars. There were toy trains and go-carts and dogs. Booze was a hobby, too, as well as prescription drugs.

Uncle Dick didn't do anything halfway. When he got into dogs, he raised prize-winning weimaraners. When he built model airplanes, he competed at the Model Airplane National Championships—and won. His hobbies kept him up all night. He'd sleep until midafternoon. Dad and Granddad considered it a special occasion if Dick ever got up in time for lunch. He might eat his biggest meal at midnight. If he had a cough, he wouldn't take just a spoonful of cough syrup. He'd drink the whole bottle. Still, everybody loved Dick. He was a big kid with an enormous appetite for fun.

Dressed in his customary dark suit with big, horn-rim glasses, he borrowed Granddad's DC-3 to pursue his hobbies. Granddad never complained: Dick was Dick and he could do as he pleased. So, with his wife, Dee, and giant stock bottles of Maalox at his side, he directed the pilots of the Lucky Liz to fly him to championship go-cart races and dog shows. On the plane with Dick and Dee might be a cabin full of freeloaders or fifteen flatulent dogs or a dozen greasy go-carts.

Maybe the games were Uncle Dick's way of filling his life after tragedy. Because while both Moncrief brothers were blessed with wealth and privilege, both suffered the devastating deaths of their children. Tex lost a son, Herbie, killed at twenty-one in a motorcycle accident while home on leave from the U.S. Marine Corps. He had already lost his only daughter, Monty Francine, seven, who died after a two-year bout with leukemia. Then Uncle Dick's daughter, Elizabeth Scott, seventeen, was killed in a car accident. Uncle Dick became convinced that he was going to be next. "I'm gonna live and enjoy livin', because I'll never see fifty," he announced on more occasions than I'd care to count.

★ ★ ★

As a child, I never thought there was anything special about being a Moncrief. No, that's not it. I mean I never thought there was anything special about me just because I *was* a Moncrief. We were a family of ten, including Mom and Dad, Dickie, and Herbie, my idol, the brother I loved most of all. Bill was the quiet brother, the sports enthusiast, even put out his own tout sheet, *Wise Willy Predicts*. These were Dad's sons by his first marriage. Debbie and Harry were my mother's children. Debbie was the best big sister a boy could have. She was always there if I needed someone to talk to. There was my new full sister Monty Francine. And finally, brother Tom Oil Moncrief. There was never a dull moment with so many brothers. And of course there were the dogs. Buck the black lab, the greatest hunting dog I've ever known, and SACROC the boxer named after a giant west Texas oil field that was operated by the Scurry Area Canyon Reef Operating Committee.

My maternal grandparents died very early in my life. But I got to become close with Dad's parents, Granddad and Granddear, who lived only a few blocks up the road. Dad's brother Uncle Dick and his family lived yet just a few blocks farther. Dad and Uncle Dick weren't very close, but every Christmas Uncle Dick would stop by with a case of scotch for Dad, and they would visit in the driveway. Uncle Dick's sons, Mike and Monty, were always cordial. But they were different from us. I never could put my finger on why, but it really didn't matter.

There was another member of our family, too. "The rigs," Dad called them. The drilling rigs. Because the oil business is not an occupation: it is a way of life. There are no days off for a drilling rig. It requires constant care. The rigs are *always* calling when you're an operator. When the field hands had trouble on the drilling rig, and there's always trouble, they would call Dad. Constantly. As far back as I can remember, the rigs were constantly calling Dad. Calling with problems, technicalities, personnel problems, and, when we were lucky, news of oil and gas strikes.

Dad would take us boys to the oil field with him. Mostly West Texas and occasionally Oklahoma. The rigs were huge. Everything in the oil field was big. The trucks, the bulldozers, the pipe racks, and especially the men. The roughnecks and roustabouts, the "iron men" as they were called. Big and strong, chewing tobacco, smoking, drinking, and cussing.

Back then I wasn't interested in the oil fields for financial security. I craved excitement. One morning, Dad woke Dickie and me up early, hollering, "Let's go! We had a blowout during the night at Conroe! I told the hands to call Red Adair to meet us at the well." The three of us landed just north of Houston and drove to the Conroe oil field. It was not pretty. The noise was deafening and gas, oil, water and sand were blowing up through and well above the top of the derrick. The blowout was so strong and continuous that it had cut the derrick floor in two. Standing three hundred yards from the well, the hands were briefing Dad. But we could still barely hear our voices over the roar.

Suddenly, a red-on-red Toronado slid up next to us, kicking up a cloud of backwashed dust. Two men emerged wearing fire-engine-red coveralls and hard hats. Emblazoned across their backs was Red Adair Well Control Specialists. Without even the slightest hesitation they walked directly to the rig and disappeared under the substructure. My heart was racing. Finally, the two men reemerged and walked over to Dad. "Mr. Moncrief, I'm 'Boots' Raymond and this is 'Coots' Mathews. There's not enough daylight left to get anything done today, so let's go to town where we can talk and make plans for morning."

We all headed towards the cars. Before we got there, Boots turned towards the blowout. Glaring at the disaster, he raised his fist and shouted, "Blow, you son of a bitch, blow all you can, 'cause I'm gonna cap your ass in the morning!"

Well, that did it for me. I knew I was going to work in the oil field. I couldn't imagine anything more exciting. I graduated from Culver Military Academy and headed to the University of Texas. I already felt like I'd spent a good part of my life at UT with my Dad watching Darrell Royal's dynamic Texas Longhorns dominate the college gridiron.

I joined the Kappa Sigs and made some great life long friends. But drugs were rampant in Austin, Texas, antiwar protests were the norm, and neither held much interest for me. My head was moving in fifteen different directions and unfortunately the classroom was not one of them. I signed up for the second semester, but I could see I was spinning my wheels. So I returned to Fort Worth and landed a job as a "hot shot" with the local Coca Cola company, replenishing Coke machines and emptying the coin boxes. There was a safe in the middle of the delivery truck's floorboard.

One day, I put the money in the safe and, just to save a step, decided not to lock it.

"We only have to go one block, and we'll be at another machine," I told my partner.

That middle-aged guy stared at me. "Let me tell you something, buddy," he said. "I've been working this job for twenty-seven years, and I've finally worked up to this position, and you ain't gonna screw it up by not locking that safe."

Oh, man, I thought. This guy's been working this job for twenty-seven years and has worked up to this? As soon as we returned to the office, I resigned and went straight to the local branch of the Marine Corps. I went to boot camp in San Diego, all ready for Vietnam. But the doctors found latent nystagmus, an involuntary movement of the eye. I didn't want to sit at a stateside desk for two years. So I took an honorable discharge and headed back to college. I signed up at Texas Christian University (TCU) and began studying in earnest for a geology degree. With the Marine Corps disappointment and the memory of that Coca Cola vet fresh in my mind, I had no problem with college this time.

My older brother Dickie, who had worked for the family, had moved to New York as an investment banker for Goldman Sachs. Which left me to do Granddad's chores. And because I wanted to learn the oil business from the ground up, it was an ideal situation. Granddad called me "The Drone."

After earning my geology degree, I moved into the Moncrief Building to learn the business from Dad and Granddad full-time. Around this time, we lost our production clerk, and I inherited my first real job. We were operating approximately twenty-five wells in Texas and the monthly production had to be reported to the state each month. Dick introduced me to production, showing me how to use the tank tables, measure the crude oil, and turn those records over to our accounting department.

At the same time, in June of 1970, the discovery well for the Jay Field in Florida blew in. Brother Dickie and Kelly Young of the Marshall R. Young Oil Company in Fort Worth went to Florida to buy royalty interests for our two families. They had located a land man out of Alabama who had all of the ownership records of the area.

The land man was an alcoholic and drove an old white Cadillac with his wife at his side and an Igloo cooler full of vodka in the back seat. This was brother Dickie's first introduction to a big oil play. Several months went by. We were the first buyers in the area, but then Dickie and Kelly began to get nervous about other land men leasing or buying royalties, driving up the price.

"C'mon, Charlie, we're going down to Florida and help these guys out," Granddad told me one day.

We rented a car at the Pensacola airport, and I became Granddad's chauffeur. We had to keep him out of sight. One glimpse of Granddad by a seasoned land man and lease prices would immediately rise. Everybody knew that only the hottest of plays would bring W. A. Moncrief to town. So Granddad would get on all fours on the floorboard as we rode through town. When we'd go to the one café where everybody ate breakfast, Granddad insisted we each get a newspaper. Soon I knew why. Everybody in the café was reading the newspaper—or at least acting like they were reading. What they were actually doing is using the paper as camouflage, peering over the top of the paper to see who was in town.

It was my first taste of the big time oil business, and I loved it.

Remembering my geomorphology course at TCU, I thought of how my professor had pointed out some aerial photos showing how the Trinity River came down across north Texas, made an interesting turn around Parker County, and headed straight east toward Dallas before turning south again. All of the other rivers came across Texas in a smooth southeasterly flow. At our ranch in Parker County, the river took the turn. The highest topographical point in Parker County was on our ranch, as well. I was curious about Parker County. Wells had been drilled there for gas. There had been discoveries, but nothing big.

I pointed out this geological anomaly to Granddad and Dad not long after graduating from TCU. Dickie had a geologist working for him, Tom Brown. Because I didn't have the experience to work the play myself, Tom Brown got the assignment. I would assist. We accumulated all of the well logs in Parker County and a couple of the surrounding counties and began correlating the logs and mapping the subsurface terrain. Sure enough, we came up with some prospective leads where we might be able to drill into a pocket of gas.

Our longtime land man Duane McDaniel parked me in the Parker County Clerk's office. My job was to determine mineral and royalty ownership in the areas where we had prospects. Once we knew who owned what, we began going to the landowners and buying leases for five to ten dollars an acre, giving the landowner a one-eighth royalty.

My title search showed that the Martin brothers owned close to eight thousand acres immediately south of our ranch. Jack and Don Martin were quiet, country dirt ranchers. Already in their late sixties, they were cousins of the actress Mary Martin, who gained fame first on Broadway as "Peter Pan," and later as Larry "J. R." Hagman's mother. The brothers actually owned three ranches, measuring 4,000, 3,000 and 1,000 acres respectively. These ranches consisted of rolling hills of blue stem grass perfect for stocker steer operations. They were also perfectly situated for our gas play.

I discovered that the ranches were for sale and reported back to Dad.

"Well, if you can get them for a couple hundred an acre, go ahead," he said.

But the Martin brothers were tough. Local legend had them going to the bank to cash five dollar checks and popping their bills like they were holding hundreds. They were asking $400 an acre and wouldn't budge an inch, especially for some youngster like me. I offered $200 an acre, and they sent me packing.

I still figured I could make a deal with the brothers, but then I got some bad news: the Martins sold their ranches, lock, stock, and barrel. Someone had outbid me, paying the Martin brothers full price. I would soon learn that the man who outbid me was Coke Gage, a wheeler-dealer part-time mayor of Decatur, Texas, and full-time wildcatter oilman. I reported this to Dad and Granddad, then took the liberty of contacting Coke Gage. Gage wasn't much interested in talking to me, but his voice rose a few octaves when he heard the name Moncrief.

"Well, Charlie Moncrief, I'm glad you called," he said. "There's something I'd like to discuss with your granddaddy. I've got a deal I'd like to have him take a look at."

One morning, after a long night in the oil fields, Gage shambled into the Moncrief Building like a country W. C. Fields: heavy-set, red faced . . . and extremely well oiled.

"Y'all got something to drink around here?" he boomed in his Texas drawl after everybody shook hands in Granddad's office. "Man needs a drink before he gets down to business."

Granddad broke out the Scotch, and Gage made his pitch.

"Yeah, I bought those ranches out there, but that's not what I came here to talk about," he said. "What I want to talk about is gas. I've leased mineral rights from Decatur all the way to Stephenville."

I watched Granddad and Dad's expressions brighten. Gage was talking about a one hundred-mile stretch of land. He had begun leasing property and had butted heads repeatedly with land we'd already leased. He wanted to combine his leases with ours and start drilling wells.

"The avenue of land between Decatur and Stephenville will be loaded with gas," he said. "And I think the biggest producers will be right on your ranches."

He took a long sip of whiskey. "I know you want those ranches, so I'll sell them to you for $600 an acre but I want to keep a 2.5 percent override," he said. "I'll pool all of my other leases with the Moncrief leases and we can start drilling some wells. Oh, by the way, I'd like an override on the Moncrief acreage as well."

Dad and Granddad thought a minute. Finally, Granddad said, "We'll buy the ranches from you at your cost. The overrides are okay, plus we'll do $200,000 worth of drilling for your account."

"You got a deal," said Coke Gage.

Granddad loved the deal, even though the messenger—Coke Gage—was now even more well oiled than he had been when he first walked into the office. We made an appointment to meet later in the week. Gage stumbled to his feet. The deal culminated as Granddad's deals always did: with a handshake. No legal papers. No formal signing of an agreement. Granddad's handshake was golden. A follow-up letter outlining the deal was exchanged with Gage soon after. And that was it. The deal was done.

Coke did divulge, however, that one ranch would not be included in the deal. It was what we referred to as the Martin Ranch Proper, and he claimed that there was some kind of a title problem. This was particularly interesting to me, and I set out to find out what the problem was.

Once again, Duane McDaniel put me in the bottom of the Parker County Courthouse with a legal pad and deed records, and I went to work determining who owned which acreage among literally hundreds of individual property owners. At the same time I started pulling information on the Martin Ranch. What I discovered was very interesting. The Martin Brothers really didn't have the legal right to sell the Martin Ranch at all. All they had was a life estate. When they passed away, the ranch would be divided amongst their heirs. There were close to thirty heirs, I discovered, ranging from housewives and lawyers to truck drivers.

As a courtesy I gave Don Martin a call. "I know what you are doing," I said. "If we give you $400 an acre you are going to buy out the heirs as cheap as possible and pocket the rest."

I told Don I was going to go buy out the heirs. Then I'd come back, and maybe then we could cut a deal on his and his brother's life estates. Don was not happy, but I went ahead and bought out the heirs just as I said I would. Sure enough, when I came back to cut a deal with Don, he would have nothing to do with it.

He would have to deal with it some day, but my attention moved back to the gas play. It was time to start "leasing," the aspect of the job that every wildcatter talks tall about: rolling up to some house in the middle of nowhere in the early evening, the oilman climbing out of his car, knocking on the landowner's front door, and giving him or her a convincing enough story to guide the landowner's hand to the dotted line.

Duane McDaniel took me under his wing. "Charlie, oil is the only business I know of where you go and pay a man first to do business with you later," he told me. "I don't have any thoughts in my mind that I'm Santa Claus, but nothing happens in the way of finding oil until someone has signed an oil and gas lease. That's where everything begins."

Duane McDaniel taught me the psychology of leasing:

"Now, here's how to do the job," he continued. "First step: watch for dogs. Before I even get out of the car, if I'm in the country, I look for dogs. If you don't see any dogs, then look for signs of a dog, like where the ground will be pounded down right up to the fence where that dog has run back and forth. Once I determine there aren't any dogs around, I go up and knock on the door.

"I can get just inebriated by turning a good deal," he said. "I just get so exhilarated, when I've taken someone who may have a negative, or even a combative, viewpoint, and turned him to our way of thinking. To close a good deal is very exciting. I get hyper, I get on a high."

His line of bull was so corny. But it worked and worked well.

Once we had the land leased, it was time to drill the first well. Coke Gage took Granddad out south of Aledo to an old abandoned gas well drilled in the fifties. It had a cracked "Christmas Tree," a nickname for the valves and flanges which secure a well. The Christmas Tree was just barely leaking air—or gas. Coke Gage struck a match and the Christmas Tree ignited.

Gas.

We decided to drill our first wells right there and were successful. Then, we moved on to our Parker County ranch. Rigs were tight at the time, and we already had a couple of rigs running right there in that close-in area. One of our rigs was coming down off a well, and we didn't have another place to put it. I called Dad at his vacation home in Palm Springs, California, and told him the problem.

"'Look, I'll be back tomorrow," he said. "Have 'em rig down the rig, and I'll come over there tomorrow and pick a site to drill it."

Just off the Lucky Liz from Palm Springs, Dad walked the ranch until he came upon a curious mound of dirt in a pasture about a foot and a half tall with a prickly pear cactus growing on top of it.

"I want the bit to go right through that cactus," Dad said. So we drilled a 6,500-foot well and hit the best gas well we would ever drill in Parker County. We didn't drill any more wells on the ranch. Within a year, however, we noticed that four or five wells had lined up across the north perimeter of our ranch, the Airport Road. We drilled wells on our land offsetting each and every one of them, ten straight wells in all. Of the ten wells, only the ninth was dry. The rest roared in for as much as two million feet of gas a day. All real good wells, considering the depth and cost.

Dad and Granddad's knack for smelling oil and gas was proven once again. We drilled fourteen wells and struck gas on thirteen. The ranch, for which Dad had paid approximately $600,000 in the fifties, was paying for itself every three months.

Eventually, though, it was time for me to learn another, equally important, part of the wildcatter's business. I was transferred from the land department to the drilling department and began working as a roughneck on the wells. Our engineer, Fred Rabalais, took me under his wing, just as Duane McDaniel had in the courthouse, teaching me how to strap pipe, measure casing, measure tubing, read well logs, and perforate the wells. I loved life on a drilling rig. Land was fun, leasing was fun, but my personality was roughnecking. I respected the "Iron Men" who worked on the rigs despite the weather and slept on the rig floor at night.

I had found a home in the oil patch, the rough end, but once again it was not destined to be a permanent residence. Roughnecking was fun, but I knew there were bigger things out there for me to experience, so I went out and landed another job.

The United States marshal for the Northern District of Texas was a retired marine captain. We'd known each other for several years, and he respected my brief tour in the Marine Corps. He asked me if I'd like to become a deputy U.S. marshal and work guarding the federal courts and tracking down federal fugitives. I was young, and it sounded exciting. So I signed up for three years of part-time duty. "Sure," I answered. "I love hunting, and hunting something that shoots back has got to be fun!"

I partnered up with Deputy Marshal Larry Fowler, who was a piece of work himself. Larry was a street fighter and street smart as well. I can't count the times that Larry and I were crouched over, hidden in an alley or hedge behind some unsuspecting fugitive's house. We'd start to move in, and Larry would tap me on the shoulder and say "Hey, Charlie."

"Yes, Larry?" I would respond.

And in his ever reassuring voice he would say, "Don't forget, we're outnumbered."

Back in the oil patch, Dad and Granddad got heavily involved in a deep gas play in the Wind River Basin of Wyoming. Big deep drilling rigs were hard to come by, so they had partnered up with an old buddy in the drilling business and were going to build four big deep rigs and put them to work in the play. It was a new, exciting gamble for my family, and I just had to be a part of it.

So, when the first rig was ready to go to Wyoming, I was ready to go with it. I put my hard hat under my arm and headed to Wyoming for six years. John Bradbury, our new drilling manager, picked me up at the airport. John looked like a mean, upper middle-aged Mr. Clean. Six foot-plus, upwards of two hundred pounds, he had a shaved head, horn-rim glasses secured by an elastic band stretched tight across his skull, and his pant legs tucked inside pointy toed cowboy boots.

When we arrived at Rig #21, it was bigger than I ever dreamed. The rig floor where the roughnecks work was twenty-five feet above ground level and the massive steel derrick towered 140 feet above that. The rig I worked on in Texas would fit in the doghouse of this one. The engine room had four 1,350-horse-powered Caterpillar diesels in a row. They powered four AC generators that sent juice to a rectifier that converted AC to DC and directed power to every arm of the rig. When the rig picked up on the drill string, those four "Cats" would suck in a deep breath of mountain air and blow blue smoke fifteen feet in the air. Shit, this was heaven. Just being on the rig sent chills up my spine.

I was eager to learn, and the Rocky Mountain drilling hands helped me tremendously. On breaks in the field, I attended some of the best drilling schools in the world. First, "Blowout Control" at LSU, where you learn how to avoid calling in the "Boot and Coots" of the world. Then, Halliburton Energy Institute in Duncan, Oklahoma, where you learn how to complete oil and gas wells. Finally, Preston Moore drilling school in Houston, where you learn the chemistry and physics of drilling wells. Five years later, after arriving on the big rigs, I got my chance to run the rig at Teepee Flats #16-1.

Teepee Flats was a twenty thousand-foot wildcat. We drilled it with Texaco. Dad and Granddad let me run the show. To start out we drilled through six thousand feet of solid granite, and we ran a world record six thousand feet of twenty-inch casing that weighed over a million pounds. When the rig moved the casing down the hole you could feel the floor buckle underneath your feet. This was what the oil field was all about, what everyone called "BIG IRON!"

The big, deep gas wells were giants. Anywhere from fifty to several hundred billion cubic feet of gas could be recovered from each well. In other words, the wells could cost anywhere from $10 million to $35 million to drill, but they would pay you back anywhere from $75 to $500 million each.

I'd come back to Fort Worth about once a month to rest and take care of office business. The local hangout at the time was the Rangoon Racquet Club, Fort Worth's version of New York's Harry Cipriani (if you squinted just right). One evening at the Rangoon I spotted Kit Tennison, a dark-haired beauty with haunting eyes.

Like my Mom and Dad, Kit and I had known each other all our lives. I knew her as a girl and watched her become an incredible lady: smart, cultured, and beautiful. She was the daughter of big game hunter Harry "Bwana" Tennison and his wife, Gloria, whose family owned the local Coca Cola franchise. But she was several years younger, so our paths rarely crossed. The night I saw her, Kit was spending her first night out with some friends after recovering from a near death accident. She had been trapped in a stall with a mare and colt and the mare kicked her almost to death.

Her eyes caught mine and that was it. Almost instinctively I went over, picked her up in my arms, carried her back to my table, and sat her on my lap. It wasn't a pushy move on my part; we were friends. "You're a beautiful woman, Kit Tennison," I told her that night.

She laughed, wrestled free, and went back to her table. I just retrieved her. Once again, the visit was short, but I got my point across. I told her I was going back to Wyoming in the morning but I'd call her as soon as I got back. When I left my house the next morning to go to the airport, Kit had left me a glass of freshly squeezed orange juice on the hood of my car. Kit and I dated for several months as I traveled back and forth to Wyoming.

Back in Wyoming, we had encountered massive gas sands at 18,000 feet. Clearly the Teepee Flats #16-1 was going to make a huge well. Granddad called me and told me I was going to need to leave the rig and go buy royalty. "Charlie, looks like we may have a discovery," he said. "You've bought royalty before, so I've got a job for you."

He had already located the owners. They were in Thousand Oaks, California; Omaha, Nebraska; and Fairbanks, Alaska. I called Kit and told her to pack her bags. "We're going to buy royalty," I said. She didn't know what royalty was, but she was ready to go. We hit the ground running, knocking on doors all day long. Buying royalty in Fairbanks, we ended up spending a night in Point Barrow, Alaska. We checked in to the Top of the World Hotel where they locked the doors at 8 P.M. so the drunken Eskimos wouldn't wreak havoc with the guests. We stared out the window at the ice covered Arctic Ocean and the Point Barrow Bordello, where the Eskimos crawled in and out all night under the northern lights.

Once the royalties were bought, Kit and I took a vacation in the city we both love most, New York. There, on the twenty-fourth floor of the Carlyle Hotel, during a room service breakfast, I looked directly into those beautiful blue eyes and said, "Kit, I love you."

A big smile washed across her face and tears welled up in her eyes. Suddenly, she threw the window open, grabbed a stack of pancakes and began sailing them out the window onto Madison Avenue.

Returning home, Dad and I went to Wyoming to bring in personally the Teepee well. The eighteen thousand-foot-deep well was ready. The entire hole had been cased with five-inch pipe, and two-and-seven-eighths-inch tubing ran the full length as well, from which the gas would actually be produced. A Christmas tree secured everything on the surface. A flow line ran from the tree to the nearby sludge pit and a bucket of flaming diesel hung from the end of the line to ignite the gas when it hit the surface.

We lowered the gun on the end of a wireline into the hole. The gun was twenty-five feet long with fifty strategically placed jet shots that would blow holes in the casing allowing the formation gas to start flowing up the tubing. When we fired the gun you could feel the wireline truck move. This was a good sign, but the best sign was the instantaneous 1,400 pounds of pressure that registered on the pressure gauge on the tree. Once we got the gun out of the hole, the pressure steadily increased to 2,500 pounds. When we opened the valve, the well came in big time. The pressure immediately cut in half, but fluid started flowing out of our line into the pit. At first, it was just a garden hose stream but then more and more came out until it was blasting a hundred feet across the pit. Then, the gas hit the surface and exploded with a boom.

The well paused for just a second, then spit out one last slug of water. Finally, the diesel ignited the gas and blew a flare two hundred feet across the pit with the sound of an F-14 Tom Cat. Teepee #16 was for real! She was a big discovery flowing close to twenty million feet a day. I gave Dad a hug. When I looked back at the flow line, it had frosted over as white as snow from the force of the expanding gas.

"Let her clean up," Dad ordered. "Then, we'll move the rigs two miles west and start another one." With a smile on his face Dad turned to the rig crew and said, "Looks like we found a gas field, boys!"

I had learned a lot in my years in the oil field. But the time soon came to return home to work with Dickie, Dad, and Granddad in the office. I retired my hard hat, from permanent duty anyway, turned in my badge, and Kit and I got married.

I moved into an office in the Moncrief Building and began my career as a full-time oil operator. From my desk, I figured I was safe from blowouts and thieves.

Of course, I would be wrong about both.

★ ★ ★

Uncle Dick was forty-eight when he had a stroke. He was in his bathrobe on a boat in the summer of 1970 with his wife, Dee, in Marathon, Florida. Dee called an ambulance, but Dick refused to get in. He demanded to return to Fort Worth—and Uncle Dick always got his way. So Granddad flew to Florida and brought him back to Texas in his plane. Dick spent some time in a Houston hospital before going home. There, in a rented hospital bed, surrounded by electric trains and go-carts, Dick Moncrief died.

His heirs were his adopted son, Mike, and his two children by Dee, Richard Barto and Lee Wiley. All could live rich from their inheritance, which was good for Richard, whom everyone called Monty. When it came to honky-tonking, few could compare with my cousin Monty. He was six feet tall and 250 pounds. With an inherited monthly income of between $200,000 and $400,000, Monty was a high roller. If somebody needed a drink, no problem. If somebody needed a loan, no problem, either. He'd pull a few bills off of his wad, and the party would rage on.

"I met him in a bar," remembered Monty's bodyguard, Rule Brown, former deputy sheriff, professional boxer, and black belt. Rule's first glimpse of my cousin was typical. Monty was standing in a bar drinking a rum and Coke and surrounded by a crowd. Of beautiful women. "He got in some trouble with some guys. He was buying everybody drinks, including these guys' women. They got pissed. And Monty couldn't fight worth a damn."

Granddad once hired Rule Brown to retrieve Monty from the Woodstock music festival in 1969. "He wasn't hard to find," remembers Rule. "He was big and tall and naked with a woman on his shoulders."

"Granddaddy says, 'Come home!' " Rule shouted.

"Tell Granddad I'm havin' a party and will come home when I'm through," replied Monty.

It took Rule Brown and two hired hands to wrestle Monty into the car. They dropped him, dirty from a week without a bath, in Granddad's office.

Back home, Monty drove a Ferrari, a Porsche, and a Lamborghini and sometimes spent $1,500 a night on cocktails. We lost track of his marriages: cocktail waitresses, socialites, one-night stands. Sometimes, the marriage lasted years, sometimes months, in one case days. In the early eighties, Mike asked for my help in curbing his brother Monty's drinking and drugging. I wanted to help, but not being schooled in the science of intervention, didn't know how. Monty's appetite for the wild life continued apace.

Deep down, Monty wanted to be an oilman like his grandfather whom he adored. He founded Montco Oil company with his cousin, Stan Wiley. But they hit mostly dry holes. In nightclubs, Monty walked around with a test tube full of crude, letting everyone smell the oil. "This is what we hit today!" he'd exclaim.

Once he was on the line for a six-figure marker at the MGM Grand in Vegas. The casino sent a goon squad to Fort Worth to collect. Monty was on his boat; Rule Brown was guarding the house and immediately called Granddad. Rule took the bill collectors to the office in Monty's Rolls Royce. Granddad, backed up by a team of off-duty Fort Worth cops, determined the men were legit and wrote out a check.

Like her brother Monty, Lee Wiley lived off her inheritance, until she ran into trouble. She was driving down a South Texas highway with her two kids and her third husband, Larry Moncrief, an Austin hairdresser who adopted the Moncrief name. Suddenly, Lee opened the Winnebago's door and said to her children, "I'll see you in heaven," and *jumped*. She survived the jump, but was left mentally and physically incapacitated for life.

One of Uncle Dick's three children would come to wear the Moncrief name like some shiny crown. But the blood of his father and grandfather—Jack and Ferrell Trapp—ran deep in his veins. Mike Moncrief has the Trapp profile: big bulbous nose, smallish eyes, and a tall, rugged frame. Like his father, he never liked school, and he readily admitted it. His dreams lay somewhere outside the halls of higher learning. He wanted to work on a ranch or as a cop or oil field roughneck, like his granddaddy, Ferrell Trapp.

But, mostly, Mike just drifted, coasting through a military high school in Texas. He almost flunked out of TCU in Fort Worth. Then, considering becoming a cattleman, he sweet-talked the dean at an agricultural college called Tarleton in Stephenville, Texas, to overlook his grades and accept him. "He voted me least likely to ever succeed," Mike later told a reporter. "But he said he'd give me a chance."

Mike found his niche at Tarleton. His grades improved. But it wasn't schoolwork that excited him. It was *getting elected!* He became the school mascot and served in that role as if he'd been elected college president. Wearing a shocking purple cowboy suit, he'd race out on a horse during football games, galloping through the end zone every time the team scored.

Spurred on by this first taste of politics, Mike ran for Tarleton student body president—and won. He'd found his future. "It was more fun than anything I could remember," he said. By the time he was twenty-six, he'd been elected a representative in the Texas state legislature, the beginning of a political career that would be liberally mixed with good deeds for the underprivileged. Mike served three terms as Tarrant County judge, two terms as a state representative and, finally, his present office as state senator, gaining fame as an advocate for abused women, children and the mentally ill. "I've probably put in more long hours than they have or ever thought of," Mike once said in an interview of our side of the family. "Now it might not be on a rig somewhere or in the middle of a blinding snowstorm in Wyoming. But it might be on the floor of the Senate, trying to deal with issues like family violence. Or it might be sitting until three o'clock or four o'clock in the morning, listening to public testimony about patients being locked up for insurance money."

With his money and political muscle, Granddad was always there for Mike, with contacts, moral support, and even lending his plane to ferry politicians between Austin, Washington, and Fort Worth. Granddad could pull plenty of strings, and Mike reaped the benefit of Granddad's political largesse.

Mike and his brother and sister left the family business to our side of the family. Of course, Granddad had already made them rich. He created trusts for each of the seven grandchildren in the sixties. Then, in the seventies, the enormous Jay Field in Florida blew in. A royalty play ensued, and each grandkid was entitled to buy a part of the royalty. The Jay Field was one of the biggest strikes of Granddad's career—and each of the seven Moncrief grandchildren were on their way to becoming millionaires. By the time Granddad died, the money he invested for us had made each of us worth upwards of ten million dollars. Mike and his brother and sister were drawing one million dollars a year in interest alone.

I liked Mike. He was always friendly, always cordial. I never thought that there was anything but love between his side of the family and ours. I knew he didn't share our political views, but I could care less about his politics. Sometimes, I heard that Mike referred to our family as "the rich Moncriefs," but I never gave it much thought. There were two distinct sides to the Moncrief clan. But I never even conceived of the possibility of a family rift. We didn't see our side as any different from theirs. We were all Moncriefs. When I would see Mike and his wife, Rosie, or Monty and his wife, Jan, we greeted each other as kin. Both Mike and Monty depended on our side of the family. Monty, especially, would always ask about various wells that we were drilling. He was genuinely interested, as was Jan.

There were only two times when I felt that Mike showed dislike for our side. The first was when he came to see Dad and asked to serve on the board of the Moncrief Foundation. Dad decided against it. Why? Mike's philosophy is different from ours. We're conservative, he's liberal. We're Republicans, he's a Democrat. The second occurence of friction was much earlier, when my brother Herbie bashed Mike across the back of his head with a shovel when they were kids. The scarred area on Mike's head grew a patch of white hair in an otherwise brown thatch.

Later, Mike said he felt an "imbalance of love" between our side of the family and his. "Tex has always been possessive of my grandparents," he would later say in an interview. "It's like he says, 'That's my Mom and Dad and I can love them, but no one else can.'" On holidays, Mike would drive by Granddad's house to make sure none of our cars were parked out front before he visited.

After Granddad's death, we continued business as usual at Moncrief Oil. When there was a well to be drilled or any business decision to be made that involved Mike, R. B. (Monty), or Lee, they were invited to the office to be advised of the situation. They could make their decision to go along with the deal or to decline. Usually, they would take our advice. With the exception of their uncle Wade Wiley—Aunt Dee's brother—they never had much understanding of the oil and gas business.

Mike and Monty had a couple of trusts and miscellaneous investments on their own, which they ran out of their offices in the Fort Worth Club Tower. But we handled at least 90 percent of their income. Mike or Monty never balked at this arrangement. We even handled all of their accounting at no charge, communicating through our respective accountants: Mike and Monty were represented by Jerry Goodwin; we were represented by our in-house comptroller Bill Jarvis. All they had to do was to send a messenger twice a month to pick up their six-figure revenue checks.

When Granddad died in 1986, everything changed. Before, Granddad's word was law. He ran the family, and no one dared to dispute it. When he was gone, we became two separate families with nothing to bind us together any longer. The trouble started in early 1988. A Fort Worth attorney who had been helping Dad with Granddad's estate told us about the Gallo provision of the IRS code, named after the wine maker. The provision would let our grandmother make a cash gift to each of her grandchildren. The gift turned out to be two million dollars per grandchild or fourteen million dollars total. With the money, we could purchase grandmother's oil and gas properties at the value that had been approved by the IRS at the time of Granddad's death: $1.8 million per grandchild or a total of $12.6 million. This arrangement would let us avoid high "generation-skipping" taxes. If Elizabeth, whom we called "Granddear," lived for three years from the date of the gift, then no tax on the gift would be due.

Granddad's last will and testament left everything to Granddear for her life. Then it passed on to the seven grandchildren. All of his oil properties were to be split evenly among the seven, with one exception. Because of Louisiana law, the Louisiana oil properties had to be split equally between the two sides of the family. So our side with four grandchildren would get one-eighth each, and Mike's side with three children would receive one-sixth each. However, none of us would get anything until Granddear passed away. We ended up buying her oil properties equally among us in 1988 four years prior to her death, which effectively nullified the Louisiana deal.

"Tex hoodwinked us and we didn't holler about it," Mike's accountant, Jerry Goodwin, would later tell the press. This was, of course, categorically false. Dad didn't hoodwink anybody. The deal he made was to Mike and his family's great advantage, which I'll explain soon.

Mike said he began guarding his side of the family's business interests from then on.

★ ★ ★

Granddear died at home on August 17, 1992, six years after Granddad's death. Dad called Dr. McDowell who came over and pronounced her dead. Dad then called Greenwood Funeral Home to pick up the body. Monty and Jan learned of her death that evening as well, but they did not go to the house. Apparently Mike went by the house the day after her death.

The funeral was at 11:15 two days after her death. The coffin faced the Moncrief Mausoleum in Greenwood Cemetery. There were covered metal chairs flanking each side. Tex Moncrief and our side of the Moncrief family sat on the east side; Mike and his side of the family sat on the west side. "You could see daggers flying out of their eyes," land man Duane McDaniel said of Mike's side of the family.

We later learned that Mike was mad that Granddear wasn't taken to the hospital instead of the funeral home. He thought Tex had manipulated her properties and had gotten her to sign various wills before her death. As executor of his mother's estate, Dad was responsible for distributing Granddear's possessions. Mike felt he didn't get his share of Granddear's personal effects. Visiting Granddear's house shortly after she died, Mike told her caretaker that he felt like he'd been treated like a stepchild. He asked Granddear's employees about her state of mind when she signed her various wills. He was especially concerned about revisions that assigned her approximately $10.8 million in cash assets and real estate to a family foundation, instead of being split among the seven grandchildren, as the more lucrative oil and gas properties had been. I believe that Mike saw the foundation, which is under Dad's control, as just another vehicle to cheat his side of the family.

A month later, at 10 A.M. on September 26, Mike called Dad and asked him to meet him at Granddear's house. Mike asked Dad to sit down for a talk in the living room. He told Dad that his side of the family never had the relationship that Tex had with his father.

He felt that he'd always been left out. He told him he felt his side of the family had been treated like stepchildren.

"Well, Mike, your basic philosophy has always been different from my father's and mine," said Dad. "You've never been a businessman. Ever since your father died in 1970, most of the money you've made is due to oil deals my father put you in. And since my dad and I worked together, those deals were the result of what we did in the oil business."

These differences were important for Dad. "Mike, you've been a politician all your life," Dad continued. "You've never worked in the oil business or, for that matter, any business. Your brother never worked. I loved your father. He was my brother. But after he made some money and moved back to Fort Worth in the middle to late fifties, he never worked. We've taken care of your side of the family for years."

Mike got mad.

"You've made a lot of money, and you're just gonna die a rich, old lonely man," he told Dad.

"Well, Mike, that's your opinion," Dad replied.

Mike wouldn't let it pass.

"I know positively that you've taken properties out of Granddad's estate and put them in your name!" he said.

Dad stood up to leave and with a wave of his hand said, "This is the end of the meeting—conversation over."

They walked out the kitchen door. Outside, Dad wanted to tell Mike that he hadn't been cheated out of anything. He pointed his finger. "Mike, I wanna tell ya..." he began.

As soon as Dad raised his finger, Mike bristled.

"Don't you hit me!" Mike shouted.

"Hit ya?" said Dad. "I'm not gonna hit you. But I know you'd rather just smash my face than anything in this world."

Dad turned, got into his car, and drove away. The battle had begun.

★ ★ ★

Two months passed. Just before Christmas of 1992, Mike sent his comptroller, Jerry Goodwin, to meet with Dad and me. Jerry questioned Dad's handling of the sale of Granddear's oil properties to the seven grandchildren.

The sale to the seven grandchildren was an extraordinary windfall; had the seven grandchildren not bought the properties, Granddear would have continued to receive the oil income until her death in 1992. At this time, the properties would have gone to us grandchildren, but it would have been subject to 55 percent inheritance tax. By purchasing the properties upon Granddad's death in 1988, we were able to buy the properites at a price that paid for itself in two and a half years—and avoided all inheritance taxes. Best of all, thanks to the Gallo provision approved by the IRS, Granddear was able to loan her grandkids the money to purchase the properties—and we didn't have to pay it back. The sale made each of us grandkids a separate fortune. But Jerry saw things differently. He thought that the two million dollars each of us paid to our grandmother for her properties should have been returned to us upon her death.

"Jerry, you're kidding me, aren't you?" I asked him when he told me how he and Mike saw the situation.

Our meeting came to an abrupt halt. That was the last we heard from Mike until July 1994. Dad filed suit over gas pricing in federal court in Wyoming against Williston Basin Pipeline Co. We figured

Williston Basin owed us as much as forty million dollars. Not long after the trial got underway, the judge asked all seven grandchildren to sign on individually as plaintiffs, instead of merely filing the suit as the estate of W. A. Moncrief. We sent the legal documents to Mike and Monty for their signatures. Their response was surprising. They weren't going to sign because they didn't believe Dad owned 50 percent of the properties. They didn't abide by Dad and Granddad's forty-one-year partnership, an unwritten agreement to split proceeds on oil and gas properties they drilled together. They felt the properties belonged exclusively to the seven grandchildren— without Dad's 50 percent substantially reducing their cut.

Dad, Dickie, and I met Mike in his office. We did our best to convince Mike and his siblings to sign the papers. But Mike wouldn't budge. "The last time I signed something, I got screwed!" Mike said, staring at Dad. "I'm not going to sign something that says you have 50 percent."

We told Mike that we could argue the ownership of the properties among ourselves. But why hinder the progress of a lawsuit that could bring in as much as $40 million? Dad invited Mike to send his lawyers, accountants, and advisers to our offices to examine our books. "Just don't hold up our progress in court!" he said.

Like Granddad could smell oil while sitting at his desk, Dad can smell a lawsuit. And he smelled trouble coming from Mike. My brother, Dickie, asked, "Why don't you let me go and talk to Mike?" Dad told him to go ahead.

Sitting side by side with Dickie in July 1994, Mike let loose. He was bitter that Tex was Granddad's favorite, instead of his father, Dick. He felt his side of the family hadn't had the opportunity to participate in the family business. Dickie sensed that Mike was ready to make a move.

"I understand how you feel," Dickie said. "My Dad may be tough. But you can't sue Dad just because you're mad at him. And what you're talking about—somebody taking something that is rightfully yours—well, that just isn't true. Everybody in this family has always been honest."

Mike disagreed.

"I'm going to give you some advice," Dickie said. "All of our records are available to you. Satisfy yourself. Hire the toughest, smartest, best accountant you know. If you find something wrong, then you've got material for the lawyers to work from."

Dickie paused for emphasis. "Then, you can sue the hell out of everybody."

But Mike wouldn't listen.

"I have a responsibility to protect my mother and my brother and sister, and I've got to do just that," Mike said.

Dickie rose to leave. "Well, then, let me tell you what will happen," Dickie said. "I know we've never done anything dishonest. So you can't win. If you sue my father, you're going to be viewed as an opportunist. You're a politician, Mike. You're in the public eye. Political support is your life. All you've got is political capital. And you'll lose every bit of support you have. Every powerful, wealthy backer you have here, the people who give the money, are going to side with my father against you. You will lose. You'll ruin your life for no reason."

In August Mike filed a cross-claim in Wyoming federal court against us, claiming that Dad had no legal ownership in the Powell PMU oil and gas field. The federal judge refused to listen to a family dispute and remanded it to the Wyoming state court.

From this point on, the two sides of the Moncrief family would communicate through their lawyers.

Chapter Four

The Snitch

I REMEMBER LEAVING DEE KELLY'S OFFICE and heading home the day of the raid. It was closing in on seven o'clock. My daughter Gloria was a seventh grader at Fort Worth Country Day, and our ten-year-old twin daughters, Celia and Adelaide, were in fifth grade. How would I explain all this to them? My wife Kit and I try to teach our kids to be patriots, to be respectful of the U.S. government. B. B., one of my two daughters from my first marriage, would grow up to be a marine, just like me. How was I supposed to foster that type of faith in our country while telling my girls that the U.S. government was accusing us of a major tax crime?

By the time I arrived, Kit and the girls were having dinner in the kitchen. The house was quiet. Even the dogs, four dachshunds, an Australian shepherd, and a border collie, just stared at me. The dachshunds usually raise holy hell when I come home. But I guess my late arrival threw them. Clearly this was no time for small talk. I decided just to lay it on the line:

"Girls, this morning our office was raided by the Internal Revenue Service, the IRS. We don't know what we're under investigation for, but we haven't done anything wrong, and we're going to get to the bottom of it. This news is going to be all over the newspapers and radio tomorrow, and it will be all over your school. Knowing kids, you may be teased about it, so don't be shocked if someone says something about it to you."

I expected that to rattle them a little. "Just be tough," I continued, "and let them know that your family didn't do anything wrong."

I looked up from my little speech and stared into their faces.

"Dad, what's the IRS?" one of the twins asked me.

"It's the taxing authority of the United States," I said. "It's the people who handle the tax returns and...."

The twins nodded, as if they understood. When I tried to explain the raid and the army of armed agents, they just asked, "Why would somebody do that?"

I tried to explain. I repeated to them that we hadn't done anything wrong. I said we would soon get to the bottom of the whole mess. They finished dinner and got up to study.

That moment, looking into my daughters' eyes turned out to be the best thing I could have done for my spirits. I could see the faith they had in me. The funny thing is, they gave me strength by assuming I already had it. Kit and I talked throughout the evening, just as we always do. Kit says I was frantic, repeatedly asking, "What can it be? What can it be?" I was bewildered. I felt as if I were in a vacuum. But Kit turned out to be as strong as the girls. Kit runs some of our ranching operations. She knows how and where our money is invested, and she's familiar with our oil properties and who owns what. That night, we collapsed in bed and tried to sleep but ended up staying awake all night, going over it all again and again, asking each other, "What can it be?"

Aside from the girls, I knew Kit's biggest concern would be the "Cowgirl." She had recently been elected president of the National Cowgirl Museum and Hall of Fame, which used to be located in the little Texas panhandle town of Hereford. Then, Anne Marion, the Burnett Oil heiress and the owner of the mammoth 6666 Ranch, helped organize a group of community leaders to move the museum to Fort Worth. Anne saw the museum as a way of honoring not only the legendary cowgirls like Annie Oakley and Dale Evans and Patsy Cline, but also contemporary women artists, entertainers, and ranchers.

Anne Marion and Ed Bass, scion of one of Fort Worth's other oil families, assembled a committee of high-powered cowgirls to get the job done, and they elected Kit president. Kit had been working hard setting the groundwork to raise seventeen million dollars for the museum's new home. "I'm worried that the bad publicity might affect fundraising," she told me on the night of the raid. "Do you think I should step down as president?"

I told Kit not to worry about stepping down just yet. "Just let it ride," I said. "Talk to Anne and if she thinks something is wrong, she'll tell you."

The kids at Gloria's school didn't really care about the raid. But the teachers sure did. At Fort Worth Country Day, the Moncrief name is very familiar; the library and the science center are named in our honor. In one of Gloria's classes, the teacher said, "Gloria, why don't you stand up and tell the class about what recently happened to your family."

The teacher probably didn't mean to be harsh, but Gloria didn't know that. She stood up. "Yes, they did raid my family's office, but they made a mistake," Gloria told the class. "We haven't done anything wrong, and we're going to prove it."

★ ★ ★

IRS agents had tracked down our employees one by one, interviewing them at home. Some of the employees were brought before a grand jury, as the IRS searched for improprieties to bolster a criminal indictment against us. Kay Capps's work for us was so technically oriented that the IRS realized there was no reason to take her before the grand jury at the onset. If they had quizzed Kay in front of a bunch of citizen jurors, they wouldn't know what she was talking about. So the IRS interrogated Kay privately. This also allowed Kay to be accompanied by her attorney which is not allowed with a grand jury.

"I think each interview lasted about five hours or more, and they were something I would never want to go through again," she later told me. "At the first one there were probably five agents, and they would all ask me the same question over and over again in a different way. They didn't know anything about the oil and gas business, so that made it worse because they were trying to trip me up, and I was almost tickled about the way they talked because they weren't making any sense. They didn't even know how to ask the questions, so I had to be real careful what I was saying, because I wanted to say, 'You don't even know what you're talking about.' "

According to Kay's notes, the IRS interrogations followed six different, but not unrelated, trains of thought, each one related to a specific area of perceived criminal activity.

Meanwhile, I began writing down everything that might be the slightest bit questionable. In compiling this list, I had to figure out what the IRS was after, and I was the only one who could do it.

With the exception of Dad, no one knew the organization as well as I did. No one else had spent as much time with Granddad and Dad as I had. I knew virtually everything that had gone on behind closed doors, and I had to dig it up and get it out on the table for our lawyers to digest. For the next year, I would push myself for every shred of evidence. I became utterly obsessed. I would work when I was asleep, waking with a start, remembering, for example, something like the fact that I had always driven a company car, but never reported my personal usage of the car. I would get out of bed as quietly as possible, close the bedroom door, go to the computer and add the item to the list. I soon had compiled what I called my "List of Twenty-Five." The list contained everything that could even remotely be considered a tax impropriety.

No large corporate concern can operate without potential tax violations. Especially an oil family with a myriad of oil properties that might have a hundred ownership interests each. I had scrupulously compiled pages of possibilities, ranging from Dad's sale to me of 10 percent of his interest in the $400 million Madden-Deep unit in Wyoming, to a dozen intrafamily loans, to a set of Dallas Cowboys season tickets charged to a family corporation.

Looking at my List of Twenty-Five, I hadn't found any smoking guns, but I was also not naïve. Anything can happen in a court of law. Just as the IRS was investigating every inch of our organization, we had to investigate ourselves.

★ ★ ★

The day after the raid, Dad, Dickie, and I met in Dee Kelly's office with his top trial lawyer, Marshall Searcy, and the distinguished tax lawyer Clive Bode. The first step was to get an accounting firm to begin examining our tax returns in an attempt to discover what the IRS found troubling. Dee Kelly suggested Price Waterhouse, and we said, "Done."

Next, we began to consider lawyers. There are the top five criminal tax lawyers in the country, followed by a big step down to the next twenty or so. We didn't need to drop below the top five; whatever had driven the IRS to a raid of this magnitude deserved the best defense money could buy. The best criminal tax lawyers were in Washington, D.C. Their fees averaged $500 an hour. The first names on Dee Kelly's list were Jim Bruton of Williams & Connolly and Robert S. Bennett of Skadden, Arps, Slate, Meagher & Flom. Bruton was a "facts man" and a former Justice Department official. Bob Bennett was the number one criminal trial lawyer in the world, the personal attorney of President Bill Clinton. Back then, he was representing former House Ways and Means Committee chairman Dan Rostenkowski.

"Bob Bennett is the best there is," said Kelly's associate Marshall Searcy. "I've worked with him, and he's the man for the job!"

But Kelly was hesitant about Bennett, whom he described as about as laid-back as a grizzly bear. "He's damn sure high priced, and Skadden will charge you an arm and a leg," he said. "The press also follows Bennett everywhere he moves. If we brought him to Fort Worth next week, the newspapers would cover the arrival like the marines climbing Mount Suribachi."

"Get in touch with him and see if he'll take the case," said Dad.

"Charlie, what about Bruton for you?" Kelly asked me.

"Sure, that's fine with me," I said. But how the hell was I supposed to know? I was lost. Maybe Dad and Dickie felt the same way, but they didn't express it to me. The names—Bennett, Bruton, criminal tax attorneys—had me spinning. I felt as helpless as on the day of the raid. The attorneys were brainstorming. I was just a visitor.

On September 22, three weeks after our initial meeting in Kelly's office, Bob Bennett arrived in Fort Worth. The purpose of Bennett's visit was to see if there was "chemistry" between us. We later learned "chemistry" was a prerequisite for Bennett to take on a case. Maybe he wanted to see if we were innocent, too, although I don't think that was the most critical question.

Bennett was hardly a grizzly. He seemed more like a big, over-grown, all-American teddy bear: brown haired, round faced, pleas-antly disheveled, with his socks falling down around his ankles and his shirttail half tucked. We liked him immediately. He was solid. He already knew the particulars of the case. After lunch, Bennett stood for a moment, habitually flopping his necktie or hanging his hands alongside his ample belly. He spoke in a brassy Brooklynese.

"Mr. Moncrief, or, rather, Tex, I'd like you to come to Washington to learn something about your business and to get to know you better," he said at last.

★ ★ ★

A week later, Dad flew alone to Washington in the Lucky Liz. He walked into Skadden Arps's offices in the shadow of the Capitol. Bob Bennett took Dad into a conference room with his right-hand man, Ed Ross, and a young assistant. "They didn't know a drilling rig from a horse rig," Dad recalled later. So they grilled him for hours about the oil business. And Dad gave them a lesson in Wildcatting 101.

"Oil is different from any other business in the world," he began. "Especially when you're talking about wildcatters. Wildcat-ters like us are a dyin' breed."

"What's a wildcatter, Tex?" Ross asked.

"I guess the best way to put it is that we're not corner-shooters," Dad answered. "A corner-shooter is an independent producer who is always snugglin' up to someone else's oil well. You've heard of slant-hole drillers, haven't you?"

He looked at the attorneys' faces: totally blank.

"A slant-hole driller would move a rig in right on the fence line of someone else's producing well, then, if he still wasn't close enough, they'd just drill at an angle, until they got into the other man's oil," he said. "They outlawed that a long time ago, but corner-shooters are still out there. They try and pick up a lease in the midst of other activity. They may not hit it big, but they can always make a livin'."

He paused for emphasis.

"A wildcatter's a completely different breed. We're elephant hunters. We're drilling rank wildcats, remote exploratory wells absolutely out in the middle of nowhere. We might be a hundred miles from the nearest producing well. We might put nine million dollars in a well. If we hit, it can be a bonanza. If not, we pump cement into it and move on down the road."

Ross looked incredulous. "You're telling me that a well can cost you nine million dollars to drill? Nine million dollars, Tex? Most people never see nine million dollars in a lifetime. But if a well is dry, you pump cement down the hole, weld a steel cap on top of it, and just move on?"

Bennett jumped to his feet. "Goddamn it, Tex, that's just crazy!"

"No, it's just part of the business," he said. "It makes you sick to your stomach. But you gotta face facts: eight out of nine wildcat wells are dry holes. I've easily drilled a hundred and fifty million dollars' worth of dry holes. I can remember a couple of dry holes costing about twenty million apiece."

"Okay, let's move on," said Bennett. "The search warrant discusses the transfer of properties between family entities. How does that work?"

Dad leaned back in his chair. "First of all, there's never been any transfer of properties between the entities," he said. "We've owned our percentages of the properties since their inception. If the IRS is saying I'm transferring interest in wells to my kids, or moving these properties around in some illegal fashion, that's just not the case. There's never been any transfer of ownership that's not completely aboveboard. In other words, the children and I all have owned our interest before the well was drilled."

"What's your relationship with your boys, with your family?" asked Ross.

"Charlie's my right-hand man," he said. "He's been in the business with me all along. Dickie's in the business and participates in our exploration efforts, but for the most part he has his own operations. He's not involved in our day-to-day activities. Tom isn't involved in the business to any extent at all. He has his own investments that he handles. Same goes for my oldest, Bill. So it's really just Charlie and me in the day-to-day operation, just like it was with my dad and me."

"Then, who owns the wells?" Ross asked. "To what extent do you participate with one another and in what percentages?"

"Historically, Dad and I split all of the deals we did together fifty-fifty. But oftentimes, one or the other of us would take a larger percent or the entire part of a deal. How we let the grandchildren in on the deals—whether it was my kids or my brother Dick's kids—was completely arbitrary. Most of the deals they weren't in on at all. By and large, the oil, gas and mineral leases that we took were taken in the name of my dad, W. A. Moncrief, and the wells were drilled either in his name or in my name. And one of the two of us would be the owner of record. The ownership percentages of anybody else in the well—grandchildren or any outsiders—might not be reflected in the county records or tax roles, only in our own accounting records."

"That just doesn't even sound right," said Bennett. "You mean you go out and drill a well for nine million dollars, and you got fifteen partners, and there are no legal documents that show what percentage a person owns in the well, except for what's on your books?"

"Yeah, but that's always been enough," he said. "We'd have a letter agreement or a handshake. And, between you and me, I'd just as soon have a handshake. My dad and I have drilled many wells with major companies on a telephone call—without even the handshake—and then, later, maybe months later, when the well was either plugged or a producer, the paperwork would be done."

The lawyers looked pale as sheets.

"That's the way we've always done it in our industry," Tex said, shrugging. "That way, if we drill a dry hole, we just walk away from it. We haven't put all of these deeds of records in the county courthouse and done all this title work in making assignments of ownership. Because who's gonna claim a percentage of nothin'? Now, if the well's a producer, that's a different story: then each person's interest is put on record and formal assignments are made of each and every mineral lease to the respective owners. But in a lot of cases, especially with family members, we *never* made formal assignments—until Dad died."

"You mean, in some cases, you didn't even make assignments to your kids?"

"No, why should we get involved in all that paperwork when the interest was shown on our accounting records?" he said. "We're wildcatters, not bookkeepers. We've just never made assignments to the grandchildren. By the same token my Dad never made assignments to me, and I never made assignments to him. We just handled it in-house. And our in-house records are correct to the penny."

They scanned the search warrant. "What about the estate of your mom and dad?" Ross asked. "Has it been handled in the same casual, in-house fashion?"

"Some of it was," answered Dad. "But the values of the oil and gas properties were appraised by a team of outside petroleum engineers, and the values of the estate were reviewed and approved by the IRS. And the grandchildren have each received one-seventh each of the oil and gas properties of the estate of W. A. Moncrief."

"But believe me, Bob," he added. "There's absolutely nothing in that estate that's out of order."

After the two-and-a-half-hour interview, lunch was served. They led Dad into Bennett's office, where he saw a brown trout mounted on the wall.

Dad read the plaque: "If I'd'a kept my mouth shut I wouldn't be here."

Bob Bennett took our case. "I'd just love to take this case before a jury in North Texas," he said. "I'd eat 'em up!"

Dad thanked him for the vote of confidence. "But I'd just as soon we don't have to take the case as far as federal court," he said.

By the time Bennett and his associates returned to Fort Worth, they would know our organization upside down. Meanwhile, our own in-house investigation was also in high gear. An army of Price Waterhouse accountants set up shop in our offices, systematically organizing our files and searching for improprieties. Attorneys from Washington and Dallas began heading into Fort Worth, racking up hourly wages that would end up totaling $5.5 million in the first eighteen months.

★ ★ ★

As the days after the raid rolled by, Kay "Kansas City" Capps, our division order analyst, became our most valuable asset. She had been with us a long time, and she knew our properties from top to bottom. She felt certain that she knew who had triggered the IRS raid. She had been repeatedly warning us about our former accountant, Billy Wayne Jarvis, for months.

Jarvis had been with us from 1978 to 1993. He'd come from the Dallas accounting firm of Bright & Bright. Dad and Granddad had hired the firm to handle our off-site accounting, because our methods were more than a little outdated. Being an oilman, Granddad didn't believe in elaborate accounting systems. Dorothy Price, an old-fashioned, sixty-something bookkeeper, more than fit the bill. She kept the documentation of working interest in oil wells on 3-by-5 index cards. She kept these cards in a small green schoolmarm's card box. Every time Granddad made a deal, he'd write out the ownership interests on a sheet of paper, sign it, and hand it to Dorothy. She would transfer the particulars onto an index card, staple Granddad's signed paper onto the back, and put it in the box.

Knowing the system had to be updated, Dad turned to Bright & Bright, who dispatched Jarvis, an accountant, to work for us twice a week. He was an affable, red-haired, freckle-faced young man from a politically active family in Sherman, a small town to the north of Dallas. He seemed to be smart, concientious, and diligent. Dad and Granddad took to him right away.

In the beginning, Bill Jarvis was all business. He always seemed to be hard at work, either at his desk or circling our accounting department. He was courteous. He would answer any questions we might have about taxes, run down any reports we needed, and sit down individually with each of us to review our returns.

In 1979, after two years of contract work, Bill Jarvis was hired as the full-time comptroller of Moncrief Oil. Kay Capps came to know Jarvis well. While keeping track of royalty and working interest ownership in Moncrief oil and gas wells, and setting up divisions of interests to be paid, Kay can quote the ownership percentages in any of our wells. Having worked for three Fort Worth oil companies before joining ours, Kay knows the oil business.

She could tell immediately that Bill Jarvis did not. She immediately sensed Jarvis was the complete antithesis of the standard oil company comptroller: not a team player, not a seeker or sharer of information, and, most importantly in the close confines of an oil company, not a pleasant person to be around—except, in later years, when it came to another Kay on our staff.

Kay Martin was our joint interest billing manager, responsible for billing working interest parties their share of costs in oil wells. She was very much married, although she would subsequently divorce. She was a young, attractive, brown-eyed woman who wore somewhat revealing dresses to work. First, Kay Martin depended upon Bill Jarvis; he was, after all, her supervisor. But then things apparently turned romantic.

"Your troubles all began when your dad broke up Bill and Kay's little playhouse," Kay Capps later told me.

Dad told Kay and Bill to knock it off. But that wasn't the only thing that pushed Bill Jarvis over the edge. When he came to work for us, Jarvis's allegiance was with Granddad. He was indifferent to Dad. Admittedly, there were transactions on which Jarvis wasn't consulted. Maybe that upset him. Jarvis was having troubles of his own, especially in his third marriage, which, at the time of his office romance, was deteriorating fast. In later depositions, Jarvis would go on and on about Tex Moncrief being "mean." One employee would later tell me that Jarvis was "ill-tempered," and "so red-faced you'd think he was going to pop."

He began arguing with Kay Capps that Dad's fifty-fifty agreement with his father on all wells didn't really exist. He didn't realize that this is a standard procedure in family oil companies, where handshake deals are done without the formal transfer of title. (Back then, the deals were still detailed on those 3-by-5 cards.) Behind our backs, he began accusing Dad of manipulating ownership of oil and gas properties after the well's success or failure was determined.

"Well, Tex doesn't have *equitable title* to that property," he told Kay one day, regarding the Powell Pressure Maintenance Unit. This was a block of federally owned land encompassing dozens of oil and gas wells. Dad and Granddad were operating this block in Wyoming. Kay knew that Granddad hadn't transferred the title to the 50 percent interest in the unit into Dad's name due to the mountain of paperwork it would have entailed. But the specifics of the deal weren't important; it was the language that Jarvis used that caused Kay's already sensitive antenna to quiver.

Equitable title. That's a *real estate* term for the ownership of a real estate property, Kay thought to herself, not an oil and gas business term. The oil and gas term for assuming ownership is *record title.* Although the two terms are essentially the same, there is a distinction in terminology among seasoned oil business personnel. At that moment, Kay Capps knew that Bill Jarvis had been talking to somebody outside our company about the oil business—and whoever he was talking to sure didn't know much about oil, either, or they would have used the right word.

In the end, Bill Jarvis, our $120,000-a-year comptroller, was keeping our books in an even less appropriate fashion than our previous schoolmarm. Our business accounting was in total shambles. Our personal accounting wasn't much better. Our longtime and most trusted assistant, Mary Ellen Lloyd, had worked for my family for seventeen years. But lately she'd been acting strange, flying regularly to Las Vegas and returning with stacks of $100 bills, which she claimed were her winnings.

Jarvis never looked twice at Ellen's change in attitude and activities. But he had a big problem with computerizing our organization. He wanted his department—which consisted of one bookkeeper, two assistants and himself—to stay separate from the rest of our organization, which was already computerized. His logic? "To keep controls in place," Jarvis told us. So when Dad expressed a mounting concern to me in the summer of 1991 about the business, a vague feeling that someone, not anyone in particular, might be stealing from us, I thought the best way to strengthen controls was to put every Moncrief Oil employee on a computer.

I knew our business systems were dangerously antiquated, and the thought of a comptroller running a multimillion-dollar company without a totally integrated computer system was ludicrous in 1991. We never suspected Jarvis of anything. We trusted him completely. But when he said he didn't think it necessary to computerize our accounting department, due to the need for "internal controls," we lost confidence in his judgment.

"There's not a thing wrong with our computer system!" Jarvis said on numerous occasions. This was a big red flag for us. We had trusted him, but now he just seemed unreasonable. When he said he thought it would take three years to get all employees on computers, I knew damned well I could walk down the street and buy oil company software for $20,000 tops. Our relationship with Jarvis began to unravel. We didn't know that he had told Kay, "I hope the Lucky Liz goes down with Tex Moncrief on it!"

What were we doing with a $70,000-a-year, in-house computer programmer, if we weren't computerizing the entire organization? We let our in-house computer technician go. That's when, two weeks later, the building was broken into—or out of, since the window was broken from the inside out—and only our former computer programmer's hard drive was stolen. We didn't think much about it. By then, we had turned to our in-house engineer to find a software company to install an oil and gas accounting system. As companies arrived to interview for the contract, Jarvis refused to interview them, scoffing at the entire process.

★ ★ ★

At the office, everyone, especially our lawyers, soon began asking the same thing: Did we have any disgruntled former employees? An employee not just mad—but disgruntled? Someone so disgruntled that he or she would not only bad-mouth us to friends, but take grievances to the top: the IRS?

It happens more often than you'd think, merely because the long arm of the IRS touches everybody. Ordinary citizens rarely have contact with the FBI or Secret Service, but everybody files a tax return. And the IRS's doors are always open to citizens with tales to tell. When employees go to the IRS for a conversation, they are seeking revenge or money, or both, because the IRS pays substantial rewards to informants. Normally, the limit is $100,000. But bigger deals can be negotiated. Informants can reap sizable rewards if the case is big enough. The criminal prosecution of a $350 million Texas oil family would be considered big time, indeed.

"Well, I can make some recommendations of things to consider," said Max Wayman, a former IRS special agent turned Fort Worth private investigator contacted by our attorneys. Wayman had heard about our IRS raid on the radio and immediately knew it had to have been triggered by an inside informant. He knew that "probable cause" is a prerequisite for any search warrant for an IRS raid. Probable cause doesn't just materialize from thin air. Probable cause requires someone from the "inside," an informant. In almost every case the informant is a disgruntled employee or, even more dangerous, a disgruntled *former* employee.

Wayman, a highly decorated former IRS agent, met with our defense team. Bennett and Bruton flew down from Washington. Dee Kelly drove across town to Wayman's offices. They discussed defense strategies—what might be the IRS's next move and what we could do to counter those thrusts and parries.

If Bill Jarvis was indeed the informant, then, Wayman suggested, we should consider conducting an "impeachment investigation" against him. He said that impeachment investigations typically involve three investigative methods: "Number one, searching the suspect's background for any history of criminal activity. Number two, searching the suspect's civil background for any history of lawsuits. And, number three, searching the suspect's trash."

He leaned back and smiled.

"*Garbology,*" he said. "It's just amazing what you can find."

The three attorneys didn't have to be told about garbology. Nor did they have to question where Wayman learned the technique. He learned about garbology from his days with the IRS. Special agents from the IRS and FBI dig through people's trash all the time.

Wayman told us that an IRS agent's goal in every raid is simple: They're seeking indictments. But there are two kinds of agents:

those who seek the truth regardless of indictments and those who seek indictments regardless of the truth. The latter is the more dangerous. IRS agents, like accountants, become jaded. Many have what Wayman calls "a preconceived notion of guilt." They believe the whole world is guilty of some sort of tax crime; it's just a matter of catching 'em at the right time. They only seek evidence that will lead to an indictment; anything that contradicts that evidence is ignored. Honest people are indicted. Or they'll spend their last dime defending themselves, only—when they're found innocent—to be financially and emotionally destroyed in the process.

"Frankly, those kinds of agents make my job easier," Wayman said.

But Wayman had never heard of a raid involving sixty-four agents. The biggest raid he'd heard about involved twenty-four—and that was for three different medical clinics suspected of selling illegal narcotics. That raid, which had been triggered by a disgruntled former employee, ended without an indictment. He figured that the IRS must have had some powerful evidence to strike us with such velocity and force. We needed to find out the facts, and we needed the facts quickly!

Early one morning in late 1994, two months after the raid, an investigator from the firm of Max Wayman and Associates drove to 829 S. Saddlebrook in Bedford, Texas, one of a dozen bedroom communities halfway between Dallas and Fort Worth. Amid a skyline littered with the signs of fast-food franchises, Bill Jarvis lived in a small, pleasant, redbrick, Tudor-style house with charming bulbous windows and large trees shading approximately twenty feet of green lawn.

We would never know what actually happened in that house. But we would know exactly what came out in the trash. For while

Bill Jarvis's home was his personal property, the street was ours. "Most people think that when they throw something in the trash, it's gone," said Wayman. "But the reality is that when they throw something in the trash, it becomes public record."

A single phone call to the Bedford Sanitation Department was all it took to determine garbage pickup times for Jarvis's street. Twice a week, Jarvis would place a couple of black garbage bags on the curb. These garbage bags gave us a blueprint into Jarvis's activities nearly as precise as the blueprints the IRS agents had of our offices. The second the door slammed behind Jarvis, the detective down the street would walk over to the curb, grab the bags, and take them back to the office where the detectives would pick through the trash, assembling clues.

Late night and early evening surveillance gave the detectives plenty of license plate numbers to check out, too. Cars were lined up outside Jarvis's house night and day. From various sources we learned the stinging truth: We knew next to nothing about the man who served as our comptroller.

Detective agency data from 1981 to 1993, when Jarvis served as comptroller of Moncrief Oil, revealed two divorces, an annulment of a third marriage, a DWI charge reduced to a misdemeanor conviction of public drunkenness, and charges of beating his first wife—which the court did not mention in the final divorce decree, though it did warn both parties against "causing bodily injury" to the other and issued a restraining order against Jarvis.

We didn't know any of this at the time. We would come to learn that there was a lot we didn't know about the accountant we had completely trusted for fourteen years with our finances and tax returns. Our lack of knowledge would prove to be our undoing.

Chapter Five

Self-Examination

THE SATURDAY FOLLOWING THE IRS RAID was September 3, my forty-fifth birthday. I went over to Dad's house and found him putting on his camouflage for dove hunting. We were going to our attorney Dee Kelly's house to discuss the case and then head out to the ranch for my birthday and our postponed family dove hunt.

So when Dee Kelly opened his door, he found three Moncriefs—Dad, Dickie, and me—standing there in our hunting clothes, which, being the third day of dove season in Fort Worth, was not unexpected apparel.

"Come on in, boys. Have a seat; make yourselves comfortable," Kelly said in greeting. But before we could even get near a chair, he began jabbering. "This has to involve gift taxes, mark my words," he said. "You've got to scour your memories for any transfer of property between family members. Anything that might be construed as a gift."

Dad responded immediately. "Well, Kelly, there's only one thing that I can think of that could possibly be questioned by the IRS, and that's Charlie's purchase of 10 percent of the Madden-Deep unit."

The Madden: a huge gas field in Wyoming where Dad purchased the right to drill for natural gas. In the 1970s and 1980s, the Madden had generated a profit. In 1988 Dad decided he wanted me to have a 10 percent interest in the property to repay me for the work I'd done on the project over the years. The value at the time of my purchase was $180 million.

But for how much money? And under what terms?

I could not remember!

This was just the sort of thing that worried Dee Kelly. After I bought into the Madden-Deep deal, the gas market collapsed. The Madden only returned to profitability in 1993 and 1994. Then, it turned out to be a very lucrative investment, worth hundreds of millions of dollars. If I assumed ownership of my interest without paying Dad what it was worth, the gift tax involved would be significant, and the whole transaction would look very suspicious to a judge and jury.

When we adjourned at Kelly's, Dad, Dickie, and I joined the whole family at the ranch for the dove hunt. Kit and I were still concerned about Gloria, Adelaide, and Celia, but kids just seem to roll naturally with the punches.

All through the dove hunt, I could not get the Madden-Deep unit off my mind.

When we finished the hunt, we mixed Crown Royal—as always—for everybody, and Dad made a toast to the memory of Granddad and to Kit's late mother, Gloria.

Then I went home to look for records of any payments I'd

made to Dad on the Madden. I went straight to the bathroom closet where I kept all my business diaries.

I wrote in my diaries daily, a practice I started at Granddad's insistence. "See this diary?" he'd asked me on my first day of work. "I want you to go out today and buy one. And everything you do, write it down. In business deals, there are always questions. If you write down what happens when it happens, you'll always know exactly what you said and did."

I remembered the year Dad cut me in for a percentage of the Madden, and I went through that diary page by page until I found an entry outlining the deal Dad and I had made. It described how Dad and I went to Dallas and had lunch with our accountant, Gilbert Bright.

I remembered the conversation. "I want Charlie to have a 10 percent interest in the Madden," Dad had told Bright. "How can I carve that out for him?"

"Well, he's gotta buy it from you," Gilbert said. "You could just give it to him and pay the gift tax. But there's a better way to structure it."

We followed Bright's suggestion for a "production payment" deal. I agreed to pay Dad 75 percent of the "runs," or gas revenues over and above expenses, until the sale price of $4.5 million, which represented 10 percent of the deal, was paid similar to an installment plan.

At least, that's how the deal was outlined in my diary. But one question remained: Had I unwittingly been collecting revenue off the Madden without paying Dad his share?

When I got to the office the following Monday, I asked our bookkeepers to find what the books showed my cost to be in the

Madden. Their answer was, "Zero." Because of complications in the gas market's collapse, and the considerable costs for deep drilling in the Madden-Deep, the Madden had yet to produce a profit. So I still didn't owe Dad anything: not yet, anyway. If the Madden issue turned out to be one of the main contentions in the criminal investigation later, as we suspected, then my diary had just closed the case, in my mind.

The zero cost on my books for the Madden would be of critical importance during the ensuing investigation.

On September 9, 1994, five days after the IRS agents had cleaned out every cranny of our business offices, Mike Moncrief made a play that alerted us to the depth of our problems.

Mike's attorney sent us a "149A accounting request"—really more of an order than a request—requiring us to provide a detailed accounting of Granddad's estate and its various oil and business interests. We had sixty days to respond. Under normal circumstances this would have been a standard request—it happens with family estates fairly often—but the timing confirmed our suspicions about a connection between Mike and the IRS raid. "Tex, I told you Mike was involved in this thing," Kelly said when he called to inform us.

Dad hung up and turned to me.

"You know what my daddy used to say was the worst thing you could call someone?"

"No," I responded.

"An ingrate," he said. "Someone who turns against his family."

The 149A request asked for information about each and every piece of property that Mike's side of the family might have inherited from Granddad and Granddear. But it was clearly focused on a single, very lucrative issue: the Powell Pressure Maintenance

Unit, or "PPMU" for short. The request was for an accounting of the PPMU from its inception.

A pressure maintenance unit is a special kind of oil field. When there's gas associated with the oil, the gas will lift the oil, like steam lifting coffee in a percolator. When you start to run out of gas pressure, you can actually add gas back into the oil field, to continue lifting oil out. If you maintain a certain pressure, the gas will lift a much greater percentage of the oil. We drilled the Powell well with Woods Petroleum Corp. back in the seventies. It was one of the most profitable deals we ever made, worth tens of millions of dollars.

For years, Mike and his lawyers had been trying to find a way to prove they were entitled to more of the PPMU revenues than we were giving them. And now they were asking for a full and complete accounting of the PPMU from its inception.

I could clearly remember the very day that the deal was made. It was 1972, the year I graduated from college, in my office in the Moncrief Building. Al Freshauer, top dog at Woods, came down to visit Dad and Granddad and show them the deal. He rolled out a big map on my desk that had sketches of the old channel sands meandering their way across the Powder River Basin. Both Dad and Granddad took special notice of the huge amount of acreage involved in the play.

Al said, "Monty, we just want to drill a few wells up here. If you pay for two of them, you'll earn a half interest in the acreage around both prospects."

Granddad looked over the paperwork and took Dad aside. "Tex, this looks like a hell of a deal," he whispered. "Let's get in on as much of this as we can."

Turning to Al, Granddad asked, "Just how many wells do you intend to drill in the entire Powder River Basin?"

"Twelve wells," he answered.

Freshauer was pretty surprised to hear Granddad's response: "We'll drill all twelve wells, for half interest in all the acreage you've leased in the entire Powder River Basin."

Granddad's initial gut feeling turned out to be correct, as usual. We discovered a huge amount of oil throughout the entire block of acreage, and it happened at the perfect time, contemporaneous with the Arab oil embargo. We found ourselves owning half of a vast reserve of oil right when the price went to $40 a barrel!

Mike had argued that, contrary to Dad's claim that he and Granddad had split the PPMU deal fifty-fifty, he felt the Moncrief family interest in the PPMU was owned entirely by Granddad's estate. Having purchased all of Granddad's interest in the PPMU, Mike and his family believed they were owed a lot more of the PPMU revenues than they were getting.

Just two months before Mike's 149A request, we'd convinced a Wyoming judge that Mike and his lawyers were wrong about their PPMU contentions, and now it looked like we'd have to do the same thing again in a Texas state court.

Mike's 149A request basically forced us to trace the financial records of the PPMU deal from the inception, to prove that Dad actually did own half and Granddad owned the other half. Trace it we did; proof we soon had.

★ ★ ★

Now that the IRS agents had finally cleared out of our offices, we replaced them with a team of Price Waterhouse accountants. We borrowed long, wide, collapsible tables from Hogan Office Supply and set them up end-to-end in an open area next to my office. There were neatly dressed CPAs with laptops and ten-key adding machines. This team was going to review Dad's and my tax returns for the past ten years and look for any obvious violations.

The second team set up on the first floor and was assigned the task of fulfilling Mike Moncrief's 149A request.

At first, our accountants didn't have much to work with, since our file cabinets were still in storage at the IRS offices in Dallas.

Dee Kelly dispatched lawyer Hugh Connor to a warehouse in the Earl Cabell Federal Building in downtown Dallas. Our production clerk, Patsy Holcomb, went with him, carrying a list of vital documents we needed. They parked in the basement and went up to the IRS offices where they were greeted in a secured anteroom. After checking their identification, the IRS agents allowed Hugh and Patsy to enter the office. Posted on a bulletin board was a copy of the front page of the *Dallas Morning News* announcing the raid on our offices. "They were proud of themselves," Patsy told me when she got back to the office.

Hugh and Patsy were escorted into a warehouse by two armed officers who watched their every move. The warehouse contained the entire contents of the Moncrief Building, stacked in numbered white boxes. Our filing cabinets were lined up against the walls. There were roughly a million documents: revenue and royalty reports for the hundreds of oil wells we had been operating, checkbooks, Rolodexes, files, telephone logs.

It took Hugh and Patsy all afternoon to find what we needed to resume our operation. But we could only get so much.

A week after the raid, we filed a petition with the federal court to force the IRS to give our documents back to us. The IRS agents refused to do this on their own, claiming they needed the material for evidence. The judge spent a few moments looking through the IRS regulation book, then turned to the U.S. attorney and said,

"Well, sir, you ARE going to give those records back. Not only are you going to give them back, but you're going to give the *originals* back and pay for your own copying."

This order would end up costing the IRS $100,000 in copying charges.

Combing our tax and bookkeeping records for anything that might be interpreted by the IRS as a matter of tax evasion, we experienced something strange. As soon as we began to explore an issue in our internal investigation, IRS agents would start questioning our lawyers, and, later, our employees, about the same thing. The pattern of IRS questioning followed our own internal inquiries too closely to be coincidence.

Employee raises were one example. Just before the raid, we were planning to give overdue raises to several employees, and we did so within three weeks after the raid. As soon as we gave the raises, IRS agents asked our lawyers about them, trying to twist the story to look as if we were giving our employees "hush money."

The pattern could only point to one thing: Either the IRS had an expert psychic on their payroll or someone besides Bill Jarvis was providing them with information—someone still employed by us.

Despite the evidence, we were reluctant to start regarding our employees with suspicion and mistrust. That sort of paranoia would be another step toward turning Montex into the kind of soulless corporation we'd always despised. But gradually, our lawyers started convincing us that you're not being paranoid if someone really is out to get you.

★ ★ ★

By October 12, the accountants had finished their job. From the "upstairs team" which was examining Dad's and my tax returns for any obvious violations, we learned that there were no "smoking guns" in our tax return records. It was nice to hear, but no real surprise.

Meanwhile, the team down on the first floor, which was fulfilling Mike's 149A request, determined that Granddad did in fact own half of the Powell Pressure Maintenance Unit in Wyoming, not all of it as Mike was claiming. Those accountants traced every penny that had gone into that unit since its inception in 1972, starting with the $800,000 check Granddad wrote out to Al Freshauer on the day of that fateful "twelve-well deal."

The day after Granddad wrote Al's check, Dad wrote one to Granddad for half of the amount. From that moment forward, Dad and Granddad owned the PPMU fifty-fifty all the way through. This meant that Mike and his side of the family were entitled to exactly the amount of PPMU revenue we'd been giving them all along.

The continuing coincidences between our investigation and the IRS's compounded the stress level. To protect ourselves from intruders and to afford our late night employees some security, we installed high-security magnetic door locks, and then put high-security lights and cameras on the exterior of our building. We also had our phones checked for wiretaps and had a scan performed for electronic surveillance. Our in-house counsel, Mel May, was paranoid about an old, beat-up Winnebago that kept showing up—sometimes for days in a row—parked next to or within a block of the Moncrief Building.

We were under siege, and the strain was starting to show on everyone. My blood pressure shot up, requiring a daily dose of two-and-a-half milligrams of Altace. The stress was so intense I took out an additional life insurance policy. But my life was a cakewalk compared to how things were going for Dad and Mother. To this day I don't know how they took the pressure.

"Do you think I'm gonna have to pull a Mike Tyson?" Dad asked me one morning over coffee. I knew what he meant. Mike Tyson had just been sentenced to two years in jail.

"Absolutely not!" I said. "The IRS is going to have to prove conspiracy, and we both know there's never been one!"

Despite the family's efforts to put his mind at ease, Dad's age and stress levels were taking a crippling toll. He'd been suffering for years from occasional heart palpitations that Digitalis kept under control, but now the pressure was stronger than the medicine. Within a few months of the raid, he suffered three episodes of heart palpitations in a row. Even worse, his nervous state gave him a constricted esophagus, making it hard for him to eat. At any given meal he would excuse himself and go to the bathroom, where he would force himself to vomit food lodged in his throat.

And the worst news was yet to come.

Never did a day go by at the Moncrief Building that I didn't amble into Dad's office and take a seat to chat about what was going on and what we'd been working on during the day. November 7 was no different from any other day.

"What are you working on?" I asked.

"Close the door there for a minute," Dad responded.

I knew this wasn't good. Dad took a deep breath. "Your mother has a lump in her breast."

Oh, God, don't tell me this, I thought. Timing is everything in life, but there is never a good time for death or disease. Dad continued.

"We plan to go to M. D. Anderson next week, and the surgeons there will go in and take a look. If it is malignant, we'll remove the breast. Your mother and I have discussed this, and that is the decision we have made. She'll go under anesthesia not knowing how she'll wake up."

Dad leaned back in his chair with a lost look in his eyes. Everything that he had in life was now on the line. "It seems like everything is happening at once," he remarked grimly.

★ ★ ★

Kay Capps never had to testify before the grand jury, but she was interrogated by the IRS twice. On February 10, 1995, she presented us with a set of detailed notes describing the IRS's questions, and it proved to be crucial to our understanding of the case.

Suddenly, it became easy to read the case the IRS was trying to build, through their questions to Kay. Our speculations turned out to be largely accurate.

First, they were planning to claim that we purposefully used informal "family transactions" to hide reserves of cash and other wealth from the government, and then buried our tax evasions through sloppy record keeping.

Secondly, they seemed to be claiming that we artificially reduced estate taxes by undervaluing or hiding the property left by Granddad and Granddear.

Finally, it seemed they were even considering charging us with having paid bribes—in the form of gifts and loans—for the purpose of retaining and silencing employees who knew we were lawbreakers.

Watching these charges emerge from Kay's notes was both a shock and a relief. It was a shock to see such accusations against me and my family in black and white, and yet it was a relief to see how baseless the IRS's case was against us.

As the early months of 1995 rolled by, the IRS brought a few of our current staff before the grand jury, questioning each exhaustively. Frankly, the people I saw receiving subpoenas were of no concern to me. The problem was that I had no way of knowing at the time who else was being subpoenaed. I thought that the IRS would be questioning people who weren't so firmly on our side— people who might like to see us go down—like my cousin Mike or any disgruntled ex-employees.

★ ★ ★

By March 1995, six months after the raid, the IRS still had us surrounded. Agents were interrogating our employees, summoning them to their offices for hours-long interviews, and paying surprise visits to their homes. The press was sniffing around for more dirt to add to the compost pile; we were becoming a long-running, front-page Fort Worth soap opera.

Kay Capps was working more overtime than she was regular hours. On her way to work early one morning, her trouble-plagued car wouldn't start. Her supervisor suggested to Dad and me that maybe a company car would alleviate her hardship. Merle Burgess, our longtime secretary, was near retirement, and we had been contemplating a gift for her as well.

"Tell them to go together tomorrow and find themselves new cars," Dad decided. "Dickie, you and Charlie can pay for Merle's, and I'll buy the one for Kay."

We had never bought a car for any employee. All the field hands and a couple of the Moncrief Building personnel, including Bill Jarvis, had company cars, but that was all. Times were tough, though, and Kay and Merle deserved to be compensated for their extra duty.

Immediately after we sent a check over to Tyson Buick to pay for the cars, the IRS summoned Merle and Kay to their offices. Afterward, Merle blew back into the Moncrief Building, fuming. "You won't believe what that IRS just accused me of!" she said. She put her hand on her hip and went into her best IRS agent impersonation: "Well, Miss Burgess, we understand that Mr. Moncrief has given you a car just to shut you up. Now, that wouldn't be a bribe, would it?"

"I showed them a thing or two!" she said. "I'll guarantee you, nobody accuses me of taking bribes."

I had to laugh at her impersonation. But the accusation was troubling: The only way the IRS could have known about a purchase we had made before our check had even cleared was through a very inside informant.

A leak.

But who was our leak? I couldn't believe that someone in our office was feeding information to the IRS. I'd rather believe that the IRS was keeping us under electronic surveillance. It was easier to cling to this explanation than consider that one of our employees was betraying us. I tried to convince myself that agents had tapped into our bank's computer system to monitor our financial transactions. But we had checked our system completely for wiretaps, and the speed at which the IRS was on our trail made bank surveillance unlikely. It had to be the work of an insider.

My suspicions soon fell on Mary Schneider, one of Kay Martin's subordinates. Mary had worked directly with Bill Jarvis on Moncrief books just before he was fired, which made me think they might have been in cahoots. I went by Mary's office to visit but she had taken the day off. For some reason, her Rolodex caught my eye, and I noticed that it was open to Jarvis's phone number.

Mary Schneider had always been hard to figure out. She was nervous and very emotional, never showing the kind of loyalty I was convinced I saw in Kay Martin, Kay Capps, and the others.

Mary had worked for us once before but had quit because of an offer to make more money elsewhere, but things didn't go so well at her other job, and she came back when Jarvis needed some extra help. Now, things were getting tough, and the way Mary handled herself after the raid seemed more than a little suspicious to me.

The biggest red flag in my mind came from one simple fact: Every single employee had signed up to be represented by Dallas attorney Chuck Meadows and his associates, with two exceptions, Mary Schneider and Kay Martin.

I asked Kay Martin, "We've got attorneys on board, why don't you want one of them to represent you?"

"Well, I just didn't like that Meadows when I sat down with him," she replied.

I didn't like Kay's response, but I let it ride. I already knew that Kay was very confused and nervous about the whole IRS investigation. Mary Schneider didn't like Meadows either, which was the reason she gave for declining his representation. Then, suddenly, Mary changed her mind and decided to let Meadows represent her.

When further evidence of leakage arose, I began thinking that the informant might not be a staff member but a family member. At the end of January 1995, I heard that Bill Eddy, one of Granddad's longtime household employees, had been questioned by IRS agents about some old pictures hanging near the staircase in Granddear's house. The agents wondered if the pictures were still there. They asked about pieces of art, rugs, and other household items—in extraordinarily specific terms.

The more I thought about it, the more significant these questions became. Bill Jarvis had never been in Granddear's house at 313 Rivercrest, so could not have seen any pictures; more than likely he would never have even heard of them. So how did the IRS know about the art? Someone who had been in Granddear's house would have to be involved—someone who knew a lot about her belongings.

We thought that cousin Mike might be influencing the IRS investigation in some way, perhaps even feeding information to Jarvis, and this instance involving the pictures pointed directly toward him. After all, Mike had been in Granddear's house all his life, and he always had a problem about how Granddear's personal possessions were distributed after her death. Still, something didn't add up. Mike could have easily advised the IRS on these particular items, but how could he have known about Merle's car or about the employee raises?

★ ★ ★

About this time, Clive Bode told me, "When this is all said and done with, you won't believe how poorly your accounting records have been kept." He was right. I realize there's no excuse for this, but our records had been in bad shape for years. "The Moncriefs are beautiful, generous people," one of our secretaries, Joan Barnhart, would later say. "But they've hired some ding-a-lings. With all of their millions, I wonder how in the world do they have any money left with such ding-a-lings handling it? Bill Jarvis didn't know the oil industry. And even if he did, he would have had trouble understanding this place."

When the IRS stormed the offices of employees like land lady Joan Barnhart, they got what she calls, well, "crap." "I even had a folder marked 'Stuff.' They took reading files from my office. Tons of papers, all of which they made copies of, even copies of the Post-It notes. When I think of the tons of copies they made of all that crap! Our files were helter-skelter. They could be in two or three places. We understand them—ho, ho!—but the feds? They didn't know what they were looking for, so they just took . . . stuff. It would have been simpler to secure the whole building and ask us to help them."

During my review of our files and records, we discovered that Bill Jarvis had been submitting incomplete reports to our auditors, Bright & Bright. It was their job to ensure that our bookkeeping was accurate and legal. But they based their accounting on material provided by Bill Jarvis.

Jarvis had been very careful to cover his tracks, but there was one document he failed to destroy.

One day early in 1995, Clive Bode called Dad and me into his office. "Gentlemen, I've got something you'll be very interested in," he announced. "Take a look at this!"

The IRS had audited the Moncrief Foundation back in the mid-eighties. Clive had found a copy of Jarvis's notes from his meeting with the auditors, as well as a copy of the memorandum that he had sent to Bright & Bright about the results of the audit. There was a glaring discrepancy between the two. When Jarvis visited with the IRS examiner, he made meticulous notes of five issues raised by the audit. The very next day, Jarvis sent a memorandum to Bright & Bright reporting the results of the audit, but it included only four of the five issues. The agent pointed out that our procedures for giving out scholarships needed to be formalized. Of the five issues this was the only one that needed serious attention—

and it was the one missing. It seemed that Jarvis had been setting us up for a long time.

The more we learned about our previous head accountant, the more obvious it became that we needed to get aggressive about our myriad bookkeeping lapses. "You're going to have to have someone at your office to head things up, coordinate the staff with the lawyers and with Price Waterhouse," our attorney Dee Kelly had told us a couple of months after the raid. "That's going to be a tough job, so you've got to have somebody very strong in there to help you."

We agreed with Dee in principle, but we knew that the person we hired would have to do a lot more than coordinate the staff for IRS-related matters. Now, it was five months after the raid, and it was perfectly apparent that our whole accounting system needed to be rebuilt. We needed an executive financial architect: someone smart and cool-headed enough not only to spearhead our battle against the IRS but also to redesign the entire accounting end of the Moncrief operation.

"I think I know somebody," Dee Kelly told us one day.

Dad and I are in the business of hiring and firing, especially hiring. When we met Vikki Pier in Dad's office, it didn't take long to tell we were talking to someone special. We just sensed that she knew how to get in there and kick ass. Short in stature with wire-rimmed glasses and a sharply tailored business suit, Vikki spoke in a high-pitched, gale-force voice about reorganizing our company systems. By the end of the week, we had offered her the job of CFO for $150,000 a year.

It turned out to be one of the smartest hires we ever made, even though she only stayed with us for a year. When she started working for Montex, Vikki might have intended to stay forever, but she just wasn't the Kay Capps type, someone happy in a family environment. Our laid-back attitude wasn't what Vikki saw for her future. She loved that big, bustling corporate structure, Monday morning meetings and all that. When she left here she eventually ended up involved in a start-up bank with some stock options that made her a small fortune.

But in the short time she spent with us, Vikki whipped our place into shape. Unable to figure out where such a small person got so much energy, we decided she was the first example of atomic energy in the oil business. I secretly nicknamed her the "U.S.S. Vikki."

Vikki was charged with three primary duties:

- To seek out any and all discrepancies in our books and records and to rebuild the organization to whatever extent she found necessary to make things run right;
- To coordinate the staff and records in order to provide all needed information and records to both our attorneys and to Price Waterhouse in their battle against the IRS;
- To make sure the Montex and Moncrief companies were handling business effectively.

She moved into Bill Jarvis's old office, but from the start, Vikki filled the space in a way no one ever had before. She immediately started moving from one department to the next, breaking each one down piece-by-piece, going through the books to find out how they were organized.

Old family-run companies like ours fall prey to a special kind of malaise when habit is mistaken for tradition, when clinging to the safe and familiar path is mistaken for "faith in the tried and true."

The U.S.S. Vikki's most important service to the Moncrief operation was to break that inertia, shake up our all-too-complacent waters, and expose the sharks swimming in our own sheltered harbor. And yes, we had sharks.

Some of them were our oldest, most trusted employees. They saw the U.S.S. Vikki headed their way and decided to get out quick.

★ ★ ★

The first to seek shelter was perhaps the most unexpected: our beloved longtime family clerk, Ellen Lloyd. Since 1978, Ellen had worked directly with Granddad, Granddear, and Dad in charge of several personal accounts. Prior to that, she had been a pro shop assistant at Shady Oaks Country Club, where she was always friendly to many of the older men, especially Granddad. When Granddad heard she might be laid off at the club, he gave her a job at the Moncrief Building.

Ellen was an average-sized woman, maybe 5'5", but she looked taller in her short skirts and high heels. She was always considered quite a character around the office. But to my family she could do little wrong. She was almost a member of the family, outgoing, funny, and always willing to help. My grandparents adored her. Whenever Granddad would leave the office for the day, he had a ritual: He'd go into Ellen's office, close the door, and emerge a minute later with a smile on his face. We guessed he'd gotten a quick hug and a kiss, as that's about all that his brief time behind the door would have allowed him. After Granddad's death, Ellen would spend hours talking to Granddear, taking checks to the house for maids and nurses.

One Monday, after an early morning return from Vegas, Ellen showed me a stack of hundreds she said she had won. The women in the office knew she had a lot of cash, because they would see her counting stacks of it. They all assumed the cash came from the casinos.

In the middle of 1995, Vikki came into my office and said, "Charlie, I'm reconciling the books in various departments, and I'm about ready to reconcile the Moncrief rental account. Would you please let Ellen know, so she's not too surprised when I come in there next week?"

The rental account paid the delay rental and shut-in gas royalties. If you take a mineral lease for, say, five years, you pay an initial lease bonus of $10 an acre. Then, you'd pay an annual "delay" rental fee of a dollar an acre to keep the lease in full force. If you drilled a good well but could not get the gas to a pipeline for some time and a year would soon lapse, you would have to pay a dollar an acre "shut-in gas royalty" to keep the lease in force. Keeping the rental account had always been Ellen Lloyd's main job, but her role was limited. She had the authority to write checks but could not sign on any accounts.

I called Ellen into my office to give her the news. She always entered my office the same way, leaning against the door casing with the edge between her breasts and her cheek against the side. "Next week, Vikki's going to start reconciling your accounts," I said, "so expect to see her in your office."

Ellen's face flushed.

"What's the matter?" I asked. "Are you okay?"

"Oh, I'm fine . . . ." she said, but she looked as if she was going to get sick.

I wasn't surprised when Ellen called in sick that following Monday. I heard she came in Tuesday for a couple of hours but left again. When a few more days went by with no word from her, Dad and I began to worry about Ellen's health. When she didn't return our calls or answer her phone, Dad looked up her doctor to find out if she was in the hospital. The doctor said he hadn't seen her.

Now I was getting suspicious. The question of our office leak was still very much on my mind, and I began thinking that Ellen Lloyd might be our spy. I really couldn't believe I hadn't thought of her before. She had been privy to the raises that caught the IRS's attention, and she definitely would have known about the purchase of Merle's car ahead of time. Unlike most of our employees, Ellen had been out to Granddear's house many times over the years, first to deliver checks to my grandmother, and then later, when my brother Tom lived there, to visit with his wife, Therese. She might easily have noticed those pictures the agents had been asking about. But the real clincher was that Ellen had worked directly under Bill Jarvis for many years, so he would have had countless opportunities to recruit her for mutiny. And now, most incriminating of all, after seventeen years with our company, Ellen had left without so much as a goodbye.

I called my brother Tom. He was at the ranch in Gunnison, Colorado. "Tom, I'm starting to think our leak is Ellen," I said. "Goddamn it, think about it; she's been in your house jillions of times, even upstairs. The IRS knows so many specifics about your home. Ellen could have made mental notes of its contents and told the agents. Now, she's disappeared completely!" My suspicions seemed justified when Vikki went to work on Ellen's records.

"Charlie, I'm in Ellen's office," she said. "I found a check written to the rental account from Tex's personal account for $25,000. Is there any reason that should have been done?"

"Absolutely not!" I said. "The money for the rental account always comes out of our business account. Something is wrong."

"I should probably look into this, don't you think?"

"I sure do!" I said. Dad wouldn't have signed that check.

That $25,000 check in the rental account led Vikki into Dad's personal checking. She looked through Ellen's books on that account, then looked at the cancelled checks themselves, and called me into her office a few days later.

Vikki was sitting at her desk. In front of her, she had about a dozen checks lined up in straight columns. She picked up one of the checks.

"Look at this check," Vikki said. "It's made out to Texas Electric Service Company. It's got Tex's meter number and Ellen's meter number typed in right under it. It looks like Ellen would make out your dad's check to the electric company, let him sign it, then lift the dollar amount, probably with Scotch tape, and add her meter and dollar amount due."

I couldn't believe my eyes. Dad had been concerned for years that someone might be stealing from the company, which is why we had Bright audit us back in 1991–92. But they obviously didn't catch it.

"And that's only one of her methods," Vikki continued. "There're lots of others here, too. There's no telling how much money she got out of here with."

Under normal circumstances this revelation would have knocked me down, but I had grown accustomed to abnormal circumstances. "Well, we've got to find out," I replied.

Vikki recommended that we hire a couple of former FBI agents turned private investigators to go through all the Ellen Lloyd–associated transactions to determine exactly what she had done.

The agents were Clint "C. B." Brown and Mike Connelley. I had met Mike years before when I was at the U.S. courthouse visiting some of my old friends. Mike and Clint took our records and put together the case against Ellen. There wasn't much to be said; it was obvious what she had done. "She got better and bolder as time went on," Mike told me. "When the bank statements came in every month she'd just throw them away."

We believed the check for $25,000 must have been Ellen's first experiment with embezzlement. She apparently then began writing checks to pay her own bills. She never deposited the checks directly to her bank account. They all went to credit card companies and to pay her utilities and other bills. A few went up to the Franklin Mint; I guess she was buying gifts or gold or something. Within the four-year time frame covered by the statute of limitations, our FBI agents figured Ellen had taken at least $300,000.

Once we discovered the embezzlement, I decided that Ellen wasn't our leak. She had a different reason for absconding so quickly when Vikki announced that she was to look at her books: She was stealing from us! Other employees were not so sure that she wasn't also passing information to the IRS. Kay Capps pointed out that Jarvis was Ellen's immediate supervisor and would have been the first to uncover anything suspicious concerning the books. This would have given Jarvis a lot of power over Ellen; he could have forced her to provide information to him after he was fired. Under normal circumstances, I would have said Kay's explanation was way too elaborate to be realistic, too much like something out of a movie. But considering the way things were going lately, the idea seemed about right.

We eventually filed a criminal embezzlement complaint against Ellen Lloyd, and she was indicted by a grand jury. The case went on for a long, long time, and the result—as I discuss later—was mind-boggling.

★ ★ ★

Meanwhile, insider information continued to leak to the IRS. Within days of Ellen's disappearance, the IRS agents were trying to track her down. So much for my idea that Ellen was the leak.

One day, Dad and I went down to our payroll office to discuss a few things with Kay Martin. Another bookkeeper, Alice Anderson, would be absent for a few months to undergo cancer treatment. Dad and I wanted to continue paying her salary while she was gone. Dad asked Kay if those payments had to be reported as income.

"It doesn't have to be," Kay snapped. "I guess you can do whatever you want."

Kay's comment pissed me off. I turned on her. "Why would you say something like that?! We don't do things the wrong way, and we're damn sure not starting now!"

The comment was completely out of character for Kay; it was the first time Kay had ever taken that tone with us. I walked Dad back up to his office and then came back downstairs to pop Kay good.

"With everything hitting the fan around here right now, I can't believe you'd make such a smart-ass comment!" I said.

Kay didn't have anything to say in her defense, so I just let it drop. But it all seemed strange, and it continued to bug me in the following weeks. I began watching Kay Martin more carefully and paying more attention to what other people were saying about her.

In the winter of 1995, Ted Harter, a college graduate, cowboy who manages all our ranches in Texas and Colorado, came to my office for his weekly visit. He had something special to show me. He closed my door and handed me a fancy little bound booklet, filled with color-coded maps of our Texas ranch, including the names of all the pastures. I thought it was some kind of a present at first.

"Charlie, Kay Martin asked me to make this," he said, handing me the booklet. "But I got to thinking about it, and I wanted you to see it before I gave it to her."

I looked at the booklet and one word resounded in my brain: Why?

"Kay asked you to do this?" I asked Ted.

"Yeah," he said. "She said she needed a map showing all the parts of the ranch, ownership of the different parts, where the houses are located, what improvements have been made, and various other things."

"This is more than strange," I replied. "Kay and her staff have been coding the ranch invoices into their books for fifteen years now. They've never asked for this information before, so why the sudden interest?"

"I was sort of wondering the same thing," said Ted. "That's why I wanted you to see it."

I stuck the booklet in a drawer. "Well, thanks, Ted. I'll just hold on to this. Don't give Kay anything else."

I sent that book right up to the attorneys for safekeeping. I never said a word to Kay about it, and Kay never mentioned the booklet to me. I started scrutinizing Kay Martin even closer.

Could Kay be our leak? I thought about it a long time. Her attitude had been just a little "off" since the raid. She wasn't highly educated, but she collected a pretty good salary after working her way up to the head of a staff of Montex bookkeepers. She had been one of only two employees not to have signed on with attorney Chuck Meadows to represent her when we brought him in for the employees after the raid. And there was her strangely hostile remark to Dad about Alice Anderson's income taxes. Now, with her request to Ted Harter, the more I thought about it, the more Kay looked like the leak. After all, she had been involved with Bill Jarvis. In addition, many of our leaks were related to payroll issues, and payroll was Kay's main area of interest.

I remembered going down into the staff area a week or so after the raid and asking the same question to each employee: "If you can think of anything whatsoever that's out of sorts that we haven't handled properly, I don't care what it is, I need to know about it."

Only Kay Martin was ready with an answer. "The only thing I know about is Gregory's salary," she said. "He works in here and at Tex's house about half the day, and his salary's billed 100 percent to the ranch."

"Good point!" I replied. "We need to change that."

Within days, the IRS indicated that they knew we were changing the allocation on some salaries.

Kay was also in a perfect position to know about most of the other leaks, especially employee raises, the first thing that made us suspect that we had a spy. Then there was the question of how the IRS found out that we were buying cars for Merle Burgess and Kay Capps before we had even sent the check to the dealership. And . . . Kay Martin was the one who typed the check!

Of course, I had already incorrectly convinced myself that Ellen Lloyd was our leak, so I wasn't taking myself too seriously this time. But all the pieces fit with Kay. She had the emotional involvement with Jarvis. She had access to all of our information. And lately she'd been acting weird.

She was about to get weirder, because the U.S.S. Vikki was heading Kay's way. Vikki had already paid for her salary by uncovering Ellen Lloyd's embezzlement, but she was only just getting started.

Her next target? The Joint Interest Billing Department, the bailiwick of Kay Martin.

Early one morning in July 1995, I found a note from Kay Martin waiting on my desk.

"I'm going to resign in two weeks," the note read in its entirety.

I thought, "This woman's been here fifteen years, we sent her to school, put her daughter all the way through college, and this is how she quits?"

I picked up the note and made a beeline to her office. "Kay," I said, "what the hell is this?"

She didn't even raise her head from her work. "Well, I'm resigning," she said.

"I noticed, but come on, one measly sentence?" I asked. "What's the problem?"

Her reply was brief: " I decided to get out of here while I still have a reputation."

Chapter Six

Telling Tales

IT WASN'T UNTIL MUCH LATER that we could begin to see how Bill Jarvis had assembled his team and created his strategy to take our case to the IRS. Here's what the Informant's Agreement laid out:

> The IRS will pay to the Informant amounts per the below-outlined schedule of the net taxes, fines and penalties (but not interest) collected from the Taxpayers as a direct result of information provided by the Informant that caused the investigation and resulted in the recovery:
> 10 percent of the first $10,000,000
> 15 percent of the next $10,000,000
> 20 percent of the next $10,000,000
> 25 percent of the amount over $30,000,000
> with a maximum not to exceed $25,000,000.

It was undeniably money, big money, that spurred Jarvis to plead his case against us before the IRS. Sure, his hatred of Dad loomed large in the equation. But it must have been the inconceivable assemblage of zeros—*"with a maximum not to exceed $25,000,000"!*—that made the $120,000-a-year CPA and corporate comptroller yearn to become an IRS informant. His reward would be sweeter than the choicest oil deal: gig us for $10 million and he'd take home a cool million; gig us for $30 million and he'd walk away with $4.5 million.

The only thing that stood between him and the cash was the proof.

We learned in court and through depositions that he took what he thought was proof, and when that wasn't enough, he tried to manufacture proof.

Jarvis began assembling his case while he was still an employee of Moncrief Oil. He was still overseeing our books and interacting with our employees. He had access to every inch of the Moncrief Building and the trust of our company's employees. He was still governed by the ethics of his profession, which required him to maintain client confidences no less than a doctor or lawyer. He would later say that he decided to approach the IRS to save his own hide; he was concerned "about being held responsible for the possible illegal actions of Tex and his CPA firm."

In the year before he left Moncrief, Bill made copies of almost all of our personal and business files—our tax returns, our bank accounts, records of property transfers, our check vouchers—everything, in short, that could help him build his case. Jarvis later contended that he didn't "steal" anything from my family. He simply did not return the documents when he packed up his office upon his termination in June of 1993. In his testimony he stated,

"I didn't ask if I could take them, and he [Tex] didn't ask me to give them back."

He kept these boxes of files in a spare bedroom in his home on Saddlebrook Lane in the suburbs between Dallas and Fort Worth. The boxes contained not one but two copies of every pertinent paper and tax return of his years at Montex.

One set of our documents would eventually go to the IRS. The destiny of the second set, when revealed, would turn the entire case on its head.

To Jarvis, the boxes must have seemed precious. They were, in a sense, Jarvis's *real* severance pay after fourteen years of service to us—the bounty that would make the five months of his $120,000-a-year salary and the Lincoln Continental Dad gave him upon his termination seem paltry by comparison.

"Not to exceed $25 million"!

Of course, the Informant's Agreement contains some important fine print, a couple of obstacles that Jarvis should have read carefully and heeded from the start.

First: The informant gets nothing if he or she "participated substantially in the evasion scheme or prepared the returns for the taxpayers with the knowledge that taxes were being evaded."

Secondly and particularly pertinent to Billy Wayne Jarvis's case: "This agreement may not be delegated or assigned to others."

In other words, the informant must act alone; any collusion with others outside of the IRS would make the Informant's Reward Agreement null and void, resulting in the informant's receiving *nothing.*

Jarvis said he began expressing his concerns over our tax liabilities with his brother, attorney Don Jarvis, in October 1991—almost two years before being fired from Moncrief Oil. But he soon chose not to discuss his concerns with the Moncrief family. Rather, he took his grievances against us to the IRS.

Between Bill and his reward stood two major obstacles: First, he didn't have the faintest idea how to approach the IRS; second, he was terrified about being discovered—especially by Tex Moncrief, who, he believed, had the power and influence to end his case before it began. Jarvis decided to surround himself with an arsenal of attorneys and advisers pledged to secrecy. He called them "the group."

"The group recognized the need to protect themselves as much as possible from physical and financial retaliation by the Moncriefs, who are one of the wealthiest and most influential families in the country," Jarvis would later say in depositions. "The group realized that Tex had demonstrated that he had significant power in the federal and state court and government structure in the Metroplex area and therefore there was concern that confidentiality could not be maintained if we tried to deal with the IRS in their Dallas/Fort Worth offices."

He said the group was assembled in the beginning to "consult" about Bill Jarvis's "potential liability for the wrongful acts" of his employer, meaning Dad and our CPA firm, Bright & Bright of Dallas. But attorneys and accountants do not work for free. What did the soon-to-be-unemployed accountant have to offer them? Since he obviously didn't have the funds himself, their fees would come from a contingency: a slice of Bill's IRS informant's reward, if they could help him haul us in before the IRS.

"Bill Jarvis and his advisors decided the best course of action, under the circumstances, would be to inform the IRS now about the alleged illegal acts while Bill Jarvis might still be in a position to show how things really happened, rather than wait until [Tex] and the Brights had eliminated or changed the documentary evidence," he would later say, referring to himself in the third person, in his brief prepared for the IRS.

But, he added, contacting the IRS is no simple task.

"There's no magic to approaching the IRS, is there?" Jarvis was later asked by our attorney Marshall Searcy.

"It's magic to approach the government when you are dealing with a situation where you have a billionaire on one side that can harm you in many ways in retaliation or to seek revenge," he replied.

His brother, Don Jarvis, was the key. Don had contacts in the legal profession. He turned first to his longtime friend Sam Graber, now an attorney based in Sherman, Texas, and a former IRS attorney in the seventies. Graber was retained without formal contract or fee, at least "not a formal fee agreement," according to Don Jarvis. Don then contacted a friend he'd known from elementary school—James Rolfe, a former U.S. attorney practicing law in Dallas. He retained Rolfe without formal agreement or fee. The troika was finally joined by an accountant, Jim Keller, yet another high school friend of Don Jarvis who was also a former IRS employee, to act as CPA for Bill and his growing battery of advisers, all without formal agreement. However, they would soon sign a fee splitting agreement that would not only be unusual, but unethical*—and it would be signed in urgency before Don Jarvis was sworn in as a Grayson County judge.

---

* In January 2000, a disciplinary committee of the State Bar of Texas cited the participants for professional misconduct. In September of that year, a federal judge declared that the agreement violated rules governing attorney ethics.

This group of school buddies turned attorneys decided that "because of Tex's influence in the North Texas area" they couldn't go to the IRS in Fort Worth. Not even Dallas, they felt, was far enough for their activities to go unnoticed by Dad. "We were concerned about what would happen to us if Tex Moncrief and his family learned that we were going to tell somebody...," Jarvis would later say in depositions. "... If we were going to become an informant, how to do it without getting ourselves hurt."

Sam Graber had a sterling connection: David Jordan, an old friend who worked alongside him as an IRS attorney in Dallas in the seventies. Graber recalled that Jordan was last stationed in Atlanta where, the growing party concluded, the iron grip of Tex Moncrief did not reach. "We thought that might be far enough away that we might be able to divulge information without it being leaked back," said Jarvis.

So in March 1993, three months *before* he was fired from Montex, Billy Wayne Jarvis interviewed for another job, a job that would pay him more than the measly $120,000 a year he was getting from us: the job of full-time IRS informant.

★ ★ ★

That Atlanta connection turned out to be solid gold: David Jordan had ascended the ladder to the agency's headquarters in Washington, D.C. He was now the chief counsel of the IRS.

Graber, Keller, and Rolfe flew to Washington to meet with Jordan. Their intention was "to provide the agency with information of alleged criminal tax violations by the Moncriefs that would lead to a criminal tax investigation," Rolfe later recalled in depositions. "We also wanted to convince the IRS to give Jarvis an informant's

(Top) Sixty-four armed agents from the Internal Revenue Service ransacked the Moncrief Building and confiscated our files on September 1, 1994. They promised our disgruntled accountant up to $25 million if he could help them find something wrong with our books.

(Left) The IRS could pack up all the files its agents could carry. It was never going to prove the Moncriefs were tax evaders.

Three generations of Wildcatters—independent and unincorporated—made Moncrief Oil a success. The University of Texas recognized my dad, Tex, as a distinguished engineering graduate for his hard work. Standing by his side that day were his father, "Monty" Moncrief (left), my brother Tom (second from left), my brother Dick (second from right), and myself (right).

Our family business is run out of this downtown Fort Worth building on the corner of Ninth and Commerce. Imagine how painful it was to see the business my family built from nothing torn apart by the IRS, a disloyal employee, and a bitter cousin.

Dad (left), Dick (second from left), Tom (second from right), and I (right) decided to prove our innocence. We fought back against the IRS. Here we are leaving the Tarrance County Justice Center.

Without my wife Kit's support and the good job done by our team of lawyers (including Dee Kelly, to the right of Kit), Moncrief Oil would have been unjustly punished.

Monty Moncrief and his brother, State Sen. Mike Moncrief, are my first cousins. Unfortunately, deep-seated resentment and suspicion got the better of Mike when he sued us and joined forces with our disgruntled accountant, Bill Jarvis.

After Monty passed away, his wife, Jan, told me about Mike's scheming with Bill Jarvis to bring down Moncrief Oil on tax evasion charges. Thank goodness Jan helped me understand what was going on.

Artistic Visions Photography

The biggest heroine in this story is Kay Capps, Moncrief Oil's long-time division order analyst who knew our properties from top to bottom. Before the rest of us suspected anything about our quiet accountant, Kay knew Bill Jarvis was up to no good.

Deposition Photo

First I suspected Ellen Lloyd as the IRS leak. She was a longtime employee trusted by my grand-parents, and she began to behave strangely around the time of the raid. But the reason, it turned out, was that she was taking nearly a half million dollars from my dad's checkbook to pay her personal debts.

Tanya Habjouqua

Bill Jarvis (at left, standing with attorney David Stagner) was making six figures as our longtime accountant. At first he was all business and very courteous. But as time went on, he grew territorial and unfriendly, and developed a grudge against Dad. So he started keeping copies of our files in his spare bedroom, and eventually approached the IRS.

Deposition photo

Jarvis's brother Don, a lawyer and judge with contacts in the legal profession, was key to approaching the IRS. He had a friend who was once an IRS attorney.

Deposition photo

That former IRS attorney was Sam Graber, and he joined the Jarvis brothers in their unethical fee-splitting agreement.

David Woo, Dallas Morning News

So did Don Jarvis's friend James Rolfe, a former U.S. attorney practicing law in Dallas.

Deposition photo

Jim Keller, another former IRS agent and friend of Don Jarvis, joined the conspiracy and signed the fee-splitting agreement.

Deposition photo

Linking Jarvis and Co. to my cousin Mike was Gary Richardson. Richardson was already representing Mike in his lawsuit against us when he employed Jarvis!

As Wildcatters, my family would much rather be producing oil than book-keeping and quibbling with the IRS. Here I am (left) with Dad (center) and my brother Dick (right), drilling for oil in Louisiana.

The oil business is no nine-to-five desk job. Here I am (left) with Moncrief Drilling Superintendent Jack Binkley, in the snows of Wyoming.

fee for assisting the IRS and for testifying in any prosecution of the Moncrief family." He added that he realized Jarvis did have an "obligation" to Tex Moncrief and his relatives as their employee and accountant, but apparently the promise of a "fee" outweighed those responsibilities.

Two matters would have weighed heavily on their minds. First, turning us in to the local IRS wasn't good enough. Their fear was that all the IRS would do was audit our books. Jarvis's group knew that a criminal investigation was essential. They had to be sure to sell the IRS agents on the potential for a conviction to assure themselves a settlement of some sort.

Second, the standard reward agreement that would have come out of North Texas was not good enough. The standard IRS reward agreement calls for a maximum of $100,000; this case would require higher approval. The group needed influence out of D.C. to assure a lucrative agreement.

So on March 8, 1993, the threesome attended a meeting at the IRS headquarters in Washington, D.C. Before Jordan and at least two other "top IRS officials" who were taking notes, the group kept both the identity of the informant and the accused taxpayer confidential.

But they presented a document that Jarvis would later say took him more than two hundred hours to complete. Most of it would turn out to be, according to one IRS official, "figments of Bill's imagination just to, I guess, make it sound sexy to the government that, wow, there's something going on here and we'd better take a look at it."

But in the beginning his brief was more than enough for Bill Jarvis to become an IRS informant:

To: David Jordan
Acting Chief Counsel
Internal Revenue Service

What follows is a narrative describing how a wealthy
family has systematically evaded federal taxes for fifteen
(15) or more years. The family's real estate business
involves three (3) generations and spreads through some
forty (40) taxable entities, including corporations, part-
nerships, trusts and individuals. Although the IRS has
audited the principle [*sic*] individuals, it has been approximately thirteen (13) years since a comprehensive audit
was performed, and even then the audit failed to turn up
the manipulative procedures being used to evade taxes.
The procedures have since grown more numerous and
bolder, involving tens of millions of dollars.

—From Bill Jarvis's letter presented
to the IRS in Washington

It started out so anonymously—with neither writer nor the family being named and the family's occupation changed from oil to
real estate—but Bill Jarvis's initial complaint to the IRS was certainly tantalizing. The charges were spelled out in detail, charges
that, although unsubstantiated, would make any IRS official take
immediate notice:

The surviving principal is presently engaged in
installing computer systems which will make further
manipulation easier to hide and, at the same time, elim-
inate systems that would make detection of past malfea-

sance impossible. Employees knowledgeable of past transactions and accounting systems are being terminated. This is being done in the clandestine environment involving only a few, relatively new, employees, key family members and consultants with the family's CPA and law firms.

—*From Jarvis's letter to the IRS*

There was a sense of urgency to Jarvis's brief: *Act immediately or they'll destroy all the evidence!* And there was plenty of evidence, the letter suggested, all in the author's possession. Jarvis's group served him well; the letter helped "the group" make a great entrance before the IRS:

The family consists of the patriarch, who died during the 1980s at age 90, the mother, who died recently at 91, one (1) living son (another son died in the 1960s) and seven (7) grandchildren. Three (3) of the grandchildren are children of the deceased son. Since the mid forties, father and son were fifty-fifty partners in the real estate business. Each has been mentioned as among the wealthiest people in the United States. Estimates of wealth range from $250,000,000 to $300,000,000 each. When the father reached his late seventies, he began allocating the bulk of partnership expenses to his son and, later, his grandchildren. The practice both reduced the value of his estate and effectuated substantial transfer of property to lower generations without the imposition of transfer taxes. Ownership of real properties was usually taken in either the father's or son's name, but expense sharing and revenue was determined internally, without record title, and was dictated by overall incidents of taxation within the family.... The family has connections at the highest levels of government.

Then came the "examples" of malfeasance, which, Jarvis contended, "are but a few of the transactions the family has used to evade taxes." They were listed as both examples and "comments" from the informant—and the "comments" promised tantalizing backup information to support the claim. On and on the so-called evasions went, thinly disguised but immediately recognizable:

- My 10 percent purchase from my dad in the Madden-Deep gas unit, which, Jarvis contended, was done without gift tax penalties
- Our family's purported loss of $7 million in farming and ranching activities over the past seven years, which, according to Jarvis's comment, should have been disallowed
- Manipulation of payroll costs of approximately one hundred people through charging off "household help as office building maintenance"
- Charging off the salary of "the family's investment advisor, who earns $750,000 per year," and "charging off ranch employees to real estate activities to reduce ranch losses"
- Maintaining a fleet of more than one hundred cars, by which, Jarvis contended, we schemed to "make personal vehicle costs tax deductible"
- Manipulating income from non-oil-producing business

activities, illegal deductions of the family jet, evasive operations of the family's private foundation, the $40 million bailout of a broke grandson and even manipulation of my grandmother's will to evade taxes.

Jarvis's claims painted "the family" as a pack of brazen tax cheats. His letter spewed forth for six full pages, ending with:

> While many more incidences could be cited, and I am confident that your auditors will uncover other abuses, the above examples illustrate that the family has continuously and methodically circumvented the United States tax laws by use of fraudulent procedures in order to enrich themselves and cheat the government out of millions of dollars in income, gift and estate taxes.

The letter created a dramatic effect. Jarvis's group flew back to North Texas fully expecting the case would be immediately investigated in Washington at the highest levels of the IRS—and, most importantly to Jarvis, away from the tentacles of Tex Moncrief.

Instead, they waited months before hearing from the IRS again.

Meanwhile, Bill Jarvis went to work every day at Moncrief. But in June 1993, Dad, convinced that Jarvis wasn't happy working for us anymore, called Jarvis into his office. "Now, Bill, I think things just aren't working out here for you anymore," Dad told him. "I've decided to just pay you for the rest of the year, and give you the Lincoln Town Car you are driving, and just let you move on. How 'bout that?"

We had no reasons to suspect him of anything but lack of interest in his job. We just thought he'd run his course and was ready to move on. Looking back now, I can see that he wanted to get fired. We let him hang around the office for another three weeks. During this time, I heard rumors floating about that he was threatening a wrongful dismissal suit, but I couldn't believe he would challenge the fact that he obviously wasn't happy working for us anymore.

★ ★ ★

Finally, in September 1993, Jarvis's attorneys were contacted by the IRS, not from headquarters in Washington, D.C., but from the agency's Dallas office, headed by Don Wanick, chief of the Criminal Investigations Division, and his assistant, Murray Neighbors, to whom the case had been assigned.

"We were not happy that the service had chosen to assign the case to a group in North Texas," Jarvis would later say in depositions. "We continued to warn the IRS of our concern about the ability of the IRS to maintain confidentiality in the local area and were hoping they would be able to recognize that the government would be at a disadvantage trying a case against Tex Moncrief in the Fort Worth area."

Be careful! Be cautious! Be confidential! These were the sentiments Bill Jarvis seemed to repeat like a mantra in briefs and depositions. But the agency sent the case like a boomerang back into Dad's own backyard, which must have kept Bill up at night. He wouldn't dare meet with the Dallas agents, nor disclose the identity of his family of tax cheats—not until he had his reward guaranteed in writing. Once again, he dispatched Graber, Keller, and Rolfe to do his bidding. "I was still trying to maintain my confidentiality," he would later say in depositions.

But the time soon came for the day of reckoning, when the informant would have to reveal himself and the identity of the family that, he was so sure, had defrauded the government of so many millions. The setting of his face-to-face meeting would be appropriate, in a place far enough away from Dad to be considered absolutely safe.

★ ★ ★

On November 9, 1993, five months after his termination from Montex, Bill Jarvis sat with his brother, Don, in a former funeral home just off the town square in McKinney, Texas, a small-town-turned-Dallas-suburb. The Dream Team had leased this office space on a month-to-month basis.

Once Sam Graber got what he wanted out of the local agents— an agreement that could ensure Bill a reward of up to $25 million for information leading to an indictment—the Jarvis brothers were "invited" into the meeting. Bill Jarvis probably extended his hand to the three IRS agents in attendance and said, "I'm Bill Jarvis, and I worked as comptroller for the Moncriefs for fourteen years."

Jarvis signed the Informant's Reward Agreement so fast, he later said in depositions, that he really didn't take time to read it. Then, Bill produced his bounty: the boxes of tax returns and other records he'd taken from the Moncrief offices before his termination.

Up to that point, Jarvis had done nothing illegal. A person is allowed to give information to the IRS if the information can prove that a crime had occurred. If he had simply handed over his testimonial listing our alleged offenses, signed the IRS agreements, and walked away, Jarvis might have gotten away with something—something like $25 million.

But he didn't.

He signed his Informant's Reward Agreement, with its clauses swearing his confidentiality and his pledge not to disclose anything to anyone about my family or the IRS's investigation of us. He also agreed in writing that he would not assign his resulting bounty to anyone.

Then Jarvis quickly broke both promises.

Jarvis has never admitted to participating in a conspiracy, nor have any members of his group. As for his brother, Don Jarvis, and the others, their actions, detailed in later depositions, spoke for themselves: "Our primary motivation was money," Don testified. As Don and others described in depositions, they joined in a common course of action against the Moncriefs for their mutual financial benefit. To me, that's tantamount to a conspiracy. And that's why I use that word in this book.

Immediately after signing the IRS agreement, Bill convened his team of lawyers and agreed to contracts that would award and assign each of them percentages of his IRS bounty money, the first violation of his informant's agreement. That meeting took place on the same evening as the signing. James Rolfe, Jarvis's attorney, said in a sworn statement: "The Jarvis brothers, Graber, Keller, and I agreed that we would share in any informant's fee paid to Jarvis by the IRS. As per agreement, this was to be split as follows: 35 percent to Bill Jarvis, 35 percent to Don Jarvis, 10 percent to Keller, and 10 percent to me."

During the group's many meetings with the IRS, this reward-splitting agreement was never divulged, says Rolfe, because, if the IRS agents got wind of it, Jarvis's Informant's Agreement would be null and void, and he and his partners wouldn't get a penny for their efforts.

The conspiracy had been set into motion.

The IRS bit hard on the bait that Bill Jarvis had cast them.

★ ★ ★

As an IRS informant, Bill Jarvis was in high demand. He later estimated that he spent more than one thousand hours with the IRS in debriefings, meetings, visits, scheduling, and drawings, "involving significant costs for supplies and travel." To protect himself, Jarvis maintained his personal reference file of information about the case during these meetings. "In December 1993, Don Smith requested that Bill Jarvis find an excuse for reentering the Moncrief office and the Bright offices to determine that significant changes had not taken place since his termination," he would later say in depositions.

Somehow assured that there were no Moncriefs on the premises, Jarvis returned to the Moncrief Building just before Christmas at about 2 P.M. As requested by the IRS, Jarvis prepared detailed and accurate floorplan layouts of all three floors of the building, as well as the offices of our accountants in Dallas, even measuring exterior dimensions of the property "to assist the Criminal Investigation Division (CID) in planning a search of the offices when and if a search warrant was obtained."

During a January 28 meeting with the IRS, Don Smith told Jarvis and company that there was "sufficient evidence that criminal acts had been committed to warrant a criminal investigation by CID." Smith said he would present search warrants to the IRS attorneys on January 31. He expected approval by February 14 and the "surprise search" (raid) to happen on Friday, February 18,

1994. "Be near a telephone on that day, just in case we have questions," Smith told Jarvis, per depositions.

According to the same depositions, Jarvis's phone did not ring on February 18, either with news of the raid or with an explanation from Don Smith about a delay. Finally, almost a month later, on March 15, Jarvis anxiously called Smith. He was told that IRS attorneys were holding up the search warrant while they examined a recently decided case that might be relevant. *Had Tex got wind of the investigation?* Jarvis wondered to himself. Increasingly anxious, he called Smith again the next day. Smith told him to feel free to call his supervisor. Weeks, then months, passed without word from the IRS. It wasn't until September 1994 that the raid would finally occur and Bill's hard work would pay off. And by then, there were others involved.

★ ★ ★

We'd always expected Mike and his family to file a lawsuit against us, ever since they filed that 149A request in 1994, demanding that we account for all the interests Dad was asserting in Granddad and Granddear's estates. In March 1995, Mike and his family did file suit and, with the arrival of the *Moncrief vs. Moncrief* lawsuit we began officially fighting a war on two fronts: Mike and his side of the family on one side and the IRS on the other.

Dad, Dickie, and I happened to be at Dee Kelly's law offices when we were served with the suit. Bob Bennett was there as well. The sheriff's deputy showed up at the Moncrief Building. Betty called Kelly's office and got me on the line. I told her to send him on up to Kelly's, and he served us there.

Mike served us late in the afternoon. He would have already explained to the press what he was doing and hoped that we would fail to reach the press in time for the same edition.

But Kelly, a seasoned political pro himself, said immediately, "Get the press over here right now; this is an old political ploy by Mike."

Bennett turned to Dad. "Come on, Tex, let's you and me write a response."

In the press release, Dad stated:

> The allegations in the complaint are scurrilous, baseless and irresponsible.
>
> My sons and I adamantly deny these outrageous allegations and we will vigorously fight them. Because of my father and mother, the plaintiffs are rich men. It is sad that Mike and Monty, for reasons of greed, would make these allegations.
>
> I have always carried out the wishes of my parents to the letter and the penny. This lawsuit is an insult to the memory of my mother and father.

Based on the focus of the 149A request and on the run-ins we'd already had with Mike and his family in other courts, we had a pretty good idea of what to expect in this new lawsuit. First, Mike's suit claimed that Dad and I had figured out a way to illegally reduce their share of Granddad and Granddear's Louisiana properties and increase our own shares:

> Defendants...devised a scheme wherein the Plaintiffs' interests in the Louisiana properties were diminished from a ⅛th interest to a ½th interest and the interests of the W. A. "Tex" Moncrief children, including

Charles B. Moncrief and Richard W. Moncrief, were increased from ⅛th interest to a ½th interest, in breach of fiduciary duties owed to the Plaintiffs.

Secondly, Mike's suit accused Dad of inventing a fifty-fifty partnership arrangement with his father in order to reduce the holdings of Granddad and Granddear's estates by half:

> "Tex" Moncrief, Jr., contrary to the best interests of the Estates and Plaintiffs, asserts an "equitable interest" of 50% in virtually all oil and gas properties held in record title in the name W. A. Moncrief.... Defendants have been paying to Tex Moncrief, contrary to the best interests of the Estates and Plaintiffs, proceeds attributable to that asserted "equitable interest" during the course of the administration of the Estates.

In plain language, this would mean that Dad was cheating the estate out of half of what it was entitled to. Of course, the Price Waterhouse audit had clearly demonstrated that the partnership wasn't "invented" at all. Dad had already proven himself to be half owner in all of the properties he claimed. As far as we were concerned, this question was settled.

The content of Mike's lawsuit was no surprise, but the term "equitable interest" definitely got my attention. Before we fired him, Bill Jarvis was using these same two words when he tried to convince other members of the staff that we were cheats. *Equitable interest.* As noted, it's a real estate term Jarvis had pointedly tried to apply to our ownership of oil interests. And here it was again, coming from Mike's lawyers. The apparent coincidence waved red flags.

By March 1995, it had become clear to us that Jarvis was deeply involved in the IRS investigation. Now it was equally clear that he was involved with Mike as well. But Jarvis was officially an "anonymous informant" as far as the IRS was concerned, which meant he didn't have to account for his statements in a court of law. We couldn't depose him, and we might never have the chance to question him about the IRS case on the witness stand. However, we could legally depose him for the purposes of Mike Moncrief's lawsuit. Even though Mike's lawsuit would undoubtedly cost us yet another fortune in attorney fees, it was potentially an extraordinary blessing. It could give us, for the first time, the ability to depose Bill Jarvis and to confirm publicly what we had always suspected was going on behind the scenes.

★ ★ ★

On the morning of Thursday, August 10, 1995, our entire defense team had a face-to-face meeting with the IRS to respond to each of their charges against us. Both sides met in Richard Roper's office in the Burnett Plaza office building next to the U.S. courthouse.

As this tense hearing unfolded, it became clear that our lawyers had anticipated everything the IRS had to say. Bob Bennett, Jim Bruton, Marshall Searcy, and Clive Bode were prepared to meet each of the IRS's thirteen primary charges with a clear and logical explanation. The third item on the list was my purchase of 10 percent of the Madden-Deep unit from Dad. As I've mentioned before, according to our purchase agreement, I wasn't required to pay any money for the Madden until the field produced cash flow—and this didn't happen until 1993. This meant that even though I had made the purchase back in 1988, I had only started paying for it recently. The problem was that our purchase agreement was recorded only in some handwritten notes in my business diary. When the IRS agents predictably accused me of "inventing" the agreement, we had a sweet surprise for them, thanks to the forethought of Hugh Culverhouse, my old high school roommate.

Hugh is a criminal lawyer in Florida. His father owned the Tampa Bay Buccaneers. Right after the raid, Hugh called to say he had seen the story about the raid in the Florida papers. When I told him what was happening, Hugh said, "Well, sooner or later, you or your father will probably want to take a polygraph test." When I asked him what the test should be about, he answered, "Don't worry, you'll find out. It's just typical in these cases that you need to prove your own honesty on some important point. So this might be something you want to do."

A few months after the raid, I was talking to Jim Bruton about the diaries and the Madden deal. "Jim, why don't I take a lie detector test about this?" I asked.

"Do you want to?" Bruton replied.

"Hell, yes, I want to. I wrote that deal about the Madden in my diary, and it's going to be important in this case. A polygraph test will take care of the whole problem."

"All right then," said Jim. "I've got a guy. He's world renowned."

His name is Paul Minor, Bruton said, and he was the polygraph operator who would eventually test Detective Mark Fuhrman in the O. J. Simpson case. "Paul can give it to you in D.C.," Jim said. "But don't tell anyone about this until after it's over. Don't even tell your Dad."

"Why not?" I asked.

"In case you fail it," Jim replied.

Culverhouse had warned me that while it's nearly impossible to lie and pass the polygraph test, there are many instances where people fail even though they're telling the truth. Jim Bruton had known me for only three months, and he was probably wondering whether I might outsmart myself. Anyway, I took his advice. I did not disclose my intention to take the polygraph to anyone except Kit.

In early February 1995, Kit and I headed to Washington, D.C. Paul Minor and I met at the law offices of Williams and Connolly.

Paul had run polygraphs for army intelligence and for the FBI for fifteen years. He was one of the premier polygraph operators in the country, well known and credible. He left little doubt that he knew what he was doing. The three of us, Bruton, Minor, and I, discussed the basics of the Madden transactions and the family business in general. Then Paul excused Bruton.

Paul strapped sensors to my chest and hand and a sphygmoma-nometer cuff around my arm. Sitting there all strapped up, I thought, "There is no way anybody could lie through one of these things!" I wasn't nervous about being tempted to lie. I had come to tell the truth, but I was sure intimidated. I suddenly became very conscious of my breathing and my heartbeat. Paul turned on his machine.

"Are you ready?"

"Yes."

He asked me the questions. Once, then again. I answered simply and truthfully.

"That's it," he said.

I sat there quietly for a few seconds while he rigged down his machine.

"Well, did I pass?" I asked.

"Oh, yeah, you passed with flying colors," he replied.

Flash forward to the hearing of August 10, when the IRS agents brought up the Madden transaction. Our attorneys said,

"Gentlemen, you can just put that one out of your minds. Charlie took a lie detector test by Paul Minor, and he passed it with flying colors."

Anticipating that the agents would also claim the diary entry had been written after the fact, we also mentioned that the diary had been sent to a crime lab in Wisconsin, and the ink had been dated. Strike two!

Bob Bennett closed the meeting with a memorable speech: "Gentlemen, think about it: My clients have paid $150 million in taxes to the federal government over the past fifteen years, and you are questioning $6 million that may be due? I'd love to take this case before a jury in Fort Worth, Texas!"

I think the lie detector test is what broke the IRS's back: even though I had my diary ink dated by a crime lab, the IRS could have taken the position that I made a false diary entry on purpose back when Dad and I cut the deal. But the polygraph proved that I was telling the truth. Even IRS agent Mike Sanders applauded our foresight when he heard about the lie detector test. We felt we had turned a major corner in our fight to clear our name.

However, another battle was heating up on the Mike Moncrief lawsuit. U.S. attorney Richard Roper was adamantly opposed to letting Bill Jarvis appear as a witness in any case but his own IRS case. Jarvis was, after all, a potential $100 million man for the IRS, and Roper did not want him spilling his guts on what must have seemed to the agency to be a family squabble.

To argue against Jarvis's deposition, Roper appeared at a hearing in 342nd Judicial District Court before the Honorable Judge Bob McGrath. Outside the courtroom, Judge McGrath is laid back and Texas folksy. When he calls attorneys into his chambers for consultations, he often sends one of them off to get sandwiches from Angelo's, Fort Worth's famous barbecue joint. But when he puts on his black robe and gets up on his stand, McGrath is a judge of strict rules and traditions. On the day Roper strode in, I could tell from the sour look on the judge's face that he was not impressed with Roper's appearance or with his reason for being there. But he let Roper argue his case.

"They can't depose Jarvis, because he's a witness in a federal tax case," Roper told the court. "Federal witnesses cannot be deposed. The least you can do is delay Jarvis's deposition until after we complete our grand jury investigation."

McGrath swiftly denied all counts of Roper's motion. "Jarvis is not being deposed in a federal tax case," he said. " Mike Moncrief's lawsuit is a totally unrelated matter."

In what he surely considered a generous gesture of compromise, McGrath asked our lawyers to refrain from posing any questions directly relating to the IRS's case. That suited us just fine, since it was fairly clear that while the two lawsuits were "totally unrelated," in a legal sense, their subject matter was the same: Jarvis had just sold the same bogus story to two buyers.

We decided to take Roper's appeal as a good sign. After all, why would he be worried about Jarvis's testimony in Mike's case unless he figured his witness was shaky—or had something to hide? When Judge McGrath ordered Jarvis's deposition to proceed as scheduled, Jim Bruton was elated. "This is just incredible!" he said. "No one has ever deposed a government witness before!"

Bruton knew that the two cases were so closely linked that we could ask questions about only one, but find out information relevant to both. Mike's suit was opening a major door for us.

Just before Jarvis's first deposition, we received word from our attorney Clive Bode that the IRS was demanding to see our business diaries. We had slam-dunked the IRS at the August 10 meeting, and they were desperate for more information. But we decided not to turn the diaries over without a fight. We sent them to Clive Bode for preliminary review and left them there for safe-keeping. Even though the IRS kept pressuring our lawyers, Kelly and Bode refused to turn the diaries over. Lawyers do a lot of things as a matter of principle, especially when they are unfairly ordered to hand over personal property. I had already gone to Washington, D.C., months before, where I sat down with attorneys David Zinn and Jim Bruton and went through every one of the diaries page by page.

Eventually Clive did call us to say, "The IRS insists on seeing those diaries, and they'll go to court if they have to in order to get them in pure, unredacted form." In exchange for receiving the diaries without any more hassle from us, the IRS agreed that only IRS agent Mike Sanders, an IRS agent I used to know in college, who had distinguished himself as honest and straightforward, would get to look at them.

So in late September, Dad and I submitted our diaries for the years 1984 to 1993 to Mike Sanders for review. Some time later, after the whole affair was over, Roper would tell us, "When we went through the diaries, not only was there nothing incriminating about them, they were in fact exculpatory. What you had written down showed the very fact that you hadn't been doing anything criminal, not only about the Madden deal but your other transactions as well."

Tuesday, August 15, 1995, was the day of Bill Jarvis's first deposition. Fourteen people were crammed into a room about the size of a gas station restroom. Gerald Hilsher was there to represent Mike; Jim Rolfe was there for Jarvis; and Hugh Connor and Marshall Searcy represented us. Bill Bogle was there for Granddad and Granddear's estates, and even Mike's disabled sister, Lee Wiley Moncrief, had counsel present.

Dad, Dickie, Tom, and I all pushed our way into the back of the room. I was practically sitting on Gerald Hilsher's lap, and the woman taking the video deposition was practically sitting on mine.

Marshall Searcy began with the standard warm-up questions, and Jarvis responded with a broad but vacant smile. Obviously, he had been instructed to pretend the camera was his jury and to try and make a good impression. But when Searcy hit him with the first real question—"Who's your biggest client?"—Jarvis's strategy fell apart.

"Richardson and Stoops," Jarvis answered, staring blankly at the camera.

You could have heard a pin drop. Even the videographer, who had been involved in other depositions for this case, seemed stunned by Jarvis's answer. She turned to me with her mouth wide open—but no wider than mine. Richardson and Stoops, everyone knew, *were the attorneys representing Mike Moncrief!*

Even Marshall Searcy, who has one of the best poker faces in the business, couldn't conceal the effect of that answer. I actually saw a fleeting grin dart across his face before he returned to business. As always, Marshall's words were measured, careful, and clear, but now they rose an octave higher in pitch.

"Well, that's interesting," he said. "Let me get this straight: Richardson and Stoops? Now, those are Mike Moncrief's attorneys in this lawsuit, correct?"

"Yes, sir, that's correct," said Jarvis.

"How long have you been working for them?" Marshall asked.

"About a year," Jarvis replied.

"Who hired you?"

Jarvis said Gary Richardson had hired him.

"Do you have a written agreement?" asked Marshall.

"No," Jarvis said. "Just an oral one."

"Have you ever told the IRS that you're on Mike Moncrief's payroll?" asked Searcy.

"Well, no, I don't believe I did."

By now, Jarvis was staring wild-eyed at the camera. Every now and then, he would glance nervously at his lawyer. I don't know how much he was paying Jim Rolfe, but Rolfe didn't do much work that day. The least he could have done was ask for a break. I only remember watching a Styrofoam cup full of water in Rolfe's hand, passing up to his lips and down again. The more questions Jarvis answered, the faster that cup moved. Obviously, both Jarvis and Rolfe were in a state of shock. They surely knew these questions were coming, but I think that Searcy lowered the boom so fast that they lost all composure.

Things were getting hotter at the back of the room as well. Judging from the little chair dance he was performing next to me, Mike's attorney Gerald Hilsher wasn't enjoying Jarvis's testimony nearly as much as I was. Earlier, I had wondered why Hilsher wasn't sitting next to Jarvis, and now I was about to learn why. Hilsher was there to protect Mike *from* Jarvis. So when Searcy asked: "Tell us the oral agreement that exists between you and lawyer Richardson," Hilsher jumped to his feet.

"I would object at this point in time!" he said. "I don't think that's relevant."

Then, he turned to Jarvis and said, "Don't say anymore!"

It's highly unusual for an attorney who doesn't represent the witness to tell him what to do in a deposition. But in this case unusual was the norm. And it would quickly get stranger. Marshall Searcy, who has a master actor's style of dramatic delivery, slowly turned and addressed the cramped little room and its sweaty occupants. "Did I hear a voice?" Searcy asked.

Hilsher eventually convinced Jarvis's attorney Jim Rolfe to do something!

"Don't answer any more questions about this!" Rolfe told Jarvis.

Searcy wanted to make the record absolutely clear about which questions Jarvis was being instructed not to answer and why. He spent about half an hour running down an impromptu list of questions concerning Jarvis's employment at Richardson and Stoops, forcing Rolfe and Hilsher to object to each question and to forbid Jarvis from answering:

Searcy: How much were you being paid?

Hilsher: I'll object to that question on the grounds of privilege as we previously stated.

Rolfe: I'll instruct him not to answer that until the judge orders him.

Searcy: Are you refusing to tell me how much you're being paid by Mike Moncrief's lawyer in this matter?

Jarvis: Yes.

Searcy: What were you being paid to do?

Hilsher: I'll object to that question on the grounds of privilege.

Searcy (to Rolfe): Are you instructing him not to answer?

Rolfe: Right.

Searcy (to Jarvis): Are you refusing to answer that question, sir?

Jarvis: Yes.

When he finally got through his list of questions, Marshall adjourned the deposition and went to call the judge's clerk. "We need to come over there for an emergency hearing," Searcy said. "The witness is refusing to answer any questions."

The clerk wrote us into Judge Bob McGrath's schedule for that afternoon. Marshall immediately called U.S. attorney Richard Roper.

"Richard, I just wanted to let you know that your key witness is over here," Searcy told Roper, a point man in the IRS investigation. "We were taking his deposition, and we found out a couple of things that might interest you. Number one, he's on Mike Moncrief and Gary Richardson's payroll. Number two, he's getting ready to plead the Fifth Amendment!"

Roper's only comment: "SHIT!"

Eventually, the whole contingent from the deposition room marched over to Judge McGrath's chambers. If he was stern in the earlier hearing, Judge McGrath was now fully annoyed, not only at Jarvis's refusal to answer, but also at the behavior of his growing phalanx of attorneys. The judge ordered Jarvis to return to the deposition and answer Marshall's questions.

As we straggled back to our cramped deposition room in the Kelly, Hart and Hallman offices, I wondered how Jarvis would get out of this one. Surely he wouldn't admit to entering a business agreement with Mike and his attorneys. It would be improper on Jarvis's part and unethical on the part of Mike's lawyers. You can't put a potential fact witness on your payroll, nor could Jarvis be handing out our tax return information to whomever he chose.

Rolfe certainly wasn't stupid enough to let his client do that! On the other hand, it wouldn't be a very good idea for Jarvis to perjure himself either.

When we got back to our little deposition room, the short-term answer to Jarvis's situation became clear to me. When Jarvis and his attorney disappeared during our return to the deposition, we just thought they had left to get a cup of coffee or have a short conference. Looking back, I have to admit I was surprised and impressed with the simple elegance of their tactic: *Jarvis and Rolfe had left altogether!*

Marshall Searcy had the video camera turned back on. He convened the deposition—even though there was no one to depose! Then, speaking directly to the camera, Searcy explained the situation in detail:

> We have just been in a proceeding before District Judge Bob McGrath where the claims of privilege asserted by Mr. Hilsher and subsequently by the witness were overruled. We are now at the reconvened deposition of Mr. Bill Jarvis, which is being held pursuant to Court Order. Mr. Jarvis is not present to continue the Deposition. We have waited a decent interval for his reappearance at this proceeding and we must assume now that he is not going to come back....

It must have been one of the shortest depositions in legal history, ending with a camera pan from Searcy's face, barely suppressing a grin, over to Jarvis's empty seat.

About a week later, Judge McGrath held a hearing to determine two things: First, he needed to know what Bill Jarvis was trying to hide. Exactly what kind of relationship had been established between Jarvis and Mike Moncrief's lawyers? The key witness in that question turned out to be Mike's accountant Jerry Goodwin, who first presented Mike with Jarvis's information about us and who acted as a go-between for Jarvis and Mike's lawyers in the early stages of their partnership. Second, Judge McGrath needed both sides to make arguments about the legal significance of Jarvis being on lawyer Richardson's payroll. For that purpose, the Judge would hear from several experts.

The day after the hearing, the *Fort Worth Star-Telegram* (also derided as the "*Startlegram*") ran an article about the meaning of Jarvis's botched deposition. The article explains the whole mess a lot better than I can:

> In a tense hearing yesterday in state district judge Bob McGrath's court, documents and testimony by Mike Moncrief's accountant revealed that [Bill] Jarvis was offered the consultant position in July 1994, two months before the Internal Revenue Service raided Tex Moncrief's offices based on allegations of tax fraud.
>
> Jarvis now figures as an important witness in two cases involving one of the state's best-known oil families: the lawsuit that Mike Moncrief filed against his uncle in March, claiming Tex Moncrief defrauded him out of his rightful share of the family's oil and gas earnings; and the ongoing federal criminal investigation into Tex Moncrief's taxes....
>
> "Today's testimony destroys Mr. Jarvis as a witness in the criminal investigation," said Bob Bennett, who has represented President Bill Clinton and former Illinois

congressman Dan Rostenkowski and now represents Tex
Moncrief in the criminal case.... "It is clear that he is a
disgruntled ex-employee terminated by Mr. Tex Moncrief who later went on the payroll of Mike Moncrief's
lawyers...."

Also yesterday, the senator's accountant, Jerry Goodwin, testified that Mike Moncrief has reimbursed his
lawyers for Jarvis' services.... "I almost fell out of my
chair when I heard Mr. Goodwin testify," said Marshall
Searcy Jr., Tex Moncrief's lead attorney in the lawsuit.
"Bill Jarvis should not...go down the street and sell his
client's confidential information."...

One of the expert witnesses, University of Pennsylvania law professor Geoffrey Hazard, said Jarvis violated
state law by "giving any information at all" to Mike Moncrief's lawyers.

He also said Mike Moncrief's lawyers violated legal
ethics by paying Jarvis as consultant, which he said could
be grounds for dismissing the lawsuit or disqualifying
the lawyers.

At that hearing, McGrath got fed up with Jarvis's stalling. If he
was going to plead the Fifth, so be it. If not, it was time to start
answering questions. He issued an order that Jarvis would be
deposed again on September 12. To ensure that Jarvis and his
lawyer would show up this time, Judge McGrath ordered the deposition to take place in his courtroom and in his presence.

At this same time we began to receive suggestions from the
IRS of the possibility of a "global settlement" as well as some type
of a corporate plea to help them save face. This would be a *nolo*

contendere plea. You're not really admitting guilt, but it certainly has that appearance. One day, Dee Kelly had run into U.S. Attorney Roper at the federal courthouse in Fort Worth. As a way of getting this whole orderal behind us, Kelly suggested that our family pay the IRS three million dollars. Roper responded that the tax penalties they had against us were worth more like $300 million, at which Kelly headed back to his office.

That same day, Kelly called Dad and me to his office. "I ran into Roper today and we talked settlement," he said. "Now, don't pay any attention to these figures; it's just loose talk."

We said okay.

"I suggested three million, and Roper mentioned three hundred million," he said. "With that, I hit the door."

My heart sank at the figure. Dad looked at me and said, "Good gosh almighty."

We'd been in enough legal skirmishes to know that these early settlement volleys are wildly exaggerated, just to give the lawyers some room to wrangle. But Roper's response was many zeros higher than we ever dreamed. If his tactic was to put the fear of God in us, he had succeeded.

For his second deposition on September 12, Jarvis showed up dressed in the same padded gray suit and blue shirt. He answered every question Marshall Searcy asked him by replying, "I am going to invoke my constitutional right against self-incrimination."

To this, the judge would say, "Because this is an inappropriate application of your Fifth Amendment rights, I'm instructing you to answer."

Then Jarvis would repeatedly respond, "I continue to claim my Fifth Amendment right."

It went like this for three hours.

When Marshall finally ran out of questions, he said: "Your Honor, at this time the defendants, W. A. 'Tex' Moncrief and others, move that Mr. Jarvis be held in contempt for his refusal to answer questions the court has instructed him to answer."

Judge McGrath turned to Jarvis. "I will give you one last opportunity, if you wish, to change your response to the questions I have instructed you to answer," he said.

"I continue to claim my Fifth Amendment right," Jarvis repeated.

"All right," said the judge. "I will then finally adjudicate you in contempt of court and order you confined to jail until such time as you purge yourself of that contempt by answering the questions that have been duly posed and to which you have been instructed to answer."

For a minute there, it looked like Jarvis was headed to jail. But then Marshall Searcy stood up and asked Judge McGrath to release Jarvis "to the recognizance of his attorney." Of course, the judge agreed. Searcy was merely trying to extend at least some professional courtesy to the opposing lawyers. But this was one of those moments when that courtesy got a little irritating to Dad and me.

I turned to Searcy's young associate, Hugh Connor, and whispered, "Hugh, why the hell won't Marshall let the bastard go to jail?"

Connor reminded me that no matter how angry I felt at the moment, the satisfaction of jailing Jarvis was definitely not worth the trouble of jeopardizing our case and our standing before the court, the public, and the legal profession. I chalked it up to lawyer B.S. Whenever we look back on that moment, Dad and I always wish we had let Jarvis spend at least a weekend behind bars while we had the chance. But Marshall assured us that setting him free would more than pay for itself in the respect of the judge and Jarvis's attorneys. I supposed he was right.

At the end of the hearing, Jim Rolfe requested that the transcripts to this hearing be suppressed from public access. The judge asked why. "Because [the press] could basically portray an invalid picture of what this is all about by picking and choosing some of the questions that were asked here and then his invocation of his constitutional right," said Rolfe.

In other words, Rolfe was afraid that Jarvis's use of the Fifth Amendment would make him look, well, *guilty*. Once again, I was floored. What the hell was so unfair about Jarvis looking guilty? If he was afraid to answer questions about the work he was being paid to do for Mike's attorneys because he thought it would incriminate him, then wouldn't he deserve to look guilty? It doesn't take a high-priced lawyer to figure that out.

Bill Bogle, the attorney for Granddad and Granddear's estates, stood up and nailed Rolfe's plea on the head: "The way to avoid that negative inference is simply to answer the question!"

The judge decided to seal the transcripts of this deposition until after a more thorough hearing on the matter. But after another hearing, the transcripts were unsealed, and to this day Jarvis's "negative inference" is a matter of public record.

One month after Jarvis pled the Fifth Amendment, we took the deposition of Gerald Hilsher, the reputable attorney who did legwork for Gary Richardson when he was retained by Mike and his family. In response to the discovery documents request, Hilsher provided us with our best evidence yet. It was an unsigned copy of an agreement between the entire group—Gary Richardson, Bill Jarvis, Jim Keller, Jim Rolfe, Don Jarvis, and Sam Graber—that set forth how all the parties intended to divide the money they made from Mike's lawsuit and from Bill Jarvis's IRS informant's fees. Simply put, it was a fee splitting agreement between lawyers and nonlawyers, which is unethical in the legal profession. According to Texas Disciplinary Rules of Professional Conduct, Rule 5.04A: "A lawyer or law firm shall not share or promise to share legal fees with a non-lawyer. . . . "

Hilsher also described how he discovered the agreement, and how this discovery caused him to urge his law partners to turn themselves in to the state bar. Hilsher confronted both Gary Richardson and Sam Graber, who told him that the "fee splitting agreement" had never been signed. Hilsher testified that it was obvious to him these men were lying.

The agreement revealed to us exactly who had been involved with Jarvis in the conspiracy. Immediately after Hilsher's revelation, we heard from Mike's attorneys; Mike and family wanted out of the countersuit we'd filed against him when he filed suit against us over Dad's handling of Granddad's estate, in March 1995. We reluctantly agreed to release them from the suit, provided that they send us a formal letter of apology. We had the letter the next day. After getting the unsigned copy of the fee splitting agreement, we sued all of the conspirators, the signatory parties on the agreement.

After our considerable advances during Jarvis's depositions, not to mention our successful hearing at the IRS, we were feeling pretty good about our case with the IRS. But we still had a tough battle ahead of us, and a lot to learn about how Bill Jarvis and Mike Moncrief came to be unlikely allies.

Chapter Seven

The IRS Settlement

FOR EIGHTEEN YEARS, KAY MARTIN WORKED at Montex, first as assistant bookkeeper, then, when our chief bookkeeper, Margie Driskill, collapsed across her desk from exhaustion, as our new chief. To the best of our knowledge, Kay was a trooper, doing her job with precision and enthusiasm. But at some point, Kay Martin began to sour on us. By 1995, she had turned so completely against us that she began providing information to the IRS. But it wasn't until October 20, 1997, when we took Kay's deposition, that we would discover the depth of Kay's discontent.

What we really wanted to know was, *Why?* Why had Kay turned her back on all those years of hard work, on all the friends she had made in the Moncrief organization, and on the secure future that would surely have been hers as a lifelong employee? Could Bill Jarvis have been so convincing? Could his promises have been that compelling? Kay had married another man since her office relationship with Bill, so the romantic connection was apparently not an issue anymore. Was it money? Was it fear?

Our lawyers had their own reasons to question Kay Martin that fall day, reasons having to do with the complex tangle of legal issues surrounding Mike's lawsuit against us and our suit against Jarvis and his coconspirators. But my brother Tom and I attended that deposition mostly out of curiosity. We just had to clear up our confusion about how this trusted, longtime employee could become an IRS double agent, to see the flipside of loyalty.

The lawyers had many different ways to ask basically the same questions. The trouble was, Kay had some weird ways to answer them. It was almost as if she were two Kays: Kay for the prosecution and Kay for the defense. In the days after the IRS raid, Kay refused to hire an attorney to prepare her for the grand jury. She just didn't trust lawyers, she said; they made her nervous. She had shown up at her own deposition without counsel. I guess if there were ever a chance for the world to discover why lawyers made Kay so nervous, now would be the time.

There were two lead questioners in that deposition. Marshall Searcy's associate Hugh Connor represented our side of the suit. A trim and fit thirty-year-old, Hugh has a brilliant mind for litigation, which he hides behind a wry, fun-loving personality and an affinity for dipping snuff. The truth is, Hugh's legal mind seems to feed off his sense of humor, as if he uses his humorous anecdotes to help him memorize and organize all the minutiae of a case.

Bill Jarvis and his brother, Don, were represented by David Stagner—"Stags" for short. Stags is Hugh Connor's polar opposite: a pudgy, prune-faced guy, partial to Big Bomber Partagas cigars. I liked Stags; he was always very courteous to me. He might drive a four-door Mercedes and smoke expensive cigars, but I know him for what he really is: the quintessential small town Texas lawyer. Stags loves to piss people off, not only with his go-for-the-jugular style of questioning, but also with his constant show of edge and attitude. He would drive two hours to one of our depositions, then just sit there sucking on a cigar and thumbing through the latest issue of *Texas Lawyer*, acting as though he weren't listening. When we appeared before the United States Court of Appeals for the Fifth Circuit in New Orleans, he brought his *extremely* young bride with him. He had his associate sit between him and her, as if hoping that the age discrepancy wouldn't be so obvious.

When Kay's deposition began, we quickly discovered that her problem with lawyers was well founded. She turned to absolute putty in each of the attorneys' hands. To Hugh Connor, she portrayed herself as a loyal employee, goaded by the government into helping the IRS fabricate evidence against her innocent employers. You'd have thought she and Bill Jarvis had never met. In the first few minutes of questioning, Kay said she never even knew Bill was working for the IRS. To David Stagner, she told the story (or at least allowed *him* to tell it) of an unsuspecting bookkeeper intimidated by her cruel, heartless bosses into repeatedly defrauding the government. The scary thing is, I believe Kay figured *both* stories were true!

When it was Connor's turn to question her, Kay claimed that she'd decided to cooperate with the IRS because they'd intimidated her into thinking that if she didn't cooperate, she'd be prosecuted along with us:

> **Connor:** So you were doing this out of, what, your belief that the federal government had been wronged?

Kay: That if I didn't, then they would—

Connor: Put you in jail?
Kay: They would come after me, yes—because the government is the government. They will delve into your personal life until they find something to bring you up against.

When it was Stagner's turn, Kay flip-flopped. First, she let him make us out as bullying, frightening employers:

> **Stagner:** In what way was [Tex] hard to work for?
> **Kay:** He was very intimidating—
> **Stagner:** Did his sons... try to intimidate people?
> **Kay:** At times...

Stagner then focused specifically on Dad. According to the portrait he attempted to paint, Tex Moncrief was a bully who forced his employees to break the law. If he ever got caught, he would turn the blame back on them:

> **Stagner:** Oh, so you didn't question what Tex did? Is that a fair statement?
> **Kay:** Yes, sir.
> **Stagner:** He's a mean old man, isn't he?
> **Kay:** Some think that he is...
> **Stagner:** Do you think he has loyalty to anybody?
> **Kay:** No, sir.
> **Stagner:** When push came to shove with the govern-

ment, do you think Tex Moncrief would ever accept responsibility for the things he told you to do?

Kay: No, sir.

Then there was the question of Kay's spying for the IRS. When Hugh Connor questioned her, Kay admitted that for two months in late 1994 and early 1995, she had been secretly meeting with the IRS in order to "explain" various documents Jarvis had given them. As those meetings progressed, she claimed, it became obvious that the government wasn't really searching for the truth—just a conviction and lots of cash:

> **Connor:** Was it your feeling that the federal government was going to attempt to fabricate some evidence?
>
> **Kay:** That's exactly right—
>
> **Connor:** In your opinion, they just couldn't grasp the accounting?
>
> **Kay:** They were trying to make something out of something that wasn't there.

These were Kay's words, not Connor's. *Make something out of something that wasn't there.* Those were welcome words to me, even coming from Kay! But before the words had a chance to sink in, it was Stagner's turn to question her. Within minutes, Kay was allowing Stagner to guide her towards a very different word: *Fraud.* Together, Stagner and Kay Martin went through a laundry list of allegations. First, they made our college scholarship fund, especially the scholarship we provided to Kay herself, look like some kind of conspiracy to extort Kay's cooperation by luring her into breaking the law:

> **Stagner:** He was taking money out of this charitable foundation and using it to pay your tuition?
>
> **Kay:** Yes, sir.
>
> **Stagner:** Which was directly benefiting one of his employees, correct?
>
> **Kay:** Yes, sir.
>
> **Stagner:** And you knew that he was not supposed to direct these monies?
>
> **Kay:** Yes, sir. . . .
>
> **Stagner:** And that certainly gave them some control over you from your perspective?
>
> **Kay:** Yes.

Regarding the scholarships, we could give them to employees, but they would have to meet the same standards set for anyone else.

Next, they made our method of allocating joint interest in oil wells, which was consistent with standard industry practice, look like some kind of orchestrated tax evasion:

> **Stagner:** Explain to the jury, the best you can, how they were directing you to manipulate those [allocations] so that it defrauded the government.
>
> **Kay:** If it were dry, then they would take the cost themselves instead of bearing it on to the other parties that did not need the write-off.

Then Stagner led Kay into a blatant distortion—a claim that we charged the payroll of our household help to the corporation:

Stagner: [Did the Moncriefs have] maids?

Kay: Yes, sir.

Stagner: And all kinds of hired help?

Kay: Yes, sir.

Stagner: And some of those people to your knowledge were being paid out of the corporation?

Kay: Yes, sir. . . .

Stagner: Did you read about Leona Helmsley? I think that's what she was doing before they sent her to prison . . . .

Leona Helmsley? The only misappropriated payroll funds I knew about were related to our "handyman" Gregory Kurilec's salary, which Kay had discovered years ago, and we had fixed immediately. Based on this one incident, Stagner made it seem as if we illegally wrote off the pay of many household employees. The worst distortions of all, however, concerned our personal character:

Stagner: What do you think would happen [to you] based upon your dealings with these stellar members of the community?

Kay: I knew what would have happened.

Stagner: What was that?

Kay: It would be me.

Stagner: You'd be the sacrificial lamb?

Kay: Yes, sir. . . .

Stagner: And you knew they had the loyalty of an alley cat when it came to their employees, didn't you?

Kay: Yes, sir.

Okay, I know what it means to be nervous, and I know how adept lawyers can be at making someone say things they don't really mean. But sacrificial lamb? Loyalty of an alley cat? Before I walked into that deposition room, I believed that our staff—at least the ones who had known us for almost twenty years—understood us better than that:

> **Connor:** At some point in time did you have a discussion with Mr. Jarvis about possibly assisting the government in their investigation?
> **Kay:** No, sir.

And then just fourteen pages later:

> **Connor:** Why would he give you a portion of his finder's fee? For your assistance?
> **Kay:** Yes.

I believe two factors motivated Kay. First was her hatred for Tex Moncrief. Second, Jarvis clearly had convinced her that there was a possibility she might be implicated.

★ ★ ★

Despite the disappointment we felt after Kay Martin's testimony, our advances during Jarvis's depositions, not to mention our successful hearing at the IRS, left us feeling pretty good about our case with the IRS.

Bob Bennett took it upon himself to initiate settlement negotiations with Roper. "What do you say to $500,000?" Bennett asked the assistant U.S. attorney Richard Roper. Having thoroughly examined our tax records, we knew that the few items we might have overlooked in the past twenty years added up to about that much.

Roper responded, "What about $50 million?"

Fifty million dollars is a hell of a lot of money, but Roper had just chopped off $250 million from his earlier $300 million offer. Bennett was in constant communication with Dad during the evening. Clearly $50 million was of no interest to us. Bennett said he would keep working Roper and get back. He upped the ante to $10 million and Roper dropped it to twenty-five. Roper immediately dropped down to $24 million, but the small drop indicated he was running out of room.

Bennett called Dad. "Tex, this is a good deal," he said. "You've already got seven and a half million dollars in legal and accounting fees. We can fight this thing and win, but it will take four years to get to trial. You will double the seven and a half and you'll be seventy-nine years old. In my opinion, at $24 million you're breaking even."

Dad gave him the okay. "You're making the right decision, Tex," Bennett said. "I'll make a deal, but I'm going to squeeze one more million out of 'em."

"Sounds good," Dad joked. "If you do, I'll split it with you!"

He thought Dad was serious. "Oh, no, I couldn't do that!"

Oblivious to the bargaining, which was now stretching toward midnight, I was home asleep. Bennett got back on the phone with Roper, while Dad waited by his phone.

A half an hour later, Dad's phone rang one more time: "Tex, I got it done; they agreed to $23 million."

Dad clearly wasn't as happy as his lawyer expected him to be. "I don't know about this, " Dad said. "We don't owe them anything as far as I'm concerned. Considering how much money we've had to spend defending ourselves against these false charges, I think *they* should be paying *us*."

The next morning, I went by Dad's house as usual. Dad was busy at the kitchen chopping block preparing breakfast for his pugs. I watched from a chair at the kitchen table sipping my mug of coffee.

"Well," he said, "we settled with the IRS last night."

"Great," I replied. "Why didn't you call me?"

"It was pretty late," Dad replied. "I figured it could keep until morning."

"Okay," I said, glancing out the window again. "So, what happened?"

"Well, we agreed to pay 'em $23 million."

"Twenty-three million?" I said. "Oh, no!"

I was shocked at the figure; $500,000 or maybe a million was all I ever thought we might really owe, if that. Dad explained to me how the negotiations went and how he decided to accept the deal. He rehashed what we already had sunk into legal costs, what it would cost to prepare and present our case in federal court, and most importantly, the amount of time it would take to get to trial.

I understood the rationale, but it just didn't make good sense to me. . . . Twenty-three million dollars? It was extortion.

"Well, who pays the $23 million?" I asked.

"We don't know," Dad said. "It was just a block sum of money that was negotiated out of thin air, but Clive thinks that each of us will have to pay some part, including the Moncrief Foundation."

It would end up that Dad would pay a little more than half of the twenty-three. The Moncrief Foundation would pay just a little less than half, and my brothers and I would take up the slack. All of this was okayed by IRS order.

"What about the *nolo contendere* plea that the IRS wanted?" I asked.

"They are still insisting on some type of a corporate plea," he said.

Innocuous? Maybe, but we all know that a no-contest plea in the newspaper looks, smells, and tastes like guilt.

Jim Bruton, Bob Bennett, and I met in my office. Bob and Jim told me that I should sign the plea and appear in court as well to save Dad the disgrace. I agreed wholeheartedly and reached for a pen. As I signed the documents, I noticed that my name had already been typed in. C. B. Moncrief. They already knew I'd be willing to take the fall.

Jim had a different angle, though. "Charlie, once you've signed everything, we are going to get it to the U.S. attorney's office immediately," he said.

"What's the hurry?" I asked.

"Well, you don't have to worry about what you are signing or about ever appearing in court, because the Department of Justice will never accept a corporate *nolo* plea in a tax case."

"So you're telling me it will amount to nothing?" I asked incredulously.

"That's right," Jim responded, and he was correct. The Justice Department threw it out the next day.

Several years later, Special Agent Bruce Mason with the Inspection Division of the IRS was deposed in a related matter, and I got to read the transcript. At one point, when Mason discusses our settlement negotiations with the IRS, I learned something new.

"By then," he says, meaning the time of the settlement, "the government had already dropped the criminal investigation."

I was ticked off, as you can imagine. It was nice of them not to tell us! When we agreed to pay that $23 million, we were still under the impression that the IRS was coming after us criminally. Dad and I knew that once Jarvis took the Fifth Amendment, the IRS's case was severely damaged—that's why we thought it was a good time to talk settlement—but we never realized that it was totally *destroyed*. Our lawyers Bennett and Bruton had figured as much: on the day Bill Jarvis pled the Fifth, I remember Jim Bruton saying, "Well, Charlie, the criminal case is gone because they don't have a witness anymore." But no one knew for sure that the criminal case had actually been closed out because of this revelation.

We finalized the settlement on January 4, 1996. I went by Dad's for coffee as usual, and then on to the office where I found that the IRS had already delivered the settlement papers. By 9 A.M., all of our key attorneys had arrived. I sent my assistant, Kathy Wright, to the bank for a $23 million cashier's check. By the time she got back, Ma, Kit, Dickie, and his wife, Marsland, my brother Tom and his wife, Therese, and my brother Bill and his wife, Anna Marie, were all present. We all gathered in the "dungeon" to execute the papers. I thought it was a fitting place, since we were about to end the nightmare that had begun in the very same room eighteen months before.

Clive Bode explained to each of us, one couple at a time, exactly what we were about to sign and what it meant. In simple language, the IRS was agreeing that all the years prior to 1994 were shielded forever from any more IRS inquiry. The IRS could never question us about those years again, and in return we could never come back after the IRS in any form or fashion about their investigation of our family. By then, we were aware that it was very unusual for the IRS to make such a stipulation; obviously they were concerned about what else the ongoing Mike Moncrief lawsuit might turn up. We all signed the documents.

By 10:40 A.M., the lawyers had packed up their precious cargo and left for Dallas to get the necessary official signatures. Right after they left, all of our employees came into Dad's office with a card and a bottle of Dom Perignon. Dad gave a very short speech, letting the staff know that the papers were all signed and on their way to the U.S. attorney's office in Dallas.

"There could be a slip-up," he cautioned "but more than likely we're all done."

The employees applauded him, and we all thanked them.

On the way to Dallas, Bruton and the other attorneys picked up Bob Bennett, who was just arriving from Acapulco. The lawyers had just one more battle to fight in Dallas: We had decided that a joint press release—including a statement from the U.S. attorney's office—was the most appropriate way to announce our settlement. But we would have to wrestle over that. Eventually it became clear that the feds would have nothing to do with the idea. U.S. Attorney Paul Coggins said the government was going to put out its own press release, and we were free to release whatever we desired. The government had to have something to save face; we could not have cared less.

At long last, almost four hours after they'd gone to Dallas, Bob Bennett called to say everything had been signed. Tex invited him out to his house that night for a celebratory steak.

Kit and I took Jim Bruton and Ed Ross, Bennett's gofer, to dinner at the City Club.

Jim told me at dinner, "While we were hashing out the press release business, I had an interesting talk with Dick Roper. It turns out, as far as Roper was concerned, the entire investigation fell apart early on. Jarvis had told them that Tex didn't own half of any of the oil properties."

From the lead U.S. attorney, Bruton had learned that before the raid, Jarvis claimed that the vast majority of the properties were owned by Granddad, and that the IRS would find they were all still in his name. If that had been true, every single tax return Dad had ever filed would have been a blatant lie. No wonder the IRS came after us with such vengeance! Roper also allowed that when the search warrant for the Moncrief Building landed on his desk, "It was signed, sealed and delivered," emanating from a higher authority. He had no choice but to let the IRS execute the warrant, but he stood firm on one issue: The IRS was planning to hit our homes at the same time. God only knows what that would have been like. Having them storm the office was bad enough!

"Roper said it took them about two months of research to figure out that Jarvis was full of bullshit." Jarvis had lied to the IRS from the very beginning, that was for sure.

We surmised that Jarvis might have invented the ownership issue just to get the attention of the government. Jarvis and his coconspirators must have decided to gamble that Dad and Granddad's fifty-fifty ownership and my Madden deal were significant tax dodges, but they also probably thought that to get the IRS to pull off a search warrant, they would have to start with some huge claim.

"There's no telling what all Jarvis swore to," I said.

"Oh, by the way," Jim added, "Roper tells me that now *Jarvis* is under investigation by the IRS. This may prove interesting."

Chapter Eight

The Truth at Last

SOME TIME AFTER MIDNIGHT on September 1, 1997—the third anniversary of the IRS raid—I was awakened by a phone call from Thomas Hill Puff. Puff is heir to the Hill Royalty Trust. An heir by nature as well as profession, Puff has always wanted to think of himself as an oilman and to move in oil circles. He's a good guy, and he certainly is an oilman in my book, but most of his income comes from the trust—a fact that Puff readily admits. "Boy, Charlie, these oil prices are really terrible," Puff told me one day. "Really knocks my monthly income!"

Anyway, when Puff woke me up that fall night, he launched into a speech about how much he hates to involve himself in family politics, and how he would hate to do anything that I considered improper, etc., etc., until I finally got fed up.

"Puff," I said, staring wistfully at my pillow, "you called to tell me something. Now get to talking or shut up, goddamn it. I was asleep!"

"I think your cousin Monty's dead!" he finally blurted. "I was coming back from dove hunting and saw an ambulance out in front of his house. I watched them wheel him out, then followed the ambulance to the hospital. That's where I'm calling from now."

Stunned, I asked him, "Are you sure he's dead?"

"I'm pretty sure. His arms and head were uncovered when they pulled him out of the ambulance, and he was all gray colored. He sure looked dead to me. But if you want me to, I'll go find out for sure."

"Yeah, see what you can find out."

Ten minutes later, Puff called back.

"Well, he's definitely dead. I managed to get it out of the nurse. She asked me if I was family and I said 'yes,' so she filled me in. It was easy to convince her that I was family, 'cause there was no one else around—no wife, no brothers, nobody!"

Later, I would learn that Monty was already dead when he was found at the house. That's probably why no one went with him to the hospital. But for a minute there, the combination of receiving this very personal family news from Tom Puff and the image of Monty all alone and dying in some hospital bed opened up a black hole in my heart. So this is what greed, and lawsuits, and high-power squabbling had brought us to. What a waste.

Monty Moncrief was a great big overgrown fun-loving kid. Big-statured and big-hearted, he was hungry: hungry for fun, hungry for food, hungry for excitement. No matter what happened around him, Monty seemed to be eternally carefree. Like his father, he was in love with his "toys": his cars, his boat, and his trips to party places like New Orleans.

Like the rest of the Moncrief boys, Monty went to Culver Military Academy, but he lasted only a year. He had the brain power, but the military style of life was definitely not for him. Although he always had a fascination for tough guy types, and probably had his own bodyguard just because he liked having that type of person around, Monty was not a tough guy himself. If anything, he was a softy—too nice and too fun loving for his own good.

I would see Monty and Jan, his last wife, at the Fort Worth Society's annual Steeplechase Ball. Since they lived on the River Crest golf course, I would occasionally see him test-driving a Ferrari or a Harley, but that was about the extent of our contact.

Monty was married three times, and all three wives were sweet and honest women. I think his innate instinct was to be a good, solid man, to have a respectable wife and raise good children. But like his father, he remained a slave to the kind of lifestyle that comes around with an excess of money and an absence of work. It was obvious that when his third wife, Jan, married him he started turning his life around. But for years and years before that, Monty had enjoyed the good life, and I guess it eventually caught up with him.

For about five years prior to the raid, Monty would call or come by to see Dad a couple of times a year. At one point, he wanted Dad to relinquish control of one of his trusts, which Dad was happy to do, but mostly his visits were strictly social in nature. Of all the people on his side of the family, Monty was always the one we got along with best. Even after all the troubles started, it was obvious that Monty still had a basic respect for us. He was the only one to call us personally after we dropped them from the lawsuit. He was the only one to make any gesture of reconciliation.

★ ★ ★

In the months following Monty's death, it became clear that even though we had settled with the IRS, and even though Mike, Monty, and Wade had dropped their lawsuit against us and apologized in writing, our courtroom battles were not over. We had not yet gotten justice against the conspirators nor finished the fight to clear our name. Even though we had dropped Mike and his family from the lawsuit, we had added all of the conspirators, Bill Jarvis, Judge Don Jarvis, Jim Rolfe, Gary Richardson, Sam Graber, and Jim Keller. We felt we had to go after them to find out what really went on—and we were desperate to learn the truth.

To do that, we had to gather as much information as we could about the men Bill Jarvis had enlisted to help him come after us. Over the next two years, the information came to us in pieces: First someone would slip up at a deposition and give us a key piece of information; then we would put that information to use in the next deposition to draw out a little more evidence. In fragments, the story was hard to comprehend: a scrap here, a shard there, an opportune slip of someone's tongue. Watching the whole thing unfold turned out to be more than fascinating. Once the puzzle could be assembled and the whole picture seen in full, it was an amazing tale.

The conspiracy had its tenuous birth many years before the IRS raid, and long after Dad broke up Bill Jarvis's interoffice love affair, which occurred soon after he arrived at our offices. Soured by that experience, Jarvis began holding a series of lunches with Jerry Goodwin—Mike Moncrief's CPA. At first, these were casual lunches. But as Jarvis's dislike deepened, he began voicing claims that our side of the family was somehow cheating Mike's side. Then, two years prior to the raid, Bill's brother, Don, began making connections on Bill's behalf with a few old friends and a group was assembled, sharing their expertise in dealing with tax crimes.

All were former employees of either the IRS or the Department of Justice. These attorneys and accountants in turn began making contacts with their friends in the IRS. Before long, Jarvis was signing witness agreements with the IRS and "consulting" agreements with Gary Richardson, who would soon become Mike Moncrief's attorney.

Mike contended that he and his side of the family had no idea Jarvis was acting as a witness for the IRS at the same time he was consulting for their attorney. Mike also said he had no idea his own attorney had entered into a financial agreement with Bill Jarvis. This was apparently part of what Mike later referred to in the letter of apology he and his family sent us as "an incredible web of secret agreements."

According to Mike, neither of the two armies attacking our side of the Moncrief family had anything to do with the other. Two undeniable facts suggested otherwise. First, timing. Mike's lawsuit came too closely on the tail of the IRS raid to be mere coincidence. Second was the matter of Bill Jarvis. We knew that before he started working for Mike Moncrief, Gary Richardson had already been in cahoots with Bill Jarvis and his bunch. To put it simply, Mike was asking us to believe that his own attorney and chief witness never told Mike or his family about the IRS raid. It made no sense, but we had no way to prove otherwise—not yet anyway.

A month later, we deposed Mike's accountant, Jerry Goodwin, who revealed that six weeks before the IRS raid, Bill Jarvis invited him into his home to inspect our tax records. Improper? Very. Goodwin also detailed a series of meetings that Mike and his side of the family conducted with Gary Richardson, Jim Rolfe, Bill Jarvis, Don Jarvis, and Goodwin himself. Goodwin essentially described the development of a conspiracy: Together, the group devised a way to use Bill Jarvis's testimony as a means to wrest millions of dollars from our family in the form of a settlement.

In less than two months of discovery, we had everyone dead to rights. The "conspiracy" had gone from a mere suspicion to an undeniable fact. When did this plan originally hatch? Who exactly were all of these people listed on the fee splitting agreement and what roles did they play? Where was the signed copy of the fee splitting agreement? Finally, and most important, how exactly were all of these characters connected to the IRS investigation?

In an attempt to block us from learning anything more, the conspirators pulled every legal maneuver they could think of to put off the day of reckoning. One appeal made it all the way to the Texas State Supreme Court. In another, they tried to claim that Jarvis was a government employee while acting as a government informant, which made its way to the Fifth Circuit where it was denied *per curium*—that is, by one or more of the appeals court judges rather than by the full court of judges. Clearly not pleased with the decision, they asked for a rehearing, which was summarily denied. But every delay they invented only played into our hands, providing us with more and more knowledge of what had been perpetrated against us.

We deposed most everyone at least twice. In the first wave of depositions, Jarvis and his cohorts took the position that they were prohibited by Jarvis's status as an IRS witness from disclosing any information about his involvement with the IRS. It didn't take us long to get past that roadblock. The courts quickly decided that only the IRS itself was able to enforce Jarvis's immunity from questioning, and by now the federal government had no reason to protect him. No matter what the question might be, the flavor of each answer in these depositions was always the same: Dad and I were a couple of mean, vicious, vindictive, tax-dodging crooks. The second wave of depositions held more of the same, except this time the court ordered the conspirators to respond to any and all questions about their involvement with the IRS or the United States attorney's office. Armed with this order, we were able to glean a much clearer understanding of the overall plan and of each individual's role in it.

The best evidence, of course, was the unsigned fee splitting agreement obtained from Gerald Hilsher, who worked with Gary Richardson. Eventually the conspirators were forced to admit that they had signed the agreement; but they all took the position that it was only a rough, nonbinding document. They said they intended to correct the agreement at a later date. We have never uncovered any attempt to correct or rescind what the Texas State Bar disciplinary committee has said was an unethical agreement.

By now, the two trains originally under Bill Jarvis's control—the IRS investigation on one track and Mike's lawsuit on the other—had collided in a cloud of courtroom papers, scandal, and even potential prison time for some of the parties involved. But there was a new train heading down the track—one that, this time, Dad and I were driving—and Jim Rolfe wanted to get out of the way. A former United States attorney for the Northern District of Texas, Rolfe pleaded for us to let him out of the suit. He said he'd sign an affidavit for us, and he did. Paragraph 28 of the "Sworn Statement of James A. Rolfe" contained the most critical statement in all of our discovery:

> During this time (1994 and 1995) I was having discussions with Richardson, Don Jarvis, Bill Jarvis, Graber,

and Keller regarding the contingent fee arrangement between Richardson and Michael Moncrief and the sharing of that fee among us. We entered into a written contract to split both Jarvis's informant's fee from the IRS and Richardson's fee. Attached hereto as Exhibit 1 is a true and correct copy of a document entitled "Contract and Agreement of Employment." The cover letter is dated August 31, 1994 [two days before the execution of the search warrant by the IRS] and is signed by Carla Jones, an assistant of Richardson. This contract indicates that Richardson would be entitled to 10% of any amounts received from Bill Jarvis's, Don Jarvis's, Graber's, Keller's and my portion of the expected IRS informant's fee. Exhibit 1 also calls for Richardson to receive ⅓ of the fee obtained for representing Michael Moncrief. The proposed signatories on the agreement include Richarsdon, Bill Jarvis, Don Jarvis, Graber, Keller, and myself. I signed this document. Neither Keller nor Bill Jarvis are attorneys. I was to receive a percentage of the Richardson contingent fee. I never represented Michael Moncrief in any manner relating to this case. This percentage was then to be split among Keller, Graber, Bill Jarvis, Don Jarvis, and myself. I do not recall Don Jarvis, Keller, Graber or Richardson ever contacting me to attempt to amend, modify or opt-out of this agreement at any time.

This one paragraph confirms many things: First, it provides a specific connection between the two legal battles we had been forced to fight. The conspirators, including all the individuals involved in the fee splitting agreement, fully intended to play the IRS raid and Mike's lawsuit off one another to their own advantage. Second, the conspirators intended to lump all the proceeds from both endeavors together, and then divide the take according to their agreement. Third, and possibly most damning, Rolfe's confession indicated that somewhere there existed a fully signed and executed copy of the agreement. It would give us everything we needed to expose everyone involved. But where would we find that signed copy?

The answer came from Gary Richardson's former paralegal Carla Jones Sousa, whom Connor deposed in Dallas. When shown an unsigned copy of the fee splitting agreement, she acknowledged familiarity with the document. When asked if she had seen a signed copy, her answer was, "Yes." When asked if she might know where a copy of it was, she responded that she did.

"In fact," she said, "I found the original and turned it over to my lawyer for safe keeping. Would you like to see it?"

★ ★ ★

The rest of our discovery work was mostly fine tuning, with the exception of a deposition given by an IRS special agent by the name of Bruce Mason. Mason testified as to how Jarvis had exaggerated the possible tax violations to the IRS, and more:

"He's working two sides of the fence, he's wanting to get paid by the government, he is getting paid by the senator, he's sharing what is believed to be a great deal of the same, if not more information, and secretively."

Both Bruce Mason and IRS special agent Tom Davis referred Bill Jarvis for prosecution for lying to the federal government. One of Mike's attorneys, Fort Worth lawyer David Broiles, and I both reported the attorneys involved in the conspiracy to the State Bar of Texas, and I reported Bill Jarvis to the State Board of Public Accountancy as well. Broiles not only has a high ethical reputation; he taught a course called "Business and Legal Ethics," which I took from him in college.

But Jarvis was still pushing for his IRS reward. He filed suit in the Federal Claims Court in Washington, D.C., in an attempt to get the $25 million dollars he still thinks is rightfully his. The U.S. attorneys for the Northern District of Texas recused themselves because of an obvious conflict of interest. Because of this, the IRS referral of Bill Jarvis for prosecution landed in the hands of the Fraud Division of the Department of Justice in Washington, D.C., but so far no decision has been made as to whether Jarvis should be indicted.

We knew the secrets of the first train—Jarvis's and his conspirators—but what about the second? Had the conspirators kept the IRS raid a secret from Mike and his side of the family, as Mike contended? That would be a much tougher question to answer. How could we possibly find out what Mike, Monty, Dee, and Wade *really* knew, and when they knew it? For information like that, you'd have to be a fly on the wall at one of those initial meetings between Gary Richardson, Bill Jarvis, and my cousins.

The revelation that Bill Jarvis was on Mike Moncrief's payroll and Hilsher's production of what was clearly an agreement to split fees between lawyers and nonlawyers was devastating evidence. Dad and I, without hesitation, decided to pursue the culprits. At the time, however, we had no idea that the answer to our quest would come from yet another family member: a young lady by the name of Carolyn Jan Moncrief, wife of Monty, sister-in-law to Mike, and a godsend to us.

★ ★ ★

In the middle of December 1997, I thought it might be a good time to visit with Monty's widow, Jan. I had wanted to give her time to get her life together after losing Monty before seeing her. After leaving Dad's house one morning, I drove a little out of my way to pass by her house to see if her car was there. I figured it would be way too early to knock on her door. But then I saw a moving van being loaded in her circular driveway. I called Jan from my cell phone and left her a message. Shortly after I got to the office, Jan returned my call.

The minute Jan and I started talking, it was obvious that Jan was still very upset about Monty. Her voice—and her thoughts—kept breaking the entire time. At some points in our conversation her speech was so disjointed that I had a hard time even understanding her.

"After Monty died, I wanted to keep the house that the two of us had lived in, but Wade Wiley wouldn't stand for it," she said, as the movers packed up around her.

I knew what she meant. Wade Wiley controlled Monty's trust, which owned the house from which Jan was now leaving.

"You mean Wade just kicked you out?" I asked.

"He gave me until January 31, but my lawyer advised me to just go ahead and move out of the house now," she said.

"What do Dee and Mike have to say about this?" I asked.

"I haven't heard from anyone since three weeks after Monty died," Jan replied.

She told me that Wade and Dee had given her $50,000 and Monty's boat and basically sent her packing.

"What am I supposed to do with a boat?" she asked.

"I don't get it," I replied. "Didn't Monty leave you anything?"

"Of course he did," she answered. "He left me his 99 percent interest in Montco."

Montco was a pretty much defunct oil company that Monty had created with Wade's son, Stan.

"Just the other day, most of Monty's business records were dumped on my doorstep," Jan said. "Just left them there in a heap. I guessed the family just didn't want anything to do with me. I believe, to them, Monty is dead, and so am I."

I told Jan I wanted to talk with her about what all had transpired over the years between our two sides of the family, but she acted as though she wasn't quite ready.

"I'm going to have to do a lot of praying first," she answered, and then she started rambling on about how she was going to make it no matter what. Like I said, I had a difficult time understanding her. Eventually Jan suggested that she'd be better in a couple of weeks and that we could visit at that time.

True to her word, Jan phoned me in early February.

"You know, I'm meeting with my lawyers on Monday," she said. "We're going to talk about how the family has been treating me, and how they've been handling Monty's estate. My lawyers think I should sue them. What do *you* think I should do, Charlie?"

"Whoa, now," I replied. "I'm not going to give you legal advice, Jan. Your accountant—what's his name? He's a pretty good hand. You need to stick close to him."

Jan was, after all, the executrix of Monty's estate. So she had the authority to do anything she wanted. Our conversation shifted again, this time to Mike and Monty's relationship, and the relationship between Monty and his mother, Dee Faxel.

"You know, Charlie, Monty didn't like Mike or his mother and yet he still loved them, you know what I mean?" Jan remarked flatly. "He always hated what went on between the two sides of the family."

Knowing I wasn't inclined to believe what she was saying, Jan proceeded to tell me a story. After our conversation, I was finally able to figure out how Mike Moncrief and Billy Wayne Jarvis became unlikely allies.

Chapter Nine

The Lady Sings

"MIKE'S INVOLVED IN THIS THING," our attorney Dee Kelly would say repeatedly after the IRS raid.

From the beginning, our thoughts pointed straight toward Mike, the professional politician and state senator from Fort Worth. Mike's entrance into Billy Wayne Jarvis's life started innocently enough—at lunch with Mike's accountant, who oversaw Mike Moncrief and his family's business interests and investments. Once a week (sometimes twice) for at least ten years, Goodwin would have lunch with our then comptroller. It began as a noontime ritual between two accountants taking a break from their world of crunching numbers and landscapes of business forms for a quick bite and some conversation.

By the fall of 1992, the same season in which Jarvis had hired three attorneys and a consulting CPA for his personal counsel, the lunchtime conversations began to change. Jarvis would drop tantalizing hints that implied that my Dad and I were cheating Mike out of portions of his inheritance. I'm sure Goodwin wasn't hard to convince on this subject. Mike had obviously griped about my side of the family for some time, and he was looking for a fight.

In the spring of 1994, Jarvis, technically unemployed but working undercover as a full-time IRS informant, met with Goodwin.

"Bill Jarvis and I had lunch," Jerry Goodwin would later say under oath. "He said there were some things that had been handled incorrectly by the defendants [our side of the family] with regard to the purchase of the properties that Mike and Monty bought from their grandmother in 1988, and he wanted to talk to Mike with regard to the situation."

Jarvis wouldn't go into detail about his allegations, but they were tantalizing enough for Goodwin to take them back to Mike. Mike was eager to hear more and sent word to Jarvis, via Goodwin, that he'd meet him anywhere, anytime. But Jarvis wouldn't meet with him—not yet. It was income tax season, he explained, and he couldn't possibly fit a meeting into his schedule.

Busting Tex Moncrief was Jarvis's top priority, and he didn't want anything to interfere with that. He knew the animosity harbored by Mike Moncrief against our side of the family. In fact, he would later say in depositions that Mike's accountant, Jerry Goodwin, told him that Mike and his family were preparing to challenge and possibly sue us for, as he would later put it, "various wrongs that they believed Tex had done to their side of the family."

Jarvis was ready to help Mike. Mike would be dealing with the same issues as the IRS, Jarvis later testified. "While the government was looking at illegal tax reporting, Mike Moncrief would be looking at the civil fraud perpetrated against him and his family."

But if Mike beat the IRS to the punch—if his lawsuit was filed before the IRS raid—then Jarvis feared that Tex might destroy precious evidence, and Jarvis's reward would disappear. Jarvis and his men apparently wanted to be sure that the IRS raid hit before Mike did, because it was the more lucrative of the two trains headed toward our side of the family. So Bill had to stall Mike, telling Mike's accountant that by waiting for Jarvis's help, the case against Tex would be greatly strengthened.

Mike agreed to wait, Jarvis said in depositions. But when the IRS's target date of February 18 passed without a raid on our offices, or even a word of explanation from the IRS about the delay, Jarvis became alarmed. He called investigator Don Smith in February, then again on March 26. The April 15 tax season deadline passed and still "no indication of what the schedule might be for conducting the search," Jarvis remembered later in depositions.

This was the height of the unemployed accountant's discontent. Now it seemed that the IRS train, the one carrying his informant's bounty, had temporarily stalled on him.

So he began stoking the other train: the one carrying Mike Moncrief.

★ ★ ★

"Mike Moncrief was very insistent on getting a meeting," Jarvis remembered in depositions. "He said he would meet wherever we wanted to meet.... We did not have any idea how much longer we would need to try to delay Mike Moncrief in order to allow the IRS-CID to have a good chance for a successful search of Tex's offices."

So on the afternoon of April 29, 1994, Bill Jarvis agreed to meet with Mike, but only in Dallas, in the office of one of his attorneys, James Rolfe. Mike and Jerry Goodwin drove to Dallas and found Bill Jarvis accompanied by attorney Rolfe and his brother, attorney

Don Jarvis. Mike's first question was, "Why do you have all of these lawyers here, Bill?"

Jarvis claimed it was because he was considering a wrongful termination suit against Tex Moncrief.

Mike's accountant, Jerry Goodwin, began the meeting by reading "a list of things he thought [Mike's] uncle had beat his family out of...." Don Jarvis said in depositions. "And he wanted to know whether or not Bill had any knowledge of these things."

Jarvis said there had been fraud involved with regard to the handling of the W. A. Moncrief Sr. estate and the oil and gas properties of the Elizabeth Moncrief estate in the way that the properties were sold to the seven grandchildren after Granddad's 1986 death. He said he would be available as a witness to testify against Tex Moncrief if and when Mike filed suit.

That's all he said, but that was enough. It was as if he could stare into Mike Moncrief's soul and see the place where he was hurting. Mike had long been telling people that he felt like a second class Moncrief, and it was from that vulnerable place that he exploded at Dad after Granddear's funeral in 1992: "I know you've stolen properties from Granddad's estate!" The lawyers poured gas on the fire. "You're looking at actual damages, and if you don't settle out of court, we'll be asking for punitive damages," they said in depositions.

"How much do you think that could be?" Goodwin asked.

"Probably in the fifty to one hundred million dollar range."

The numbers were, to use Mike's favorite term, "stronger than a horseradish milkshake." But then Jarvis suddenly clammed up. He wouldn't say anything more, wouldn't get into the details. He had said the extent of what he was ready to give up in the meeting—and he wasn't saying anything else.

"Why not?" Mike implored.

"We just don't want to go into detail until you hire an attorney to handle the case," Bill Jarvis said.

That shouldn't have been difficult. They were, after all, meeting in a roomful of attorneys, in the middle of Dallas, where there are more than enough attorneys to represent every man, woman, and child thrice over. But Jarvis's attorney Jim Rolfe said that not just any attorney would suffice. If Mike and his family wanted to know more, they had to hire a *specific* attorney: Gary Richardson of Tulsa, Oklahoma.

"And we said, '*Who the hell is Gary Richardson?*'" Goodwin testified.

Rolfe explained that Richardson was a "longtime personal friend," a former U.S. attorney now working as an extremely competent plaintiff's attorney. Richardson was ""someone who could chase down Tex Moncrief and "chew his butt good." Richardson had the credentials, Rolfe bragged. You could see them if you visited his office, where favorable newspaper articles about him were prominently displayed. "He has received substantial notoriety for large contingent fee awards in Texas and Oklahoma," said Rolfe. But Richardson didn't come cheap, Rolfe added; he required a 50 percent contingency fee.

Richardson's contingency fee would also include a piece of any IRS informant's reward received by Bill Jarvis. Likewise, Jarvis and his group of attorneys and advisors had already agreed to split Richardson's contingency fee.

Mike was more than suspicious about Jarvis. He would later say he could tell that Jarvis was working with the IRS. He had already begun to "visualize the big picture," and his "suspicions were solidified." There were two trains (his own lawsuit and the IRS proceedings) colliding head-on with Tex Moncrief squarely in the middle of them.

In this first meeting, Mike really just wanted Bill Jarvis to tell him everything so that they could each pursue their separate endeavors against Tex. But according to Mike, Jarvis and his advisors gave him an ultimatum: Hire Richardson, or no more information would be forthcoming.

Mike said he'd have to run all of this by the other members on his side of the family. "We'll get back to you," he said.

Soon after, Mike and his wife, Rosie, held a family meeting that included his mother, Dee Faxel, as well as her fourth husband, Ralph, Mike's brother, Monty, his wife, Jan, and Mike's uncle, Wade Wiley. He told his family that he had real reason to believe that Uncle Tex had cheated them out of inheritance money, and he was ready to sue. The family agreed in principle to join in on the lawsuit.

★ ★ ★

Across forty-five miles of prairie from where Bill Jarvis was conducting his conspiracy against us in Dallas, Monty Moncrief was most likely sitting in the big, black easy chair in his Fort Worth living room. The son of my Uncle Dick Moncrief, Monty dabbled in the oil business, but, like his stepbrother Mike, the majority of Monty's income came from oil royalties handled by our side of the family.

Monty was happy with this business arrangement. All he had to do was cash the checks. Monty was, of course, the only real Moncrief on his side of the family. His mother was a Moncrief by marriage; his brother, Mike, a Moncrief by adoption. However, his mother constantly railed at Monty for what she considered his outrageous expenses. "You're spending too much on charity!" she would say. Or Lear Jets. Or vacations. But Monty was headstrong. Someday, he swore, he would show them all. "I hope I'm a success someday, because then I can prove to the family that I'm not just some nobody," he'd say.

Mike and his mother encouraged Monty to attend their meetings, Jan Moncrief told us. Maybe, it was out of self-preservation. They surely wanted to keep him on their side and ensure that he didn't slip and tell us anything. But Monty, like his father, hated meetings. The Monty I knew came across as being a very smart man. But judging from Bill Jarvis's testimony about the meetings Monty participated in—testimony later confirmed by Jerry Goodwin—the Monty Moncrief at these meetings was a different person, numbed by painkillers from recent surgery and perhaps affected by his decades of dabbling in booze and dope. Jan later explained to me that Monty had long since quit drinking. But in the last few years of his life he had taken blood pressure medicine and was virtually dependent on painkillers for back pain.

According to Jan, the numbers discussed at these meetings sounded like lottery winnings: fifty million, one hundred million, and all they had to do was sue Uncle Tex! Monty was summoned to attend a June 3, 1994, family meeting in Dallas—perhaps by his mother, perhaps by Mike. But from the beginning, Monty had second thoughts, according to Jan. Something just smelled funny about the plans Mike and his relatives were brewing with the attorneys and accountants in Dallas and with Tex's former comptroller, Bill Jarvis.

Walking into the meeting in the Dallas office of Gary Richardson, Monty could see the whole group. There was Mike with his wife, Rosie, at his side. He would jump up and down, depending on his level of rage at his Uncle Tex, shouting, "We're not going to take this! We're going to get our money!" while Rosie held his hand and quietly attempted to keep him tethered. Equally exuberant was Mike's mother, Dee, a small woman with gray hair and an ancient "pill box" hat, literally surrounded by attorneys.

Jan later told me she was shocked by Mike's actions. The veins stuck out on his throat as he jumped to his feet to exclaim, "I want a complete divorce from Tex's side of the family!" Jan claimed that Mike and Dee's hatred for Tex Moncrief, festering for years, was beyond her belief.

But the real purpose of this meeting, according to Jerry Goodwin, was to introduce "Mr. 50 Percent," Tulsa attorney Gary Richardson, who was eager to take on the case. "When I was interviewed, I was told that Mr. Jarvis was going to work with us and furnish the information that was needed to have a successful progression of the lawsuit and in essence that it was an open-and-shut case," Richardson would later say.

Jarvis's two attorneys, Jim Rolfe and Don Jarvis, hoped to convince Mike and his family to hire a third attorney for 50 percent of whatever he won in his lawsuit against our side of the family. One thing was for sure: Richardson took control of the meeting. Jan Moncrief called him "Tall Boots," and that's the impression she remembers: a legal gunslinger standing tall in his boots and waving a flashy gold Rolex. He talked for a full fifteen minutes, even handed out a videotape which touted his abilities, the cases he'd won, and the juries he'd swayed.

The verdict? Well, Richardson at least won the chance of a third meeting in Dallas, where Mike and his family presented their decision: The 50 percent contingency was too high, fraud or no fraud.

Mike would say later in depositions that he figured the fee could be whittled down when the actual contracts were drawn up.

After the meeting, Mike began using Jerry Goodwin to negotiate a more favorable contingency fee. But Goodwin wasn't instructed to negotiate with Gary Richardson directly. He was told to deal with Bill Jarvis's brother, Don. Believing Don Jarvis was in close communication with Richardson, Goodwin negotiated away. But, he would later learn, Don Jarvis was handling the negotiations on his own—without Richardson's input. "I thought that was strange," Goodwin would later say in depositions. "I didn't know who all of the players were and exactly what peg that they all fit into."

When he couldn't get very far in his negotiations with Don Jarvis, Goodwin turned to Bill Jarvis. But he wasn't the Bill he'd had lunch with for the better part of a decade. This Jarvis had a shadowy presence, never revealing his place in the jigsaw puzzle of attorneys and relatives and allegations of fraud that now surrounded him.

In a fourth meeting in the Dallas attorneys' offices, Mike and his family hashed out Gary Richardson's contract with Jarvis and his attorneys. The meeting was monitored by Mike's personal attorney, Lyndell Kirkley. Kirkley advised his client to structure the contract so that Bill Jarvis's name was never mentioned. Later, Goodwin would discuss the matter of payment of Richardson's paralegal costs, with Bill Jarvis; he'd meet Jarvis for lunch to discuss the contract's terms and conditions.

Why Jarvis and not Richardson, the attorneys deposing Goodwin demanded?

The answer was hard won, but it eventually made sense of all aspects of the surreal situation. Jarvis finally revealed it himself in his deposition: He and his brother were intensely involved in Richardson's contingency fee agreement because it was part of a "larger" contract between Gary Richardson and Mike Moncrief, "which allows for the involvement of me as a CPA, a consultant under that contract."

On June 20, 1994, Don Jarvis apparently prepared a fee agreement between the Dallas firm of Richardson, Stoops and Senator Mike Moncrief, which included a clause stipulating a $5,000 per month allowance for a CPA, who was, of course, Bill Jarvis. Jarvis's IRS agreement stipulated that he was to keep all information about the Moncrief matter confidential. Mike Moncrief was essentially paying his $5,000-a-month consultant's fee, which would eventually exceed $60,000 without itemization. "In exchange for this consultant's fee, Bill Jarvis was expected to work with Michael Moncrief and Richardson and help them to understand the nature of the relationship between the two factions of the Moncrief family and their business dealings," Jim Rolfe would later testify.

During the discovery process, our lawyers found out that on June 28, Mike sent a revised contract to Don Jarvis by way of Jerry Goodwin. In the cover letter, which was written by Lyndell Kirkley, Mike pointed out that he had deleted the language about specifically hiring a CPA for the case, but he had adjusted the language in a paragraph dealing with extraneous expenses that the client would reimburse. Mike also pushed Richardson to agree to a 40 percent contingency fee instead of his demanded 50 percent.

There was also an unusual provision in the Mike Moncrief–Gary Richardson contact that provided for a two-week "opt out" period, in which Mike and Co. would review the evidence that Jarvis said he had relating to our business. If Jarvis's records weren't convincing and inculpating against Tex Moncrief, Mike could opt out of the contract. So Jarvis had to act fast.

Once the deal was signed—Gary Richardson representing Mike Moncrief and family for a 40 percent contingency fee and Bill Jarvis as their $5,000-a-month paid consultant—the boxes of records and tax returns Bill Jarvis had taken from our offices were opened wide.

Meanwhile, according to Jan, Monty had mixed feelings about the whole deal. "I remember one time, way back in '94, we were driving out of Fort Worth in the Lincoln, on the way to Dallas to meet with Jarvis and Tall Boots," she told me.

"This was around the time we were going to sign an agreement with Tall Boots to represent us in a lawsuit against Tex. Right about where the freeway passes Six Flags, Monty just hit the brakes. He slowed way down, and said, 'Jan, I don't want to do it. I can't believe that Uncle Tex would do this to us. This Jarvis guy has to be a liar. Let's turn around.' "

Jan remembered looking over at him straight in the eye and telling him she was ready to bail if he was. But then, Monty changed his mind. He felt like the black sheep of the family already. Standing apart on this matter would certainly make things worse. "Oh, gosh, Mother will cut me out of the will," he reasoned aloud. "They'll all hate me and never speak to me again."

"Then he started talking about his new plan to back out of the lawsuit," Jan recalled in her deposition. "I could just feel the battle going on inside him, like two different people were talking out of the same mouth. 'I'll be the only one that doesn't go along with the family,' he said one minute. Then a second later, 'But what do we care? We don't need them.' Then he said, 'Mother will definitely cut me out of her will, and they'll all hate me and never speak to me again.' Finally, Monty decided that he had to go along with his mother and brother, no matter how much it tore him up. He always thought he was the black sheep of the family. He really felt it. He didn't want to do this to Tex, but he just couldn't go against his family."

Still, Monty often conveniently "disappeared" when the family was supposed to be meeting with the attorneys. July 23, the day the family once again gathered in Gary Richardson's office to sign a formal contract to file suit against Tex, was no exception. Aside from Mike's family, Jim Rolfe, Don Jarvis, Gerald Hilsher, and Mike's attorney, Lyndell Kirkley, attended the meeting. Don would later explain that his role was "to try to keep Bill...who was going to end up between two centimillionaires, from getting completely crushed in their war. We'll call that the 'War of the Titans.'"

Only one person was missing: Monty. At the moment of the contract signing, he was lounging in a bathrobe in the Hotel Crescent Court, one of the best hotels in Dallas. He was, once again, "playing sick," according to his wife, Jan.

Monty's mother, Dee, was determined to get his name on the contract—even if she couldn't get him there in the flesh. So she sent Don to fetch her son's signature.

"Somebody asked us (asked me, actually, I think) to take the proposed contract to R. B. (Monty)," Don Jarvis would later remember in depositions. "I remember saying, 'I don't know where R. B. is.' And Mike's mother said, 'My limousine is downstairs. He is at the Crescent.'...I had never been in the Crescent before. Apparently she called ahead. But when we got downstairs there was no limousine."

"It was crushing," Don said of the absence of the promised limo. "But we [he and Jim Rolfe in Rolfe's car] drove over to the

Crescent and R. B. was waiting. In his bathrobe, he sure was. And he signed that contract, and we brought it back and handed it to somebody... and I went back to Sherman." Once the contract was signed, Richardson began the process of filing a claim in Tarrant County. A month later, he had completed drafts of a demand letter to be sent to Dad and a petition to be filed.

Bill Jarvis wasn't concerned about his promises to the IRS. Because early on Sunday, July 24, the day after Mike Moncrief signed his agreement with Gary Richardson, Jerry Goodwin walked into Jarvis's spare bedroom and spent four hours poring over the fruits of Jarvis's employment at Montex. He saw our tax returns, accounting records, and other family records, which, Bill Jarvis led them to believe, would prove that Tex Moncrief had indeed defrauded Mike's side of the family while enriching his own. This information was contained in the second set of the documents that Jarvis had given to the IRS.

In his depositions, Bill would only admit that the boxes of our tax and banking information were "in the same room" as Goodwin, upon whom Bill "put no restrictions." But the IRS investigator later said, "Bill... told me there were no ground rules on what Jerry could and could not look at." Bill let Goodwin have the run of his home office and everything in it, including a wealth of personal information he had "kept"—not stolen—from our offices. For one of the four hours, Goodwin reviewed at least ten of my Dad's tax returns and at least three of mine and several others, making a total of eighteen returns.

"Did you think to yourself, Mr. Goodwin, that it was inappropriate for an accountant to steal a tax return from his former client?" Goodwin was later asked in depositions.

"Yes."

"And you looked at this without ever saying that, right?" he was asked.

"Yes."

Goodwin reported what he found to Mike, and the family was once again summoned to sign a letter notifying Gary Richardson, their brand new counsel, that "we have conducted our investigation of the claims which we may have and have decided that there are claims which should be pursued further.... Our decision is to continue forward."

By now, Don and Bill were in too deep to pull out. And they were about to sink deeper.... On August 30, 1994, one day after Dallas magistrate judge Jane Boyle signed the IRS search warrant, Richardson, with the help of his paralegal Carla Jones, drafted a letter to the group. "Please find enclosed ... the Original Contract and Agreement of Employment for the attorneys involved in the above-referenced matter [Moncrief Contract]," it began.

It was an improper fee splitting agreement drawn up by Gary Richardson's office. The agreement, signed and dated August 30, 1994, gave Richardson 10 percent of the IRS reward, which Jarvis had already agreed to split with his brother Don, Graber, Keller, and Rolfe. The agreement clearly instructed that Richardson receive one-third of the contingency fee from the Mike Moncrief lawsuit, with Jarvis and the Dream Team splitting the rest.

Apparently the agreement was circulated by hand and each individual signed and dated the wrongful agreement. The fully executed original was returned to Richardson's office, and Carla carefully filed it with the Mike Moncrief contract.

Attorneys don't compensate fact witnesses, but Jarvis, about to become a witness in Mike Moncrief's lawsuit, was being paid $5,000 a month by Richardson. The intricate web of improper fee splitting—Jarvis sharing his fees and rewards with his coconspirators, then sharing in Richardson's hoped-for multimillion-dollar contingency fee—was to remain secret, especially from Richardson's client Mike Moncrief and, of course, the IRS. Keeping it secret from Mike violated the attorney's disciplinary rules. Keeping it secret from the IRS violated Jarvis's informant's agreement.

The fee splitting agreement might have remained a secret. But then, as noted, Gerald Hilsher, the young attorney with Gary Richardson's firm, stumbled across the unsigned copy of the agreement while preparing for a hearing in Mike Moncrief's lawsuit. Gary Richardson told him not to worry; he knew that nonattorneys couldn't be paid a referral fee. That's why the document had never been signed, he said in deposition. Richardson later told Hilsher that James Rolfe "concurred that the proposed fee splitting agreement had not been signed." Two days later, in a meeting with Bill Jarvis, Sam Graber assured Hilsher that the improper fee splitting agreement had never been signed.

"My impression of Jarvis, from the look on his face, was that he was a bit surprised by this," Hilsher later remembered.

★ ★ ★

When I met with Jan after Monty's death, she said she had attended most of the meetings between my cousins and the Bill Jarvis group, not only the meetings held in Dallas, but at least two of the ones in Fort Worth, too. She had also been in on the meetings they had with the IRS. "You know, Charlie, Mike just absolutely *despises* your side of the family!" Jan told me. "I've been to several meetings where Mike would actually stand up and go into a fit about how much he hated Tex and his sons."

"I remember how he'd rant and rave," she continued. "He'd get all red in the face and say something to the effect of how it was time to 'bring them down!' Really, I was . . . totally amazed. I knew that Dee didn't care for Tex, but I didn't realize Mike felt that way, and I said as much to Monty. Monty told me that Mike always had a chip on his shoulder about you all, probably because he was not a full-blooded Moncrief."

That much I knew. But then Jan told me something I didn't know. She believed that everyone—Mike, Wade, Dee, Gary Richardson, Monty, and she—were all aware of Bill Jarvis's involvement with the IRS long before signing on with Gary Richardson.

"Why else would we have signed a contract with Tall Boots, Charlie?" she asked with a little laugh in her voice. "See, that was the plan all along. They wanted to hit you on one side with the IRS, on the other side with their civil suit, and force y'all to settle."

"Jan," I said, trying to stay calm. "Are you telling me that y'all knew about the IRS raid before it ever occurred?"

"I'd have to go through the files to tell you who all knew about it," she answered. "But I'm certain Monty knew. I was with him when he found out."

"Well, I've got time to listen to your story, if you don't mind," I said.

"I remember the moment very clearly," she said. "Monty was in his chair in his sitting room, his black chair, and he got a phone call. I don't know if it was from his mother or from Jerry Goodwin, but I doubted it was from Mike because he and Mike didn't talk very often at all. But Jerry or Dee would sometimes call and let us know what was going on. When Monty hung up, he looked at me and said, 'You're not going to believe this.' Then, he stopped. 'No, I better not tell you.' I just looked at him for a second. He would always tell me things. He would always confide in me...*always*. 'Monty,' I said, 'You know you've got to tell me.' That was about all it took. And he told me, '*The IRS is going to raid Tex's office!*'"

I continued really to push Jan on the two issues. First, Jan recalled that Mike, Wade, Dee, Monty, Gary Richardson, Goodwin, and the rest all knew about Jarvis's involvement with the IRS prior to the raid and, moreover, even prior to Mike's retaining Gary Richardson. Second, Jan noted that Mike and his bunch *had* to hire Gary Richardson, because Jarvis and his advisers gave them no choice—no Tall Boots, no Jarvis. To my amazement, Jan said she was willing to testify about her knowledge of the conspiracy to bring us down, and about how she knew of the conspirators' involvement with the IRS. Unable to detect any inconsistencies in Jan's account of those early meetings, I decided it was time to get this information to our attorneys.

A few days later, Marshall Searcy, Hugh Connor, and I visited with Jan again, to see about her testifying in our case. She continued to believe that "they" all knew about the raid well before September 1, 1994, and claimed to have a "whole stack of papers" that were relevant to our case. Searcy asked her to look through the papers and send us anything of significance.

Jan called me the next day. "I've got a whole file for you to look at," she said. "Can I drop them off at your house?"

Jan had some interesting things to say about Mike's apology letter, too. She attended the November 1995 meeting that prompted it. It was held in Mike's office in the Fort Worth Club Building, and included Mike's attorneys David Broiles and Lyndell Kirkley; Mike and his wife, Rosie; Dee and her husband, Ralph Faxel; Monty and Jan Moncrief; Jerry Goodwin; and Wade Wiley. Broiles and Kirkley were adamant about getting out of the lawsuit, but Mike and Dee were equally adamant about not wanting to sign a letter of apology.

Broiles and Kirkley seemed unmoved. Dee sided with Mike, of course; neither wanted to let Tex off the hook. But everyone in the room knew the problem. We were gradually uncovering dangerous facts. First, the conspirators had been in cahoots from the beginning. Second, they all knew about the pending IRS raid ahead of time. Third, from the start, their plan was to use the raid as the first part of a one-two punch, combined with their lawsuit, to force us to settle. The lawyers in the room may have sensed they had unwittingly assisted a conspiracy that was coming to the surface, and they weren't about to let Mike take this matter any further.

To reassure Mike and Dee that they weren't really letting Tex off the hook through the letter of apology, Lyndell said, according to Jan, "Don't worry, no matter what you sign or promise you'll always be able to come back at Tex through the Lee Wiley Moncrief Trust." This was true. The trust, which Dad had maintained for our incapacitated cousin, was open game for lawsuits.

Jan was a great witness for our side. I believe that if Monty were still alive neither she nor he would ever have told the true story. Since we would definitely have deposed him, Monty might have talked under Marshall Searcy's guidance, but then again there would have been a whole pack of lawyers and cousins—and, most notably, his mother—urging him to keep quiet. If Monty were the one who had the most respect for our side of the family and if he were the only one who opposed getting involved with Jarvis and his bunch, then it's ironic that Monty's sense of shame might have kept the truth from coming out.

Jan always suggested to me that she was not very smart, but nothing could be further from the truth. It was amazing how much information Jan was able to pull together for us. It was up to us, however, to decide what to do with it.

Chapter Ten

Three Trials

Quite a bit of sex, lies, and scandal!
Just sex and money and embezzlement!
It couldn't have been anything more fun!

THESE ARE THE WORDS JURORS USED to describe Ellen Lloyd's embezzlement trial, as though a court of law is some kind of theater and they had come to be entertained. This was a concept that Robert Hinton, Ellen Lloyd's lawyer, played brilliantly. It's too bad the prosecutors, Paul Silverman and Charles Brandenberg, weren't equally concerned with showmanship.

Ellen might have done a lot of things wrong, but choosing Robert Hinton to represent her was dead-on right. Red-headed and rapier-thin, Hinton used the courtroom as a stage, darting back and forth before the jury, employing elaborate gestures and constant eye contact to lure them into a tale that had just about everything: sex, money, greed, intrigue . . . everything except crime, unless it was crimes he said were committed by Tex Moncrief. By comparison, the prosecutors presenting our case against Ellen were downright dull: two dry municipal attorneys who thought the facts would speak for themselves.

But perhaps the most astounding character was Ellen, our former trusted clerk, who'd regularly flown off to Vegas to gamble and flashed her winnings back home in Fort Worth. Now, she stood in the courtroom, beneath the flag of Texas, wearing an all-black suit cut in a swag pattern at the bodice, seemingly innocent as a schoolmarm. Her hands hung limply at her side, and her voice was now low and flat. To make ends meet, she said she was working double shifts as a waitress in a Mexican restaurant.

We may never know just how much money Ellen got from us. But the checks we uncovered going back four years added up to nearly half a million dollars. All told, Ellen could have walked away with a million or more at the rate she seemed to be spending.

As soon as she realized the hammer was about to fall, Ellen took off for Las Vegas. Later she went to California and tried to start a new life as though nothing had happened. We brought in our former FBI agents to make the case against Ellen. Clint Brown and Mike Connelley pulled together the evidence, and we turned everything over to a Tarrant County grand jury who returned an indictment for theft. About a year later, a California police officer spotted Ellen's Dodge Stealth in a Victorville, California, neighborhood. The officer ran her plates, made a positive ID, and moved in to make the arrest. Ellen was extradited back to Fort Worth to face an indictment for second-degree felony theft. Because of the statute of limitations, Lloyd could only be charged for the money she taken from us after 1990.

Not far into her trial, Ellen dropped a bombshell. She hadn't embezzled a penny, she claimed. She had been *given* the money as a gift...by Tex Moncrief. Why? Because, she claimed, she had been Tex's mistress—trysting with him twice a week for sixteen years!

Every Moncrief mouth in that courtroom dropped to the floor.

Ellen told one hell of a story. She testified that Dad sent her to Vegas with cash to play the slots "because the odds are good." She swore he wanted her to buy designer clothes so she'd looked presentable when she gambled in Vegas. She said he authorized her to pay her own bills from his personal accounts, as long as she kept it under $25,000 a month. He wanted her to fix up her house so it would be up to "Moncrief standards"—and, she insisted, Dad was more than happy to foot the bill.

Why did Tex give a damn about her house, her bills, or her apparel? Because, Ellen swore, twice a week she'd leave her garage door open—the signal that her daughter was gone—and Tex would glide into the drive in his Cadillac, and she'd service him.

Personally, I couldn't believe it. But Ellen's possible line of defense had occurred to us before. Even when we notified our lawyer Clive Bode about Ellen's embezzlement, the first question he asked was, "Tex, were you sleeping with her?"

Clive tried to convince us that an affair with Tex would be Ellen's defense. In hindsight, I wish we had taken the idea more seriously, but the mere thought of Ellen trying to claim that she had sex with Dad seemed laughable.

That's why I was expecting Dad's answer: "Are you kidding? I've never even touched her!" he said.

Our attitude was probably more naive than it should have been. Both Dad and I had known several people who'd been in the same situation and actually did have affairs with the woman in question. In every case, there was only one way out: settle with the woman. But we could not imagine a jury thinking Dad was stupid enough—or vicious enough—to press embezzlement charges against his mistress. Besides, we had all the documentary evidence we needed to prove that Ellen had tampered with certain checks to make them payable to her credit card accounts. How much more did we need?

As it turned out, the trial was ultimately decided by the theatrics of the lawyers. Compared to the version Robert Hinton and Ellen Lloyd told, the prosecution's real life picture of a secretary with a gambling problem, gradually discovering she could get away with stealing from her rich boss's personal checking account, must have seemed boring. So, while Brandenberg and Silverman carefully set up an airtight embezzlement case, Hinton just kept pounding away at unfounded and wild alternative theories.

The jury returned a verdict of "not guilty."

Dad seemed to take the whole thing pretty much in stride. After all, there were other battles to fight. At this point, there was not much that could surprise him. So instead of focusing on Ellen, he turned to focus on the next criminal well to drill: the conspirators. Little did he know that Ellen would come back to haunt him.

★ ★ ★

In early April 1997, the buzz inside the D.C. Beltway was that Congress was getting ready to go after the IRS. Around the country, stories of dictatorial IRS activities had begun to pile up, and the Senate was finally beginning to take the stories seriously. One story that apparently stood out was ours. When Jim Bruton heard about an impending Senate investigation, and our case rising to the top, he got on the phone to Dad.

"What do you think, Tex?" Bruton asked. "Do you want to get up in front of a Senate committee, and tell them your story?"

Dad thought it over. He had been waiting for the right opportunity to make his IRS grievances known on the national level. Several options had already presented themselves. He could have gone onto some talk show or opened up to any number of journalists. But those approaches didn't fit Tex's style. Back when the IRS was in charge of the case, they transformed their investigation into a full-scale criminal raid, making certain that the media were around for maximum exposure. He wanted to show a little more restraint than that.

But was testifying before the Senate committee the right approach? Dad had been a political observer long enough to know that congressional investigations really amounted to a media circus. On the other hand, our story would never be heard if we avoided all media attention. At the very least, testifying before Congress would allow Dad to address directly the one government body with the power to change the way the IRS conducted its business. That's what really clinched it for him.

"Yes, Jim!" Dad finally answered. "If they really want me to do it, I think it's a great idea."

"All right!" Jim said. "I'll get the ball rolling."

A full year would pass—a year of intensive legal machinations, backroom conferences, and political maneuvering—before Dad would finally fulfill his decision to be heard by the U.S. Senate.

Finally, the Senate Finance Committee's special investigators were ready to hear our story face to face. Early one morning just before Christmas, Eric Thorsen and Anita Horne (Anita looked more like the late Princess Diana than a special investigator) took a tour of our offices and met with the staff. Then they announced that Dad had been officially chosen to testify on our case before the Senate in April.

On Monday, April 27, feeling like the stars of a modern-day Frank Capra movie, the Moncriefs went to Washington. Mother and Dad, Kit and I, and brother Tom all piled into the Lucky Liz. The next morning, we got a look at the room in the Hart Senate Office Building where the hearing would take place the next day. It was hard for me to believe that in fewer than twenty-four hours, that empty cavern would be filled with reporters and senators, transformed by lights and television cameras into a fishbowl of IRS abuse for the whole country to stare into. And the biggest fish of all was going to be my father.

We went back to Bob Bennett's office and spent the rest of the day helping Dad practice his responses to the senators' questions. We also listened as Dad read through his brief about five or six times. Obsessive as a school kid about to give his first book report, he was well prepared. I couldn't blame him for taking this hearing seriously. He would be speaking before the Senate and, via television and newspapers, the nation.

One way or another, Dad had been preparing himself for this hearing for more than a year. During that whole time, I watched him with a growing mixture of pride and fear. I was proud because the project had given Dad something worthwhile to occupy his time. The prospect of testifying before the United States Senate had reawakened within him the sharp, aggressive, and focused wildcatter, and it was a very welcome sight. But I was also fearful, because of the terrible toll that the IRS investigation had taken on Dad's body and spirit. I damned sure didn't want to see him go through *that* again. As the day of the hearing grew steadily closer,

I could feel Dad's excitement and adrenaline soaring, just like they did in the first days after the IRS raid. This time, however, there was a difference. This time, Dad was in command.

At the end of our rehearsal session, I overheard Dad and Bob Bennett in a quiet conversation. "I gotta admit, Bob," Dad muttered out of the side of his mouth. "I'm sorta nervous."

Bennett chuckled and patted Dad on the back. "Don't you worry Tex, I've seen a thousand of these things, and I can tell you'll do just fine."

That evening, Dickie flew in from Fort Worth and met Dad, Tom, and me at the hotel. Before dinner, we all convened in Dad's suite and had our usual Crown Royal. We were celebrating in advance; we were all confident. Still, I had some concerns.

"How you feeling, Dad?" I asked. "A little more relaxed now?"

He knocked back his Crown. "Don't worry. I was just teasing Bennett. I'm not the least bit nervous."

Early Wednesday morning, Bob Bennett rousted us out of the hotel, and we all took a limo to the Hart Building. We talked quietly until a few minutes before 9 A.M., when one of the "stage hands" came by to usher us into the hearing room.

As we entered, camera flashes exploded around us, and the rumble of conversation was stifled as staffers and reporters scurried to their places. The echoing emptiness I'd noticed in this room the day before was gone, replaced by the cacophony of too many bodies packed in too small a space. With the other witnesses, Dad was seated at a long table, positioned before an arc of senators. A sea of TV cameras lay between the two panels, and behind the witnesses the public was seated in order of priority. We were in a reserved seating area directly behind Dad, the journalists were seated behind us, and the general public behind them.

Three witnesses were scheduled to testify that day, and Dad was batting third. Richard Gardner went first. Gardner is a tax preparer. His Oklahoma company prepares 4,500 to 6,000 tax returns each year. One morning in 1995, Gardner came out of a meeting to find fifteen IRS agents and a half-dozen U.S. marshals in his lobby, "all armed and wearing those jackets that say in bright letters 'IRS' or 'U.S. Marshal' on the back," he testified.

Like us, Gardner's company had all its records and computers seized. But unlike us, Gardner wasn't able to get them back for two years while the IRS investigation continued. All in all, Gardner's story was a lot like ours, only he never did figure out why the IRS decided to raid his company in the first place.

John Colaprete's story was even more like our own. The Virginia Beach restaurateur was raided after a bookkeeper, fired for embezzling, went to the IRS with a wild story that included drug dealing and gunrunning.

Then it was Dad's turn to speak. When the cameras and audience turned their attention towards him, he was transformed. I had seen my father overcome many stressful situations over the years, but rarely had he given a public speech before such a distinguished crowd. Still, it only took a second to see that Dad was born for this sort of occasion. The words I had heard him practice time and time again took on a bolder, richer note:

> In my imagination, federal raids were always confined to Mafia bosses and drug lords. If you had told me that sixty-four IRS agents would storm my office, with

side arms holstered and boot heels trampling my civil rights and my business reputation, I wouldn't have believed you....

After presenting a brief background on himself, his past, and his family, he went directly into the story of the raid, with a description of the gun-wielding agents swarming into the building, "like an army landing on an enemy beachfront," shouting orders at the Moncrief employees:

> They rummaged through every inch of our building, breaking into offices, barking orders like "Open the doors, or we'll knock them down!" One special agent told my son that he could blow the hinges off his safe if he wouldn't open it. Agents even removed sheet rock from the walls, as if they were looking for illegal drugs....

He described the raid's immediate effects—how, with virtually all of our records and computers gone and our reputation severely damaged, business ground to a halt:

> My family was investigated for more than sixteen months. The Justice Department finally offered to drop the criminal investigation after I had spent millions of dollars in legal and accounting fees—roughly $5.5 million—to prove that we had committed no crime. But the IRS wouldn't go along unless we paid a large, arbitrarily determined sum, which was, in my opinion, plain extortion....

Then, he explained the details of Bill Jarvis's attempt to cash in
on our wealth and his own bookkeeping incompetence, and of
how the IRS apparently didn't question the veracity of Jarvis's
claims until long after the raid had already occurred. After describing the stress suffered by his staff and family, he reminded the Senate Finance Committee that this was but one of a thousand similar
stories. He asked them to consider the inevitable fate of the many
IRS victims who don't have the financial means to fight back:

> Although the IRS never bothered to conduct a civil
> audit to find out whether we owed one additional cent
> of tax, it called the $23 million it had extracted from us
> additional "taxes and interest." It was, in fact, nothing
> more than an amount arbitrarily demanded from me,
> various family members, our businesses, and our chari-
> table foundation to let the United States attorney issue
> a press release, praising the IRS Criminal Investigation
> Division for what it had done to us.
>
> But money and a press release weren't all it wanted.
> Despite the fact that its informer's original, highly com-
> pensated allegations were false, the IRS refused to quit.
> It demanded that we sign releases promising not to sue
> the agency itself and every government employee who
> had violated our rights. I didn't like this arrangement,
> but it was clear to me that if I didn't agree, the IRS
> would investigate our family business to its demise and
> me to my grave.
>
> When we learned the truth about our former
> accountant's extortionate plan, we asked the United
> States attorney and the IRS Inspection Division to inves-

tigate. They resisted. First, IRS Inspection took a half-hearted look at the case, but closed that investigation without taking the time to interview me or my sons to find out what had happened.

But we kept pressing. We acquired more evidence. A new investigation was opened. A new IRS investigator recommended that my former accountant be prosecuted. But no action has been taken. It's shocking that no IRS inspector has bothered to take action against the IRS case agents and supervisors who thoughtlessly accepted and viciously pursued the false accusations made by our greed-driven former accountant. Our government has consistently stonewalled our efforts to obtain internal documents disclosing the truth. A federal judge in Fort Worth recently tired of the government's effort to hide the facts. He ordered the government to give us all the information we had asked for and to pay attorney fees to compensate us for the burdens it had placed upon our efforts to seek out the truth. . . .

What about civil rights? This was a clear-cut case for serious self-examination by the IRS. But the IRS did its best to cover its tracks, protect itself from ever having to answer for its actions, and move on to another investigation, another—preferably defenseless—taxpayer.

I'm here today to ask you to call an end to this kind of abuse and ensure that what happened to us never again happens to another innocent American citizen.

After the speech, we milled around in the hearing room for a few minutes and then exited through a back corridor. As we worked our way out the back, the press began swarming over Dad, but Bob Bennett was there to shield him.

"Mr. Moncrief has already said what he came here to say," Bennett told them. "And that's it. He has nothing to add."

When we got back to the hotel, we immediately packed up and flew on home. We were all exhausted. I know Dad was especially tired, but by the look on his face I could also tell he was happier than he had been in a long time. He had finally had a chance to tell our side of the story, and people were listening.

The testimony had an instant effect that reverberated across D.C. and the entire country. Charles O. Rossotti, the commissioner of the IRS, held an outdoor press conference in front of IRS headquarters, where he admitted that the allegations needed to be taken seriously.

"Should even one of these allegations prove true, it's one too many, and I won't tolerate it," he said.

Even Senator Daniel Patrick Moynihan, a tax-and-spend liberal from New York, was moved by what he heard. "Wow," he said, "We have to be much concerned about the paramilitary performance of the IRS.... It's government violence directed against citizens."

The whole hearing had been televised on C-SPAN and Dad's testimony was broadcast on CNN as well. The next morning, Dad's picture would be in every paper from coast to coast including the *Wall Street Journal*, which would headline the story on page one.

Three months later, the U.S. Senate voted on a bill to overhaul IRS investigation practices. The bill passed ninety-eight to two. It was a victory for IRS reform, but it came too late for us. The Moncrief family name and business were blackened by abusive IRS policies, and we knew that no Senate vote would restore their shine. We had to do that ourselves. We had to prove, in a court of law, that we had been the victims of an elaborate conspiracy. A conspiracy designed by experts in the methods of the IRS, experts willing and able to wield the power of that bureaucracy for their own personal gain.

★ ★ ★

Meanwhile, I continued to watch the facts unfold about what Bill Jarvis and his group had been up to before the raid. I pored over depositions and observed continuing discovery arising from our lawsuit against the conspirators and the documents we were able to obtain from the IRS investigation. I worked with the State Bar of Texas and the Texas State Board of Public Accountancy. Soon the whole process of exposing the conspirators and bringing them to justice no longer had anything to do with restoring our business reputation. Instead, it became a matter of duty.

Although they had pulled every legal maneuver possible to thwart the coming of their day of reckoning, the group would finally stand trial. Just over four years had passed since the IRS raided our offices, and we had been deposing witnesses for three of those years. By the start of October 1998, we had questioned all the conspirators and relevant witnesses not once, but twice. Now, armed with the original fee splitting agreement and a confession signed by former United States attorney and coconspirator Jim Rolfe, we could sense victory at last. We had our strategy; we had our witnesses. And now we had a trial date: October 13, 1998.

For the week prior to the trial, we brought in a group of professional jury consultants from California. The jury pool had been selected that previous Friday, so our consultants spent the weekend sorting through the profiles of each juror to rate their desirability for our case. The *voir dire* phase—in which the final twelve jury members are selected through a process of questioning and negotiation—would start on Tuesday, and the trial itself would begin as soon as the jury was selected.

Two days before the trial, Marshall Searcy stopped by the office to let me know that he'd been talking with R. H. Wallace, the "top dog" at Shannon Gracey, the firm Gary Richardson had hired to defend him.

"They asked for a settlement offer!" Marshall announced. "Knowing how you and Tex would respond to such a question, I decided to toss them a bone that's a little too big to chew on."

"Is that right?" I replied. "So what was your offer?"

"I told them we'd want a bulletproof confession and $2 million," he answered through a wide grin. "I haven't heard a peep from them since."

Looking through my diaries, I now realize that this was the last pleasurable moment I was to have for a very long time.

I wish I'd taken a moment to enjoy it.

The next morning, I went by Dad's house for coffee as usual. When I got there I saw him walking up the sandstone sidewalk from his bedroom. He appeared to be limping, but when I asked him if his legs hurt he said, "No, no more than usual, but I do feel a little dizzy." I took his blood pressure, but found nothing unusual, so I decided to stop worrying and went to the office to continue preparing for the trial, which was starting the next day.

Dad went to see his doctor, who found that his reflexes were extremely hyperactive. "Hyperactive reflexes generally indicate some sort of spinal problem," Dr. Albert McDowell told him. "So I think we should run an MRI right away." The scan revealed a breakdown in a couple of cervical discs that might have caused the reflex problem.

On Monday night, I had my usual martini and went to bed early, but I couldn't sleep. I was just too pumped about the trial. I had never been so anxious to see something get underway in my life. If my heart was ever to give out on me, the time had arrived: In the few days before the trial began, it was pumping pure adrenaline. With a mountain of incriminating evidence on our side, I was 99 percent sure of a victory, but still there was that last, *huge* one percent weighing heavy on my mind. The bitter aftertaste of defeat still lingered in my mouth, and with it the taste of nervous apprehension.

By now, I was certain that our legal team—Marshall Searcy and Hugh Connor—were far superior to Ellen Lloyd's prosecutors, and their opponent David Stagner was certainly no Robert Hinton. But the simple fact remains that when you go before a jury, anything's possible. I got up and walked around the block in the middle of the night just to calm myself down.

The next morning I met my brother Dickie at Dad's house. We hoped to find Dad his old self again, but he was much worse than the day before: He had difficulty shaving and combing his hair, and there was a slur in his speech. Alarmed, Dickie called Dr. McDowell to schedule more tests. I was geared up for the trial, but I couldn't stand the thought of starting before I knew that Dad was okay. I got on the phone with Marshall and told him to request a twenty-four-hour postponement

After lunch, Marshall, Dickie, Tom, and I drove out to Dad's house. On the way, the conversation was so nervous that my heart starts pounding as I sit here writing about it.

One question hung in all our minds: Could we go to trial without involving Dad?

"That's a tough question," Marshall said. "Without your dad's testimony, we don't have much chance to win this."

Dickie thought it was time to get out. "How about just settling with the bastards?" he said.

Tom glared at Dickie. "Settle? Are you crazy?" he said. "Think about what that would do to Dad! I swear to God it would kill him!"

But Dickie was adamant. "Well, think about what it will do to him if we *do* go to trial, but then lose because we don't let him testify," he said. "We just can't go into trial if we know we're going to lose."

Marshall tried to calm everybody down. "I'm working the settlement angle right now," he said, "and as far as I'm concerned, if we try to settle with all the defendants in just twenty-four hours, it'll be a total disaster. I do think I could get Richardson to take a solid offer for sure—and maybe Keller and Graber, too."

"All right," I said as we pulled into the driveway. "Let's see what Dad thinks."

Dad was resting in the backyard when we briefed him on our current, ugly set of choices. The word "settlement" was not what he wanted to hear. "No settlement for anyone!" he growled fiercely. "We're going to go for it." I could see how much effort it took him to muster up his fighting face, and so could everyone else.

"We've *already* won!" Tom said, suddenly switching gears toward Dickie's side. "You already exonerated us when you appeared before the Senate. We don't need to take it any further."

But I could tell that Dad wasn't buying that argument, and I wasn't either.

I turned and looked at Mother, who hovered on the edge of the group listening intently. She looked bewildered. Like the rest of us, she knew that Dad was a fighter by nature. She knew that not fighting a battle that he had spent years preparing for—and one that he needed so desperately to win—could kill him just as easily as fighting could.

"Let's go, boys." I said, standing up. "We've got our orders. No settlement."

The drive back to the office was solemn. We knew what we had to do—forge ahead with the trial. Still, I had a sick feeling in my stomach. I couldn't think of a worse way to begin this last battle.

I sat at my desk alone and peered out through the smoked-glass windows. My mind wandered back across four years that had passed since the day of the raid and all that had transpired since. I couldn't believe that all our work and careful strategy had left us with such a harsh set of options. As things currently stood, we couldn't win the trial without Dad's testimony. And if we made him the key witness in a high profile jury trial, that would probably kill him. On the other hand, we could settle with the conspirators, but that would probably kill him, too. Couldn't we find some middle ground—some way to keep the trial going but take the pressure off Dad?

I got on the phone with Marshall. It was a crucial moment for me. For the first time in our business relationship, I was going to directly disobey my father's order. I didn't feel good about it, but I knew I was doing the right thing.

"Marshall, I know you said that we can't settle with everybody so quickly," I began, "And you also said that we can't win without Dad's testimony. But isn't there a way to make Dad's testimony a little less important to our chances?"

"Just what are you driving at?" Marshall asked.

"Remember that settlement offer you gave to Gary Richardson's lawyers?"

"Of course I do. A bulletproof confession and $2 million. They'll never agree to that."

"That's true," I said. "But what if we just push for the confession and his insurance? Do you think we could keep Dad out of this trial if Richardson verified everyone else's guilt?"

"Well, sure . . ." Marshall replied with creeping tension in his voice. "But Tex doesn't want any settlements, remember?"

"Just let me worry about that." I was pretty damned worried. "If you think we have a good chance of winning this thing on Richardson's confession, then go get it. I'll deal with Dad."

"Charlie," Marshall replied. "I agree this is the best way to handle the situation. You get your trial, and you get to keep your dad off the stand. But you have to remember, I work for Tex, not you. I need to follow his directives, not yours."

"Dammit, you'll get your directive soon enough," I said. "Just get to work on that confession."

I hung up and walked into Dickie's office.

"I'm giving Marshall the go-ahead to settle with Richardson." I told him.

To my surprise, Dickie said, "Well, that's a relief. I thought I was going to have to do it!"

It was a big relief to me as well. I didn't realize at the time, but in hindsight I believe it was one of the best decisions I've ever made in my life.

Smiling knowingly, Dickie said, "Have fun telling Dad."

Dickie and I laid out our plans for the next day. I was to go straight to Marshall's office and be there to make sure that the Richardson confession was satisfactory. I couldn't let anyone else handle that. Dickie was to go by Dad's house at 8 A.M. and stay with him. When the confession was a done deal, I would stop by to break the news to Dad.

Later that evening I received an irritating fax from Marshall Searcy, recapping the conversation we had earlier that day. He was covering his ass about me directing him to settle with Richardson against the order he had received from Dad. And I can't say as I blamed him. But by then it was too late—too late in the evening and too late in the story—to worry about details like this one.

I had a terrible night, rose early, and was dressed and ready to go at 6:30 A.M. I went on to my office at 8 A.M. Still not able to calm down, I went on up to the KH&H law offices, figuring our legal team would already be there. Marshall and I met at a stop light on the way up Commerce. Laughing, we rolled our windows down.

"Where you going at this hour?" he asked, facetiously.

"Same place that you are," I said. "Off to kick some ass!"

When we got to his office, Marshall told me that R. H. Wallace, Richardson's lawyer, had gone to Dallas the previous evening to meet with Richardson. Richardson approved an affidavit that clearly implicated all of the other conspirators. Marshall was expecting to hear from R. H. at any second.

Dickie strolled through the door. "What in the hell are you doing here?" I said. "You're supposed to be at Dad's."

"Hell," he said, "I just couldn't go by there and sit for an hour, knowing that we were settling with Richardson and not tell him. You gotta let him know yourself!"

The phone rang. It was Richardson's lawyer, R. H. Wallace.

We agreed to meet him at the judge's chambers. When we got there, R. H., Marshall and I met in a small office while I quickly read through Richardson's sworn statement in a matter of seconds. I felt good about getting someone to come clean about the whole ordeal; getting this on paper was definitely worth whatever trouble it would get me in with Dad. I knew what I had done was right. I okayed the confession, Marshall and R. H. signed it, and I was out the door, headed toward Dad.

When I got to Dad's, Mother was sitting in the breakfast room, seemingly alone and lost. She said Dad had gone downstairs to get dressed.

"How's he doing?" I asked.

"Oh, he seems to be all right," she said. But I could tell she felt differently.

"Ma," I said, "I just consummated a deal with Richardson in direct disobedience to Dad's order not to settle. But I did it anyway, and I'm glad I did."

We walked down the sandstone path to their room where we found Dad was already dressed and ready to go to court. He didn't look any better. But he was certainly a lot calmer than I.

"Sit down here for a minute," I said. "I've got a couple of things to tell you. First of all, they're bringing in the jury probably as we speak and everything is on go. Second, I settled with Gary Richardson this morning."

Dad grimaced and gazed out the window in disgust.

"Dad," I said, "you've got to calm down, or this thing is going to kill you and me both. I settled, and it was the right thing to do, so I don't want to hear another word about it. It's done!"

"How much did you get?" he asked, still gazing out the window, unable to look me in the eye.

"We got his insurance money, but we agreed never to disclose the amount."

"That's bad," he said quietly. "They'd already offered more than that."

"I can't help it; it's done—that's it," I said. "I gave a little on the money, and in return I got a rock solid confession. If worse comes to worst, Marshall thinks we can win the trial with that confession, and you won't have to testify." Since we were only settling with Richardson, we still had to try the other conspirators.

Dad still wouldn't look at me.

"Do you still feel like going down to the courthouse?" I asked.

"Yes," he said. "I feel okay." But I could tell that he didn't.

"I don't want you talking to the press," I said. "I'll handle that."

When he went to his dressing room to put on his coat and tie, Mother and I followed. As he stood in front of the mirror, I could see the right side of his face droop. "Dad, take a look at yourself," I said. "Can you see your face sagging?"

"Yeah," he said. But he continued getting dressed.

"Come on, Dad," I said. "I'm not going to lose you over this. Get back in bed. It's not worth it."

"You think so?"

"Yes, sir, that's it. You get back in bed, and I'll go back down to the courtroom."

As I headed for the driveway, I heard him grumbling behind me, "But what the hell am I going to do all morning?"

Take it easy, I hoped.

Heading back downtown, I realized that I had lost all sense of direction. After four years of civil war, where was I? The other day Marshall had said, "Charlie, tell me what to do!" And now I felt the same way, but I didn't have anyone to ask. When I entered the courtroom, all of the prospective jurors were seated in the pews of the public viewing area. Every seat was occupied. Dickie rose from a chair near the jury box and moved toward me, looking around for Dad. I walked past the jurors and through a gate into the area provided for the lawyers. The conspirators and their lawyers were there lined up at a long table, looking sullen.

Before Dickie could ask, I whispered, "Didn't bring him. He's not up to it, and he's getting worse."

"All right," Dickie replied. "Let's go back and tell Marshall."

Attorneys for both sides were huddled in a room immediately behind the judge's bench. We motioned Marshall into the hallway, and then we walked on back around the corner where we could talk. "Dad's not coming," I told him. "He's getting sicker, and we still don't know what's was wrong with him."

"What are we going to do?" Marshall asked.

I didn't have the slightest idea what to say. Marshall mumbled something about a settlement or calling it quits, then headed back to the attorney's conference.

Tom must have overheard Marshall. He grabbed my arm and whispered, "We can't give up!"

"Nobody's giving up!" Dickie said angrily.

We paced, and sat, waited, and paced. Finally, Marshall came out again. "We can't call this thing off," he said. "The other side will have a field day with the press." Then he turned around and headed back into the courtroom. We waited some more. A few long minutes later, Marshall came back and said that the judge had granted us a continuance based on Dad's health and that we'd set a trial date for probably sometime the following spring. Richardson's sworn statement went in our arsenal for trial. Although we couldn't reveal the amount of the financial settlement, we were free to use the confession in court.

Tom, Dickie, and I rushed to the parking lot. By 11:30 A.M., we had picked up Dad and driven him to Harris Southwest Hospital for another round of tests. This time, the doctors found a spot on his medulla. Dad had clearly suffered a stroke, but it was a minor one. The doctors told us to continue treating him with aspirin and rest. Strangely, this news came as a relief. We were glad finally to know what was going on.

On the way back to the house, we passed a convenience store. "Hold it!" Dad said. "Pull in to that 7-Eleven."

"Why don't you just let us take you home?" I said impatiently. "I'll go get you whatever you want later."

"No, just pull in there now," he answered. "I want to buy some lottery tickets. Pot's up to forty-five million dollars and the drawing's tonight."

The ticket turned out to be a loser.

★ ★ ★

The next day Dad came to the office, but he wasn't any better. He had to walk with a cane, and Kathy helped him clear his desk. But nothing could keep him from the office this day; he wanted to read Richardson's sworn statement, so I directed his attention to paragraph fourteen:

> Attached hereto as Exhibit 1 is a true and correct copy of a document entitled "Contract and Agreement of Employment." The cover letter is dated August 31, 1994 (two days before the execution of the search warrant by the IRS), and is signed by Carla Jones, my assistant. This agreement emanated from my office and I signed it before we sent it to the others for execution on or about August 30, 1994. This contract indicates that I would be entitled to 10% of any amounts received from

Bill Jarvis, Don Jarvis, Graber, Keller and Rolfe's portion of the expected IRS informant's reward. Exhibit 1 also calls for me to receive one-third of the fee obtained for representing Michael Moncrief. The proposed signatories on the agreement include Rolfe, Bill Jarvis, Don Jarvis, Graber, Keller and myself. I signed this document. Neither Keller nor Bill Jarvis are attorneys. To my knowledge, neither Rolfe nor Don Jarvis represented Michael Moncrief in any manner relating to this case. I do not recall Don Jarvis, Keller, Graber or Rolfe ever contacting me to attempt to amend, modify or opt-out of this agreement at any time.

We finally had the confession, but it was a hollow victory. Dad was going downhill fast. The day after we got Richardson's statement, Dad didn't make it to the office. In fact, Dad wouldn't make it to the office for quite some time. On Saturday morning, he was feeling a little better, but nonetheless he summoned me to his side at the breakfast table to give me his power of attorney. He had his housekeeper act as a witness. With his signature, the power of attorney was done. I was effectively now in charge, if and when Dad became incapacitated.

The following Sunday, we had to admit Dad to the hospital and start him on blood thinners. At this point he could no longer walk without assistance, and his speech was severely slurred. Worse yet, Dad was scared and rightfully so. He only stayed in the hospital for one night.

He seemed to lose all interest in business, even though I briefed him daily, going by his house for coffee every morning as I always had. Dickie, Tom, and I would go by for lunch every day. One day, we all three went down to his bedroom to help him up to lunch. He was sitting on the edge of his bed staring helplessly, too weak to lift his head. He looked up at us briefly and said, "Boys, this may be the end for me. I just want you all to know how much I love each one of you, how much fun it has been watching you grow up, and how much joy you have given me through the years."

Tom said, "Dad, I love you very much."

Dickie said, "Pop, we all love you."

I knew if I tried to say anything I would break down and cry. I leaned my head back, looked up toward heaven, and said to myself, "Dear God, please don't let this end this way."

Epilogue

Law and Order 2000

DAD'S RECOVERY FROM HIS STROKE was a miracle, but it was a miracle hard won. He was unable to walk without the aid of a walker, and it was next to impossible for him to hold a fork or a pen without assistance. His speech was slurred, and he had difficulty swallowing. I continued to go by Dad's house for coffee as I always had, but now I would meet him in his bathroom, where he would be struggling to shave and comb his hair. I would follow closely behind him as he made his way to the staircase with his walker, then I would hold him around the waist and help him pull his way up the stairs. As Dad gained strength, he could rise on his own. I would stand behind him and had the handrail on the stairs reinforced so it wouldn't pull loose from his weight.

It would be over two months before Dad would return to the office. In fact, he didn't even seem to want to know what was happening at the office. It seemed eerie, almost as if God had removed Dad's business mind temporarily so that his brain could devote full attention to healing his body. Dickie, Tom, and I would go by the house for lunch and watch Dad fumble with his fork and knife. He would chew every bite deliberately and follow each swallow with a drink of water so that he would not choke. Dad had even lost his desire for a sip of wine or whiskey. He went to physical therapy every day, which was painful for him.

But determination has always been one of Dad's strongest attributes, so his recovery proved to be relatively rapid. Within five months, he was 80 percent back to health. Within a year, he was 90 percent. Luckily, a few months after the IRS raid, Dad had started exercising and pumping iron to reduce stress. Without that, I seriously doubt that he would ever have made such a comeback. Still, despite his recovery, the stroke, combined with the past four years of pain and suffering, aged Dad well beyond his seventy-eight years. His face sagged, and he would walk with a limp for the rest of his life.

By 2000, it had been six years since the IRS raided our offices and nine years since our former comptroller, Billy Wayne Jarvis, began assembling his own group of conspirators. But even at that point, neither Jarvis and his band of conspirators nor Mike Moncrief has been able to salvage anything for their efforts.

★ ★ ★

Back in November of 1995, when Mike and his side of the family were advised by counsel to apologize to Dad, Dick, and me, their attorneys suggested they sign a letter of apology and do everything that was necessary to get out of the lawsuit. In that meeting, attorneys Lyndell Kirkley and David Broiles told Mike and his side of the family not to worry about signing the letter because they could always come back after Tex via the Lee Moncrief Trust. Broiles went on to tell the group that he was going to turn the lawyer members of Jarvis's group—Gary Richardson, Sam Graber, and Judge Don Jarvis—in to the State Bar of Texas. Jan Moncrief had a copy of the letter Broiles eventually sent to the bar in her files, and she gave it to me. The letter wasn't much, the bare minimum required as a report for an ethical violation.

In the spring of 1998, knowing that the statute of limitations might run out on the conspirators' deeds, I took it upon myself to provide additional information to the state bar just to sort of fill in the blanks on Richardson, Graber, and Don Jarvis. I provided similar information to the Texas State Board of Public Accountancy in regard to Bill Jarvis.

The state bar's Fort Worth office agreed that Richardson, Graber, and Judge Jarvis should be investigated. The three cases were moved to Dallas for proper venue and assigned an investigator. After several months, I received a letter stating that the investigation had been concluded; the investigator found no wrongdoing by any of the three lawyers.

I couldn't believe it. I called the investigator to express my shock. How could he find the attorneys innocent of all wrongdoing? He wasn't surprised to hear from me; in fact, he admitted that he felt sure I would appeal his decision. He told me how to file the appeal, which I did immediately via fax. If I had been astounded at his finding, though, it was nothing compared to the shock I felt when the investigator told me that he was only working part-time for the state bar. His full-time job was as an IRS agent!

That investigator's ruling was overturned by the appeals tribunal in Austin and sent back to the Grievance Committee in Dallas, where hearings were set so each of the three defendants could tell his side of the story. I appeared at each of the three hearings with my attorney Hugh Connor. The hearings were interesting. You can imagine the looks on the investigative panel members' faces when each of the three lawyers looked them straight in the eyes and said something to the effect of, "Yes, I signed the fee splitting agreement, but I knew it wasn't properly written. I only signed it because we had all agreed to rescind it and sign a new one later that was correct." Dallas lawyer Bob Shoemaker, one of the panelists in the front row, looked at Gary Richardson and asked, "You don't really expect us to believe that, do you?"

But the real clincher was the sworn statement of former U.S. attorney Jim Rolfe. It would bury the group, especially in the eyes of the State Bar. Jim's statement: "We entered into a written contract to split both Jarvis's informant's fee from the IRS and Richardson's fee.... I was to receive a percentage of the Richardson contingent fee. I never represented Michael Moncrief in any manner relating to this case. This percentage was then to be split among Keller, Graber, Bill Jarvis, Don Jarvis, and me. I do not recall Don Jarvis, Keller, Graber, or Richardson ever contacting me to attempt to amend, modify, or opt-out of this agreement at any time."

It was not until January of 2000 that the Dallas-area Grievance Committee of the State Bar of Texas slammed Gary L. "Tall Boots" Richardson, Samuel Graber, and Judge Don Jarvis. They were cited for professional misconduct, but we don't know what punishment was offered. We do know that whatever the punishment was, it was unacceptable to all three. At that point the complaint became public information. In accordance with the rules of disciplinary procedures, the three attorneys elected to stand trial in state court as opposed to being judged before a panel of their peers.

The three cases were then submitted to the Commission for Lawyer Discipline for further review, and the election for a trial was forwarded to the state bar's chief disciplinary counsel. This completely autonomous board was charged with deciding whether it was worth the state bar's time and money to prosecute the three attorneys. The board was divided on how to proceed. Eventually, they agreed to appoint two outside lawyers to make an independent review of the evidence and return to the board with a recommendation on whether to prosecute. Their choices, Lonny Morrison of Wichita Falls and James E. Coleman Jr. of Dallas, were both powerful attorneys with strong backgrounds in lawyer discipline and ethics. With the Morrison-Coleman report in hand, and despite some dissention, the commission voted six to two to proceed. I received notice from Dawn Miller, chief disciplinary counsel: "At this juncture, the commission has directed that disciplinary action proceed as to all three complaints. Beyond that, I can give no further details at this time regarding the timing of the filing of suit(s)."

Out of curiosity, I had Hugh Connor research case law on improper fee splitting. Interestingly enough, there had been no cases in Texas or any other state. Now it was clear why the disciplinary panel was so divided: We were getting ready to write the law for the entire country.

Six months lapsed without any word. The commission was then reconvened, and they voted unanimously to halt all proceedings against the three lawyers. I immediately appealed the decision to the state bar's Board of Disciplinary Appeals, but they informed me that the commission's decisions are final. I sent all the case information to the Texas State Supreme Court, but it refused to review the cases for lack of jurisdiction. I finally turned to the attorney general of Texas in the summer of 2001. As of August 2001, the cases have been under review by Antonio Alarado, the executive director of the State Bar of Texas, chief disciplinary counsel Dawn Miller, and Justice James Baker of the Texas State Supreme Court.

In May 2001, a case involving fee splitting appeared in the 285th District Court in Bexar County, Texas. In that case, the lawyers were punished with three-year probated suspensions of their law licenses for knowing that a fourth attorney in their partnership was splitting fees with a nonlawyer. They were not even actually participating in the fee splitting! What disciplinary action may or not be taken against the guilty lawyer has not been made public at this time. Likewise, we are still waiting to find out whether Gary Richardson, Sam Graber, and Judge Don Jarvis will ever face disciplinary consequences for their actions.

★ ★ ★

For Dad, the most painful battle was ahead, to be waged in state probate court. True to their word, and exactly as Jan Moncrief predicted, Mike and his mother, Dee Faxel, successfully instigated a lawsuit against Dad via the Lee Wiley Moncrief Trust. In March of 1999, Dee filed a motion in the district probate court to have Billy Jarvis removed as a successor trustee. Naturally, she never discussed this with Dad, who as the sole trustee could have removed Jarvis under the terms of the trust. Dee and Mike knew that the probate court judge would be bound to appoint a guardian ad litem (guardian for the suit) to review the situation. Judge Ferchill ruled that Dee had no standing with the court or with the trust, but, as planned, he appointed James Holliday as attorney ad litem. Holliday did not find it necessary to contact Dad at that point. Instead, he immediately visited Dee Faxel's lawyer, Allan Howeth, who promptly sent Holliday to meet Lyndell Kirkley, Jerry Goodwin, and Billy Jarvis. But the real issue was not getting rid of Jarvis. I sensed they were using Holliday to strike back at Dad.

Kirkley, Goodwin, and Jarvis resurrected the same stale accusations, just as they had with the IRS back in 1993. Awestruck by what he was hearing, Holliday returned to the court and indicated that he would need help with such a potentially huge case. The court thus appointed an additional ad litem, David Bakutis. Holliday and Bakutis were so impressed by the numbers Kirkley, Goodwin, and Jarvis were discussing that they then asked the probate court to grant them a 40 percent contingency fee for taking the case. Before Lee Wiley Moncrief attempted suicide back in 1989, she had asked Dad to be her sole trustee. From an original cash infusion in 1988 of two million dollars, Lee Wiley Moncrief's trust is now worth close to thirty million dollars. When Lee became incapacitated as a result of her failed suicide attempt, Mike and his mother, Dee, begged Dad to become guardian of her estate. In that capacity, Dad even negotiated her divorce. He was trustee of her children's trusts as well and made them independently wealthy. Then, without any notice whatsoever, Bakutis and Holliday filed suit against Dad for breach of fiduciary duty. As I noted before, neither Bakutis nor Holliday ever contacted Dad to discuss the allegations being presented by Jarvis and company. They never sent Dad a notice of their appointments, a letter of engagement... nothing except the lawsuit.

It devastated Dad. With all that he had done for Lee, it was literally beyond his comprehension that he could be accused of cheating her by a couple of lawyers he had never heard of before. Dad became unruly and nearly impossible to communicate with about the new lawsuit. I was praying that his medication was strong enough to prevent another stroke. Finally, Dad and I went to Dee

Kelly's office to discuss legal strategy with Kelly and Marshall Searcy. I knew there would be trouble when Dad asked to start the meeting.

"Now let me say a few words here before we get going," he began. I knew very well what that little introduction meant—prepare for an ass chewing. "Let me tell you something, boys," Dad continued. "You've been fighting these lawsuits for me for many years now, and we haven't won a damned thing. Seems like we're the ones getting whipped all the time, and I'm tired of it. We paid $23 million to the IRS, and looking back, I think that was a mistake. The judge in our lawsuit ruled that Bill Jarvis was in contempt of court and sent him to jail, but for whatever reason, Marshall, you stood up and let him off. You told the judge that putting him in the custody of his lawyer would be sufficient.

"All of you, including Bob Bennett, talked me into letting Mike Moncrief out of this lawsuit. All of these actions were mistakes, in my opinion. Now this Lee Wiley Moncrief lawsuit really galls me. I took care of this little girl because my daddy would have wanted me to, and I made her a lot of money. Now someone is trying to say that I cheated her, and that's just not true."

He paused and then asked, finally, "Can you beat these guys, or do I need to get someone who can?"

With that, Dad and Dee Kelly began screaming at the tops of their lungs, cussing out of control. Kelly finally overpowered Dad with his superior lung capacity. "Tex, goddamn it, shut up. Just shut up and listen," he yelled. "I'm going to win this case for you one way or another. I promise you I will. So just shut up, and I don't want to hear another word about it." The walls were literally shaking. Marshall Searcy even said later, "Hell, I just wanted out of there." As far as I'm concerned, it was the greatest thing that Dee

Kelly ever did. Dad took his word for it and pretty much put it out of his mind. If it weren't for Kelly, I think that Mike and Dee's lawsuit might have been the end of Tex Moncrief.

When the ad litems filed suit against Dad, he was actually in the final stages of turning the Lee Wiley Moncrief Trust over to Chase Bank. Obviously, that process came to a halt, since no bank is going to take over a trust that is mired in litigation. The ad litems asked for a full and complete accounting of the trust, which we started immediately. We subsequently sued Dee Faxel to see how she'd been handling Lee's personal finances as guardian. Judge King (because he knew the family, Ferchill recused himself at this point) decided that the ad litem suit should go to mediation. I attended the mediation on Dad's behalf. The ad litems informed me that they would take thirty million dollars and settle the case. I told the judge that was crazy; by our calculations, the Lee Wiley Moncrief Trust might actually owe the other grandchildren money. The judge promptly accused me of negotiating in bad faith.

At that point, I began to think that maybe I should just sit down with Dee Faxel and her husband, Ralph Faxel, and clean up the whole mess once and for all. Unfortunately, that wouldn't be the case. I shook both their hands, but before I could even take a seat, Dee's head began to shake with rage. "Why are you suing me?" she said in a deep, growling voice. There was clearly no room for negotiation. I thanked them both for their time and left.

We dropped our case against Dee as the guardian of Lee Wiley Moncrief's "person" so that we could devote full time to our problems with Bakutis and Holliday. Judge King asked us to attempt another mediation, and he appointed Judge John Hughes this time. Judge Hughes is a smart man who knows the oil business from top to bottom. He read the pleadings and thought that Judge King ought to throw the whole thing out. After Hughes talked to Holliday and Bakutis, he told us, "You know, these two guys really think they have a legitimate suit." Dad and I had already decided we'd give $150,000 just to get rid of the thing, but that wasn't going to happen. Bakutis and Holliday could see some deep pockets, and they wanted their share of it. Once again, we dug in for a fight.

★ ★ ★

At about the same time, Billy Jarvis began a full blown barrage of lawsuits. But he had a different approach from Mike Moncrief. He was determined to win remuneration by attacking the federal government.

In November 1997, Jarvis filed suit in the federal claims court in Washington, D.C., asking for his full $25 million reward from the IRS. He claimed that the IRS had bungled the investigation of our family and that he should therefore still receive the full reward amount. The judge in the case threw out most of Jarvis's claims. Regarding the $25 million, the judge ruled that if Jarvis was to receive a reward at all, it would be the $1.7 million as calculated by the Department of Treasury. The defense attorneys for the government took the position that Jarvis was not entitled to anything because he had breached his witness reward agreement, but even so, they made an unofficial offer to him of one million dollars to settle the suit. When I saw the offer in writing, it literally took my breath away. Jarvis, who was out for a much bigger payday, either refused it on his own or was advised by counsel to turn it down.

Next, Jarvis proceeded to file a motion for summary judgment. Once again, the judge turned him down. In reference to one of Jarvis's affidavits attached to the motion, Judge Bruggink wrote,

"The affidavit itself has manifold problems. . . . Jarvis's affidavit contains a host of statements which would clearly be inadmissible at trial." But as requested by the government, Judge Bruggink set the case for trial. Then, Jarvis filed yet another lawsuit in federal court in Texarkana, Texas, in July of 1999. This new suit alleged disclosure violations by the IRS, claiming that they arbitrarily divulged his name as that of the informant in our case.

Jarvis kept inaccurately testifying that IRS agent Mike Sanders had told me that Jarvis was the IRS informant who had turned us in to the government. Nothing was further from the truth. When I saw what was said about Sanders, I immediately wrote a letter to the U.S. attorney handling the case for the government and told him that Sanders had never revealed Jarvis's identity as an informant and that my diary entries indicated so. In fact, what Sanders did tell me would indicate that Jarvis was not the informant:

> Mike Sanders—had not heard that Jarvis was not getting any $, but that would be his position if asked. Had heard about the "letter agrmnt" but had not seen it—I fax'd one to him. Thought may (sic) that their internal investigators were looking into Jarvis et al.
> —*Diary excerpt, February 13, 1996*

Both of Jarvis's lawsuits were designed to help Jarvis and the conspirators defend themselves in our civil suit against them. Their only defense, and it would be slim, would be to try to convince the jury that they were justified in signing the unethical fee splitting agreement because Tex Moncrief and his sons really were a bunch of crooks. If the government were to go ahead and pay Jarvis the $1.7 million, Jarvis's defense team would be able to take the position that he did nothing wrong and was justly rewarded. By the same token, if the government ruled that the IRS did in fact arbitrarily divulge Jarvis's identity to us, he could be awarded the $25 million for which he was asking. Such a decision in his favor would give Jarvis plenty of cash to defend his case and let him live comfortably for the rest of his life.

Jarvis had a third issue that he took to federal court for a ruling. He tried to claim that while acting as an informant, he was actually an employee of the federal government. As such, he felt that the U.S. government should defend him in the civil suit against us. The federal district court in Fort Worth ruled that Jarvis was in fact not a government employee. Jarvis later appealed the ruling to the Fifth Circuit Court, which upheld the lower court's ruling not once, but twice when Jarvis asked for a review of their first opinion.

At some point, Inspector Tom Davis of the Inspection Division of the Treasury Department referred Jarvis for prosecution for lying to the government in a sworn statement. Jarvis had been referred for prosecution twice before by two other investigators, but the U.S. attorneys for the Northern District of Texas had declined to prosecute. This time, though, Inspector Davis had a charge that was rock solid: a sworn statement to the government, in which Jarvis said:

> From the time I became the comptroller of Montex Drilling Company in May 1979, through the time I was terminated in June, 1993, I did not prepare a Federal income tax return for that corporation or any Federal income tax returns, gift tax returns, or estate tax returns

for the Moncrief family or their trusts. Accordingly I did
not sign any tax returns as preparer.

Whether or not Jarvis was a "tax return preparer" now became
of crucial importance. If Jarvis was not a preparer in the strict
sense, then he would have only been guilty of theft when he
turned over our records to Mike. But if he was an actual preparer,
he could be charged for a federal offense for having divulged confidential tax information.

When I saw Jarvis's statement, I called our tax accountant into
my office and asked her if she had ever noticed any tax returns in
our files that Bill Jarvis had signed as preparer. "Sure," Sharon
replied immediately. "There are lots of them."

I had her make copies of the returns with Jarvis's signature, and
we quickly turned them over to Inspector Davis. When Davis put
together his case against Jarvis, U.S. Attorney Paul Coggins could
see that he and Jarvis had a problem. Jarvis had signed our tax
returns as a preparer. But in his sworn statement to federal agents,
he claimed he'd never done that before. Because of the obvious
conflict of interest, Coggins recused the Northern District of Texas
from the case, and it later landed with the Fraud Division of the
Justice Department in Washington, D.C. As of this writing, the case
has been there for three years, and we haven't heard from them.
For all we know, the Justice Department might have even dropped
the case.

Finally, Jarvis filed suit against my lawyer Jim Bruton and the
law firm of Williams and Connolly. This suit was filed in federal
court in Texarkana as well. In it, Jarvis alleges that the government
breached its contract with him by not paying him his reward

because Bruton "tortuously interfered" in that contract. In the claim, Jarvis falls back once again on my conversation with Agent Mike Sanders, alleging that Mike improperly and illegally disclosed his name as that of the informant. It's interesting to note that as of this very day, no federal agent, U.S. attorney, or government employee has ever told my father or me that Bill Jarvis was the informant against us. We found out by virtue of discovery from Jarvis himself.

Our last blow would come from a familiar source. Mike and company filed suit against Dad in a Louisiana state court in February of 2000. His claim was that Dad drilled on a lease that he knew had already expired. Mike wanted his money from the oil well back, plus damages for fraud. The Louisiana lawsuit had been carefully calculated: If we tried to settle with Mike et al. in Louisiana, the information would be fed back to the ad litems in the Lee Wiley Moncrief case to give them more ammunition. Mike's lawsuit against us in Louisiana eventually died. In the pleadings of the suit, Mike claimed that we drilled a deep oil well on a lease that we knew we did not own. People have drilled wells on leases they did not own, but invariably they do so as a result of gross negligence. What really happened to us in the case of that well was even more bizarre, but it's a story in itself. As far as this book is concerned, it will suffice to say that the suit died on its own lack of merit.

★ ★ ★

Ellen Lloyd reappeared in our lives as well. After she was acquitted on charges of theft, she and her new lawyer, Broadus Spivey, filed suit against Dad for libel and slander. On summary judgment, Judge Lowe ruled against her, but she then decided to appeal that ruling to the Second Court of Appeals here in Fort Worth.

On Wednesday, April 5, 2000, Ellen and her attorney, Broadus Spivey, presented their cases. On December 21, 2000, the three-judge panel ruled—not totally in our favor. The previous rulings of the trial court with respect to malicious prosecution and intentional infliction of emotional distress on our part were affirmed. These two were clearly the most serious allegations brought against Dad, and now they were gone forever. However, the panel reversed and remanded the decision of the lower courts in the matter of the charges against Dad for defamation of character and abuse of process. There's little doubt that we will eventually end up going to trial over the charges.

While we fought these various legal skirmishes, the Lee Wiley Moncrief lawsuit continued to hover over our heads. The only suggestion for settlement came from Dee Faxel's attorney, Allan Howeth, who suggested that if we paid the Mike Moncrief Trust, the Lee Wiley Moncrief Trust, and the Monty Moncrief estate $750,000 each, the whole thing would "go away." We turned them down.

On Wednesday, April 12, 2000, the attorneys ad litem representing the Lee Wiley Moncrief Trust were dealt a blow. The accusations in the ad litems' lawsuit against Dad were the exact same accusations that were used by Billy Jarvis and the conspirators to secure the high profile raid of the Moncrief Building and the participation of Senator Mike and his family back in 1994. As we all know, the accusations were very compelling. Dee Faxel and Lyndell Kirkley knew that the ad litems would lap them up.

Ad litems are effectively officers of the court. Their client, Lee Wiley Moncrief, is incapacitated, so in theory they really reported to no one. They seemed focused on their 40 percent contingency fee. They were also very proud of their witnesses—Jerry Goodwin, Mike Moncrief, and, of course, Billy W. Jarvis.

The only issues that the ad litems seemed to believe would really have some teeth in court were the questions of ownership of properties between Dad and Granddad. Bakutis and Holliday agreed to go before the judge and argue the merits of the ownership for summary judgment. If they were to lose, they had agreed they would drop everything. Even U.S. Attorney Richard Roper had admitted to us that this ownership question was the paramount issue in the IRS investigation. Within four months of the raid, however, his team had realized that Dad and Granddad owned the properties exactly as was represented by their books. Even more crucial was the fact that a Wyoming state court had already adjudicated the issue and had ruled in our favor.

The courtroom battle was as short and sweet as attorney Dee Kelly had promised Dad. On April 12, Judge King ruled in our favor. Holliday and Bakutis's case vanished, as did Dee Faxel's and Senator Mike's.

As promised, the ad litems correctly decided to go home. On Monday, April 24, 2000, Bakutis told Kelly that if the Lee Wiley Moncrief Trust would cover their costs and hold the exact amount confidential (probably for fear of retaliation by Dee Faxel), he and Holliday would be gone. Dad would also be required to turn the trust over to a bank, which he was planning to do anyway. Dad had already negotiated a deal with Chase Bank because of their expertise in the oil business, but Dee Faxel wouldn't stand for it, claiming that Dad had too much control over Chase. Bakutis pleaded for any bank other than Chase, and we were more than happy to oblige by appointing Bank of America instead.

Bottom line: the Lee Wiley Moncrief Trust issue was over. However, the episode is a prime example of how the probate court and court-appointed ad litems can abuse the system that they are charged with protecting. In our case, two ad litems are hood-winked into filing suit against the trustee (Dad) of the Lee Moncrief Trust for breach of fiduciary duty. The dollars appear to be so big that they ask the court for a 40 percent contingency fee. But when they are forced to realize that there's no substance to the issues, they renege on the contingency and ask the very trust that they were appointed to protect to pay their expenses and they'll go away. All in all this cost Lee's trust over $500,000.

★ ★ ★

The federal claims court trial to determine whether Bill Jarvis should get the $25 million—or any reward—from the IRS for his services as an informant lasted three days here in Fort Worth. Assistant U.S. Attorney Ben King did an extraordinary job, while Jarvis's attorney, John Copeland, appeared to be in over his head. The first day's witnesses included the federal agents, starting with Don Wannick, then Agent Don Smith, whom I hadn't seen since the day of the raid. He had aged, but he still seemed cocky. Next was Mike Sanders, an agent who would seek the truth regardless of an indictment. He was clearly not happy about being there.

U.S. Attorney Paul Coggins was an interesting witness. He testified that Jarvis misled the government and violated his informant's reward agreement when he gave our tax information to Mike's accountant and went on Mike's lawyer's payroll. Assistant U.S. Attorney Richard Roper's testimony echoed Coggins's. Then Mike Moncrief took the stand and once again told of how his Uncle Tex had cheated him.

Judge Don Jarvis, Rolfe, Graber, and Keller took the stand in turn. Under examination, Graber insisted that the fee splitting agreement was not a fee splitting agreement at all. In response, the judge interjected, "This is a fee splitting agreement between attorneys and nonattorneys. What am I missing? There's no other way to construe it. Why did you sign it? What would a corrected one look like?"

In a panic, Graber blurted, "This was the biggest case I've ever been involved in. . . ." Copeland tried to shut him up, but it was too late.

Last on the stand—and of course, the best—was Billy Wayne Jarvis himself. Assistant U.S. Attorney Ben King caught Jarvis lying at least three times. Jarvis finally admitted that his past testimony was false, but he claimed he was now telling the truth. Billy became flustered and frustrated by King's relentless grinding. He even tried to take the position that he never gave Mike Moncrief any of our tax returns, only copies of them, which he deemed was legal.

Judge Bruggink later noted, "Plaintiff made the remarkable assertion during cross-examination that only the IRS had possession of tax information, as a taxpayer only retains file copies."

Judge Bruggink ruled from the bench and denied Billy Jarvis any reward. "If I were to give a reward in this case, I'd need to have my head examined," he mused. Bruggink's ruling would be even more damaging for Richardson, Don Jarvis, and Graber in their trial by the state bar because Bruggink ruled that they were indeed splitting fees between lawyers and nonlawyers.

As a result of Bruggink's ruling, the Texas State Board of Public Accounting notified me that they will proceed with disciplinary action against Bill Jarvis. All they needed was the court ruling.

Bill Jarvis and his group's attempts to bring down our family have been thwarted. Senator Mike Moncrief and his mother, Dee Faxel, have similarly failed to "sue us to death." Most importantly, though, the conspiracy to ruin our business and our reputation has been exposed. From Billy Jarvis's original clandestine effort to create the group while still in our employ, to his final push to influence the attorneys ad litem against us in the case of the Lee Wiley Moncrief Trust, we have prevailed over all his accusations. With the help of Carla Jones Sousa, we obtained the original copy of the unethical fee splitting agreement between Jarvis and his team of conspirators. Thanks to the honesty of former U.S. attorney James Rolfe, we have a full and complete interpretation of the agreement and its ramifications. And without Jan Moncrief, we would never have known the whole story of what happened with Mike Moncrief's side of the family and how they became involved.

When I think back to the day of the IRS raid, I remember leaving the offices of Kelly, Hart and Hallman and looking down the street at what was left of the Moncrief Building. And I remember hearing Granddad's voice in my head, saying, "Go after whoever did this, Charlie, go after those sons-a-bitches and clear our family's name."

Being a third generation wildcatter with an inherited independent streak, I set out to do just that by writing this book. Like drilling a well, a lot of time and energy has been invested in it—and no results are guaranteed. But at least we've exposed the conspirators who wanted to bring down our side of the family and the corner-shooters at the IRS who wanted to tap into a hard-dug well that wasn't theirs.

Appendix

A rare glimpse at a couple of very telling documents.

CONTRACT AND AGREEMENT OF EMPLOYMENT

The undersigned attorneys, Gary L. Richardson, Bill Jarvis, Don Jarvis, Jim Rolfe, Jim Keller and Sam Grober, all of which are referenced to in that certain "Contract and Agreement of Employment" known as the Moncrief Contract, and known therein as "the Attorneys", hereby agree between themselves and the Moncrief's; to associate with one another in those legal matters, collectively known as the "Moncrief Matters" and referenced in that certain "Contract and Agreement of Employment" known as the Moncrief Contract, referenced above.

This Contract and Agreement of Employment is for the purpose of setting forth those agreements reached among the group known as "the Attorneys" regarding attorneys fees to be shared in and between said attorneys. Those agreements are set forth below:

1. In all those legal matters referred in the Moncrief Contract (except those listed below), all parties hereto agree that Gary L. Richardson/Gary L. Richardson & Associates shall receive one-third (1/3) of the attorney fees referenced in the Moncrief Contract ("Exhibit A" hereto), under the contingency fee section. For example, Gary L. Richardson & Associates would receive one-third (1/3) of the forty percent (40%) contingency fee set forth in Exhibit A attached hereto.

2. In the certain legal matter collectively known as and referred to as the "IRS Litigation", Gary L. Richardson/Gary L. Richardson & Associates shall receive a total of Ten Percent (10%) of any recovery, said percentage to be shared from the following attorneys as set forth below:

CONTRACT AND AGREEMENT OF EMPLOYMENT
Page 1

Here's the fee-splitting agreement drawn up by Gary Richardson's office—the document that exposed the conspiracy. It says Richardson gets 10 percent of the IRS reward, which Jarvis had already agreed to split with his brother Don, Sam Graber, Jim Keller, and Jim Rolfe. The agreement clearly instructed that Richardson receive one-third of the contingency fee from the Mike Moncrief lawsuit, with Jarvis and "The Dream Team" splitting the rest.

Out of:

          Bill Jarvis' share, GLR will receive 3%
          Don Jarvis' share, GLR will receive 3%
          Jim Rolfe's share, GLR will receive 1%
          Jim Keller's share, GLR will receive 1.5%
          Sam Graber's share, GLR will receive 1.5%

For example, out of the recovery from the legal matter known as the "IRS Litigation", Gary L. Richardson will receive as compensation a sum equal to Ten Percent (10%) of that sum paid to the attorneys, with each attorney contributing the percentage set forth above to the total Ten Percent (10%).

All other agreements contained in the Moncrief Contract are incorporated fully herein as if set forth verbatim. This Contract represents the entire agreement between the parties hereto and shall control all obligations except as to any matters which may hereinafter be agreed upon by the parties in writing.

Further, the clients, known as the "Moncriefs" have the right to approve this Agreement between the attorney and may do so by signing this Agreement below in the appropriate place.

Dated this _12th_ day of _September_, 1994.

Signed:

_____   _____
Gary L. Richardson   Jim Rolfe   9/21/94

_____   _____
Bill Jarvis   Don Jarvis   9-16-94

_____   _____
Jim Keller   9/16/94   Sam Graber

CONTRACT AND AGREEMENT OF EMPLOYMENT
Page 2

GERALD L. HILSHER, P.C.
Attorney at Law

(918) 582-0660
Fax (918) 584-7681

15 E. 5th Street, Suite 3600
Tulsa, Oklahoma 74103-4307

Of Counsel To:
*Shipley, Jennings &
Champlin, P. C.*

June 30, 1996

Mr. W. A. "Tex" Moncrief, Jr.
Mr. Richard W. Moncrief
Mr. Charles B. Moncrief
Moncrief Building
9th at Commerce
Fort Worth, TX 76102

Gentlemen:

Please accept my apologies for the personal embarrassment and pain you have suffered as a result of the tax investigation and the initiation of the lawsuit.

My role in representing Mike and Monty Moncrief in their dispute with you was simply to obtain for my clients what I believed was their due, a full accounting of their entitlements under the estate administration and conveyances of their grandfather and grandmother. It was my belief that I was hired by Gary Richardson to pursue the legitimate aims of our clients in a professional and ethical manner. I did not know of and did not participate in the negotiations and intrigue with Bill Jarvis that initiated the tax investigation and search warrant. I also did not consider fully the ethical implications of using the information Jarvis had at his disposal. Nevertheless, I feel in hindsight that I should have questioned more and explored deeper into the relationships between the lawyers representing Jarvis and whether research had authorized the use of him as a consultant.

If it is any consolation, please know that I have also suffered for my naivete' and ill-placed trust in other professionals. Like you, I have tried to live up to the professional and personal standards of conduct that govern my profession. I have never been the subject of a Bar complaint or any criticism of my ethics. Now, however, as a result of my association with this matter, my friends in Fort Worth and Dallas who have read the newspapers have reason to question my integrity. They may never know that I was responsible for having "blown the whistle" over the fee-splitting agreement I discovered all too late to have saved you from this nightmare.

With my deepest regrets and best wishes for a return to normalcy, I am

Sincerely,

Gerald L. Hilsher

MON 5258

Gerald Hilsher was a young and reputable attorney representing my cousin Mike in his lawsuit against my father and me. But when he found out his law partner, Gary Richardson, had entered into an unethical fee-splitting agreement with the Jarvis brothers, Jim Rolfe, and Sam Graber, he wrote us this letter of apology.

Index

Adair, Red, 40
Alarado, Antonio, 227–28
American Airlines, 16
American Association of Independent Petroleum Producers, 29–30
Anderson, Alice, 110, 112
Angelo's, 137

Baker, James, 228
Baker Hotel, 31
Bakutis, David, 229, 231, 232, 237–38
Bank of America, 238
Barnhart, Joan ("Sarge"), 5–6, 101–2
Bass, Ed, 69
Bass family, 16
Bennett, Bob (Robert S.), 72, 73–77, 83, 130, 131, 133, 136, 144–45, 161, 162, 163, 202, 203, 208, 230; IRS settlement negotiated by, 158–59
Bode, Clive, 14, 71, 101, 102, 133, 137, 160, 162, 199
Bogle, Bill, 139, 148
Bouline, Scott, 1–2, 3–4
Boyce, A. G., 22
Boyle, Jane, 192
Bradbury, John, 50
Bradford, Daisy, 31
Brandenberg, Charles, 197, 200
Bright, Gilbert, 89
Bright & Bright, 18, 78, 102, 108, 118, 119, 129
Broiles, David, 173–74, 195–96
Brown, Clint ("C. B."), 108–9, 198
Brown, Rule, 55–56
Brown, Tom, 44

Bruggink, Judge, 232–33, 240
Bruton, Jim, 72, 83, 133, 134–35,
    137, 138, 161, 162, 163–64,
    200–201; Billy Jarvis's lawsuit
    against, 235–36
Burgess, Merle, 98–99, 101, 105,
    107, 112
Burnett Oil, 69
Burnett Plaza, 133

Capps, Kay, 6, 12, 70, 78, 79, 80,
    82, 97, 100, 109; car purchased
    for, 98–99, 112
Capra, Frank, 202
Carlyle Hotel, 53
Carter, Amon, 29–30
Casey-Swasey Liquor Franchise, 30
Chase Bank, 231, 238
Chenoweth, O. L., 36
Cleary, Jack, 27
Cline, Patsy, 69
Clinton, Bill, 72, 144
CNN, 208
Coca Cola, 41–42, 52
Coggins, Paul, 163, 235, 239
Colaprete, John, 204
Coleman, James E., Jr., 227
Connelley, Mike, 108–9, 198
Connor, Hugh, 14, 93, 139, 147,
    152, 153–54, 155, 158, 195,
    211, 226, 227
Conroe oil field, 40
Cook, Mark, 1–2, 3–4
Copeland, John, 239, 240
corner-shooter, 73–74
Crosby, Bing, 34
C-SPAN, 208

Culver Military Academy, 36, 37,
    41, 166
Culverhouse, Hugh, 134–35

Daisy Bradford #3, 31
Dallas Cowboys, 21, 71
Dallas Morning News, 93
Davis, Tom, 173, 234–35
Department of Justice, 72, 169;
    Billy Jarvis referred to by IRS
    for prosecution, 173, 174, 207,
    234–35; Fraud Division of, 174,
    235; IRS settlement and, 161,
    205; nolo contendere plea thrown
    out by, 161
Department of the Treasury, 4,
    232; Inspection Division of,
    234
deposition(s): of Jerry Goodwin,
    145, 169–70, 180, 187, 191–92;
    of Billy Wayne Jarvis, 133,
    136–37, 138–45, 146–48, 158,
    162, 181, 182, 185, 187–88,
    191; of Don Jarvis, 190–91; of
    Kay Martin, 151–58; of Carolyn
    Jan Moncrief, 189–90; of James
    A. Rolfe, 188; of Carla Jones
    Sousa, 173
diary(ies): demanded by IRS, 138;
    kept by Charlie Moncrief, 89,
    134, 136, 138; kept by Tex
    Moncrief, 138; Monty Mon-
    crief's (Granddad's) instruc-
    tions regarding, 89
Drake, Edwin L., 25–27
drilling rigs, 39–40
Driskill, Margie, 151

Earl Cabell Federal Building, 93
East Texas Field, 33
Eddy, Bill, 100
Evans, Dale, 69

Falvey, Dr., 32, 33
Faxel, Dee, 36, 38, 55, 60, 174, 175, 184–85, 186, 189–90, 194, 195, 196, 240; knowledge of Billy Jarvis's involvement with IRS and, 194, 195; Lee Wiley Moncrief Trust lawsuit against Tex Moncrief and, 228, 229, 231, 237, 238; as Lee Wiley Moncrief's guardian, lawsuit against, 231; prior knowledge of IRS raid and, 196
Faxel, Ralph, 184, 195, 231
FBI, 82, 83, 108, 198
Federal Bureau of Investigation. See FBI
fee splitting agreement, 118, 128, 148–49, 171–73, 174, 183, 192–93, 209, 219–20, 226, 233, 239–40, 241, 244–45, 246
Ferchill, Judge, 228, 231
Flemmons, Jerry, 2
Fort Worth: cattle business and, 22–23, 29; Dallas versus, 2; gossip and, 21–22; oil business and, 22–23, 29–30, 34
Fort Worth Club Building, 195
Fort Worth Star-Telegram, 21, 29, 144–45
Fort Worth Tower Club, 60
Fowler, Larry, 50
Frank Lathrop #1, 33, 34, 35

Franklin Mint, 109
Freshauer, Al, 91–92, 95
Fuhrman, Mark, 134

Gage, Coke, 45–46, 48
Gardner, Richard, 204
Goldman Sachs, 42
Goodwin, Jerry, 60, 61, 64, 144, 145, 181–82, 185, 186, 187, 188, 194, 195, 228–29, 237; deposition of, 145, 169–70, 180, 187, 191–92; Billy Jarvis showed Moncrief records to, 169, 191, 239, 240; knowledge of Billy Jarvis's involvement with IRS and, 195; lunches with Billy Jarvis and, 168, 179–81, 187
Graber, Sam, 119, 120–21, 126, 127, 212; fee splitting agreement and, 128, 148–49, 171–73, 192–93, 219–20, 226, 239–40, 244–45, 246; state bar's disciplinary case and, 225–28, 240
Granddad. See Moncrief, W. A. ("Monty")
Granddear. See Moncrief, Elizabeth Bright
Greenwood Cemetery, 62
Greenwood Funeral Home, 61–62
Gregg Hotel, 32, 33
Gunnison Country Times, 21
Gunnison River Ranch, 35, 36

Hagman, Larry, 44
Halliburton Energy Institute, 51

Harris Southwest Hospital, 218–19

Hart Senate Office Building, 202, 203

Harter, Ted, 110–11, 112

Hazard, Geoffrey, 145

Hell's Half Acre, 23

Helmsley, Leona, 157

Hill Royalty Trust, 165

Hilsher, Gerald, 138–39, 140–41, 143, 148–49, 171, 174, 190, 193; letter of apology from, 246

Hinton, Robert, 197–98, 200, 211

Hogan, Ben, 16

Hogan, Royal, 16

Hogan Office Supply, 92

Holcomb, Patsy, 93

Holliday, James, 228–29, 232, 237–38

Hope, Bob, 34

Horne, Anita, 201–2

Hotel Crescent Court, 190–91

Howeth, Allan, 228–29, 237

Hughes, John, 231–32

Hunt, H. L., 31

Internal Revenue Service. See IRS

IRS: code of, Gallo provision of, 60–61, 64; Criminal Investigation Division of, 4, 129, 206; diaries demanded by, 138; failure of, to investigate itself, 206–7; forced by court to copy and return seized records, 93–94; Inspection Division of, 161, 206–7; interrogation of Moncrief employees and, 70–71, 97–98, 99, 100; Billy Jarvis referred to Department of Justice by, for prosecution, 173, 174, 207, 234–35; Billy Jarvis's letter to, 121–25; Moncrief defense team's August 10, 1995 meeting with, 133–34, 135–36; raid on Moncrief Building and, 1–18, 21, 130, 144, 164, 194, 196, 204–5, 237, 241; Senate investigation of, 200–208; Senate passage of bill to overhaul investigative practices and, 208; Max Wayman on, 83–84; See also IRS settlement

IRS informant(s): Informant's Reward Agreement and, 115, 117, 118, 127–28, 172, 188, 191, 193, 220, 239; Billy Jarvis as, 115–30, 133, 153, 158, 164, 169, 170, 172, 173, 174, 183, 188, 191, 193, 194, 234, 236; Kay Martin as, 151, 153–54, 155; probable cause for search warrant and, 83; rewards available to, 82, 115, 121

IRS settlement: Bob Bennett's negotiations and, 158–59; finalization of, 162–63; initial suggestions from IRS regarding, 145–46; nolo contendere plea and, 161; Tex Moncrief and, 159–61, 162–63, 205, 206; Tex Moncrief's Senate testimony regarding, 205, 206

Jarvis, Billy Wayne, 60, 78–82, 83,
     84–85, 94, 98, 99, 100, 101,
     102–3, 104, 107, 109, 112, 132,
     151–52, 206; claim that as
     informant, he was federal
     employee, 234; in contempt of
     court, 147–48, 230; deposi-
     tion(s) of, 133, 136–37,
     138–45, 146–48, 158, 162, 181,
     182, 185, 187–88, 191; fee split-
     ting agreement and, 118, 128,
     148–49, 171–73, 183, 192–93,
     219–20, 226, 240, 244–45, 246;
     Fifth Amendment rights exer-
     cised by, 142, 145, 146–47, 162;
     interoffice love affair with Kay
     Martin and, 79, 168; as IRS
     informant, 115–30, 133, 153,
     158, 164, 169, 170, 172, 173,
     174, 183, 188, 191, 193, 194,
     234, 236; jail avoided by,
     147–48, 230; lawsuit against
     Jim Bruton and, 235–36; law-
     suit alleging disclosure viola-
     tions and, 233; lawsuit to
     collect reward and, 174,
     232–35, 239–40; Lee Wiley
     Moncrief Trust lawsuit and,
     228–29, 237; letter of, pre-
     sented to IRS, 121–25; lunches
     with Jerry Goodwin and, 168,
     179–81, 187; Tex Moncrief's
     termination of, 117, 125–26;
     Moncrief and Montex files
     copied by, 116–17, 189, 191;
     negative feelings toward Tex
     Moncrief and, 79, 80, 82, 116,

     118, 121, 168, 179–80; on pay-
     roll of Mike Moncrief, 139–40,
     141, 142, 144, 145, 173, 174,
     188, 189, 192, 239; referred to
     Department of Justice by IRS,
     for prosecution, 173, 174, 207,
     234–35; showed Moncrief
     records to Jerry Goodwin, 169,
     191, 239, 240; Texas State
     Board of Public Accountancy
     case against, 174, 209, 225,
     240. See also Mike Moncrief/
     Billy Jarvis arrangement
Jarvis conspirator(s): assembling
     of, 118, 119, 168–69, 179, 224,
     241; discussions with IRS and,
     118–25, 126–29, 148–49, 169;
     fee splitting agreement
     among, 118, 128, 148–49,
     171–73, 174, 183, 192–93, 209,
     219–20, 226, 233, 239–40, 241,
     244–45, 246; Mike Moncrief's
     meetings with, 169–70, 174,
     181–84, 185–87, 193–94; Mon-
     crief family's lawsuit against,
     168; professional disciplinary
     rules and, 119n, 149, 171, 174,
     193, 225–28, 240; Gary
     Richardson's sworn statement
     and, 215–16, 219–20; James A.
     Rolfe's sworn statement and,
     171–73, 209; trial continuance
     and, 209–18. See also Graber,
     Sam; Jarvis, Billy Wayne;
     Jarvis, Don; Keller, Jim;
     Richardson, Gary L.; Rolfe,
     James A.

Jarvis, Don, 117, 119, 127, 152,
    169–70, 182, 186, 187, 188, 190,
    192; deposition of, 190–91; fee
    splitting agreement and, 128,
    148–49, 171–73, 192–93,
    219–20, 226, 239, 244–45, 246;
    state bar's disciplinary case
    and, 225–28, 240
Jay Field, 42, 58
Johnson, Debbie, 39
Johnson, Deborah Beggs. *See* Mon-
    crief, Deborah Beggs
Johnson, Harry, 24, 39
Johnson, Lyndon, 7
Joiner, "Dad," 31
Jones, Carla. *See* Sousa, Carla
    Jones
Jordan, David, 120, 121
Justice Department. *See* Depart-
    ment of Justice
Justin, John, 16

Keller, Jim, 119, 120–21, 126, 212;
    fee splitting agreement and,
    128, 148–49, 171–73, 192–93,
    219–20, 226, 239, 244–45
Kelly, Dee, 10, 13–14, 16–18, 67,
    71–72, 73, 83, 87–88, 93, 103,
    130, 131, 138, 146, 179, 229–31
Kelly, Hart and Hallman, 142,
    215, 241
Kelly Plow Company, 32
King, Ben, 239, 240
King, Judge, 231–32, 238
Kirkley, Lyndell, 187, 188, 190,
    195–96, 224, 228–29, 237
Kurilec, Gregory, 112, 157

land man: defined, 28; Charlie
    Moncrief as, 47–48; Monty
    Moncrief (Granddad) as,
    28–29
"late wells," 17–18
Lathrop, Frank, 32–33
Lee Wiley Moncrief Trust, 58–59,
    196, 224; Bank of America
    and, 238; Chase Bank and,
    231, 238; lawsuit against Tex
    Moncrief and, 228–32, 236,
    237–39, 241
Lloyd, Doc, 30–31, 33
Lloyd, Mary Ellen, 81, 105–9, 110,
    112, 211; embezzlement trial
    and, 197–200; lawsuit against
    Tex Moncrief and, 236–37
Lowe, Judge, 236
Lucky Liz, 7, 38, 48, 73, 82, 202

M. D. Anderson Cancer Center,
    96–97
Madden-Deep unit deal, 71,
    88–90, 124, 133–34, 135–36,
    138, 164
Marion, Anne, 69
Marion family, 16
Marland, E. W., 29, 30
Marland Oil Company, 28, 29
Marshall R. Young Oil Company,
    42
Martin, Don, 44–45, 47
Martin, Jack, 44–45, 47
Martin, Kay, 99, 100, 110–13;
    deposition of, 151–58; infor-
    mation provided to IRS by,
    151, 153–54, 155; interoffice

love affair with Billy Jarvis and, 79, 168; resignation of, 113

Martin, Mary, 44

Martin Ranch Proper, 46–47

Mason, Bruce, 161–62, 173

Mathews, "Coots," 40–41

Max Wayman and Associates, 84

May, Mel, 95

McDaniel, Duane, 44, 46, 47–48, 49, 62

McDowell, Albert, 210, 211

McDowell, Dr., 61

McGrath, Bob, 136–37, 142, 143–44, 145, 146–47, 148

Meadows, Chuck, 100, 111

Metropolitan Hotel, 22

MGM Grand, 56

Mike Moncrief/Billy Jarvis arrangement, 133; Billy Jarvis on payroll of Mike Moncrief and, 139–40, 141, 142, 144, 145, 173, 174, 188, 189, 192, 239; Billy Jarvis showed Moncrief records to Jerry Goodwin and, 169, 191, 239, 240; lunches between Billy Jarvis and Jerry Goodwin and, 168, 179–81, 187; Mike Moncrief's meetings with Jarvis conspirators and, 169–70, 174, 181–84, 185–87, 193–94

Mike Moncrief lawsuit, 163; countersuit in, dropped by Tex Moncrief, 149, 168, 230; dropped by plaintiffs, 149, 167–68; filing of, 130; formal letter of apology from Mike Moncrief and other plaintiffs and, 149, 168, 169, 195–96, 224; Mike Moncrief's claims in, 131–32; Tex Moncrief's press release regarding, 131; Gary Richardson's contingency fee and, 172, 183, 186–89, 192, 220, 226, 244–45

Mike Moncrief Trust, 58–59, 237

Miller, Dawn, 227, 228

Minor, Paul, 134, 135, 136

Moncrief, Adelaide, 67–68, 88

Moncrief, Anna Marie, 162

Moncrief, B. B., 67

Moncrief, Bill, 39, 75, 162

Moncrief, Carolyn Jan, 59, 62, 167, 174–77, 184, 185, 186, 189, 190, 193–96, 225, 228, 241; deposition of, 189–90

Moncrief, Celia, 67–68, 88

Moncrief, Charlie: birth of, 24; buying royalty and, 52–53; car purchases and, 98–99; childhood of, 39–41; Coca Cola experience and, 41–42; courtship and marriage of, 52, 53, 54; criminal lawyers hired by, 72; as deputy United States marshal, 8, 49–50; diaries kept by, 89, 134, 136, 138; education of, 41, 42, 43; IRS raid and, 10–18, 241; Billy Jarvis reported to Texas State Board of Public Accountancy by, 174, 209, 225; as land man, 47–48; leasing and, 47–48; List of Twenty-Five and, 71; Madden-Deep unit deal and, 71, 88–90,

Moncrief, Charlie (*continued*)
124, 133–34, 135–36, 138, 164;
Marine Corps and, 8, 42, 49, 67;
polygraph test passed by,
134–36; with Gary Richardson
and, 210, 212–17; as roughneck,
49, 50–51; self-examination and,
87–113; settlement at Teepee
Flats, 51, 52–54; Texas State
Bar's action against Graber,
Don Jarvis, and Richardson
and, 173–74, 225–28, 240

Moncrief, Deborah Beggs, 9,
23–24, 39, 95, 96–97, 162, 202,
212–13, 216

Moncrief, Dee. *See* Faxel, Dee

Moncrief, Dickie, 14–15, 16–18,
39, 42–43, 44, 54, 65–66, 71,
72, 75, 88, 98, 130, 139, 162,
203, 211–12, 214, 217–19,
220–21

Moncrief, Elizabeth Bright, 27, 28,
30, 34, 39, 105, 107, 131; death
of, 61–62, 64; estate of, 62, 64,
97, 125, 130, 132, 139, 148,
182; Gallo provision of IRS
code and, 60–61, 64

Moncrief, Elizabeth Scott, 38

Moncrief, Gloria, 67–68, 69–70, 88

Moncrief, Herbie, 38, 39, 59

Moncrief, Jan. *See* Moncrief, Carolyn Jan

Moncrief, Kit Tennison, 8, 52, 53,
54, 67–69, 88, 135, 162, 163, 202

Moncrief, Lafayette Barto ("L. B."),
24

Moncrief, Larry, 57

Moncrief, Lee Wiley, 55, 60, 139,
237; injury to, 57, 229; lawsuit
against Dee Faxel regarding,
231. *See also* Lee Wiley Moncrief Trust

Moncrief, Marsland, 162

Moncrief, Michael Joseph Trapp
("Mike"), 36, 39, 55, 56, 98,
101, 168, 175, 176; adoption
of, by Richard Barto ("Dick")
Moncrief, 36, 184; controversy
with Tex Moncrief and, 59, 61,
62–66, 180, 182, 185–86,
193–94, 239, 240; family relationships and, 59–60, 61,
62–64; grandmother's death
and, 62–63; Billy Jarvis being
paid by, 139–40, 141, 142, 144,
145, 173, 174, 188, 189, 192,
239; knowledge of Billy Jarvis's
involvement with IRS and,
183–84, 194, 195; Lee Wiley
Moncrief Trust lawsuit against
Tex Moncrief and, 228, 229,
231, 237, 238; Louisiana lawsuit against Tex Moncrief and,
236; meetings with Jarvis conspirators and, 169–70, 174,
181–84, 185–87, 193–94; 149A
accounting request of, 90–91,
92, 93, 95, 130, 131; politics
and, 57–58; Powell Pressure
Maintenance Unit con-
tentions and, 66, 90–91, 92,
95; prior knowledge of IRS
raid and, 196; Gary Richardson as attorney for, 139, 144,

145, 148, 169, 172, 183, 184, 185, 186–91, 192, 194, 195, 220, 226, 244–45; Gary Richardson reimbursed by, for Billy Jarvis's services, 145; trust created for, by grandfather, 58–59, 237

Moncrief, Monty Francine, 38, 39

Moncrief, Richard Barto ("Dick"), 29, 39, 57, 184; death of, 55; lifestyle of, 37–38; marriage of, 36; Mike Trapp adopted by, 36, 184

Moncrief, Richard Barto, Jr. ("Monty"), 39, 55–57, 60, 62, 166–67, 174, 175–77, 180, 184; death of, 166; estate of, 175–76, 237; knowledge of Billy Jarvis's involvement with IRS and, 194, 195; lawsuit against Tex's side of family and, 131, 167–68; prior knowledge of IRS raid and, 194, 196; reservations about joining in Mike Moncrief lawsuit and, 184–86, 189–91; trust created for, by grandfather, 58–59. *See also* Mike Moncrief lawsuit

Moncrief, Rosie, 59, 184, 185–86, 195

Moncrief, Therese, 107, 162

Moncrief, Tom Oil, 14, 39, 75, 107, 139, 152, 162, 202, 203, 211–12, 218–19, 220–21

Moncrief, W. A. ("Monty"), 2, 10, 16, 25, 35, 37, 39, 42, 43, 44, 45–46, 48, 50, 51, 52–53, 54, 55, 56, 59, 78, 80, 105, 131, 238; death of, 19–20; diaries and, 89; early life of, 24, 27–34; estate of, 60–61, 64, 77, 90, 92, 97, 130, 132, 139, 148, 182; first oil strike of, 33, 36; grandchildren's trusts created by, 58–59; Powell Pressure Maintenance Unit deal and, 66, 80, 90–92, 95; as wildcatter, 30–34, 37, 43, 45–47, 49, 50

Moncrief, W. A., Jr. ("Tex"), 3, 9–10, 13–14, 16–18, 20, 24, 25, 29, 33, 36–37, 38, 39–41, 42, 44, 45–46, 48–49, 50, 51, 52, 53–54, 59, 61–62, 78, 80, 81, 82, 87, 88, 95, 97, 102, 103, 105, 106–7, 108, 110, 146, 154–55, 158, 167, 198; car purchases and, 98–99; criminal lawyers hired by, 72–77; diaries kept by, 138; health of, 96, 210–11, 216, 217, 218–19, 220–21, 223–24, 229; interoffice love affair between Billy Jarvis and Kay Martin broken up by, 79, 168; IRS settlement and, 159–61, 162–63; Billy Jarvis's employment terminated by, 117, 125–26; Billy Jarvis's negative feelings toward, 79, 80, 82, 116, 118, 121, 168, 179–80; lawsuit against Dee Faxel and, 231; Lee Wiley Moncrief Trust

Moncrief, W. A., Jr. ("Tex")
(continued)
  lawsuit against, 228–32, 236,
  237–39, 241; Ellen Lloyd's lawsuit against, 236–37; Madden-
  Deep unit deal and, 71, 88–90,
  124, 133–34, 135–36, 138, 164;
  controversy with Mike Moncrief and, 59, 61, 62–66, 180,
  182, 185–86, 193–94, 239;
  Mike Moncrief's Louisiana
  lawsuit against, 236; Powell
  Pressure Maintenance Unit
  deal and, 66, 80, 90–92, 95;
  power and influence attrib-
  uted to, 118, 120, 125; Gary
  Richardson settlement and,
  212–13, 216–17; testimony
  before United States Senate
  and, 200–208, 212; watched
  his daddy strike the Big One,
  33, 36; as wildcatter, 37,
  40–41, 45–47, 48–49, 50,
  53–54
Moncrief Building, 2–8, 10–16,
  18, 45, 54; IRS raid on, 1–18,
  21, 130, 144, 164, 194, 196,
  204–5, 237, 241; Billy Jarvis's
  access to, as employee, 116;
  Billy Jarvis's return to, upon
  IRS request, 129; security
  measures and, 95
Moncrief Foundation, 59, 62,
  102–3, 160
Moncrief Oil: computerization
  and, 81–82; Billy Jarvis copied
  files of, 116–17, 189, 191; Tex

Moncrief on operation of,
  75–77; self-examination and,
  87–113
Moncrief River Ranch, 35, 36
Montco Oil, 56, 176
Montex Drilling Company, 94,
  104, 111, 234; Billy Jarvis
  copied files of, 116–17, 189,
  191. *See also* Moncrief Oil
Morrison, Lonny, 227
Moynihan, Daniel Patrick, 208

National Cowgirl Museum and
  Hall of Fame, 69
Neighbors, Murray, 126
New York Times, 21
Nixon, Richard, 7

Oakley, Annie, 69
Oil Creek, 25–26

Pier, Vikki, 103–5, 107–8, 112–13
polygraph test, 134–36
Powder River Basin, 91–92
Powell Pressure Maintenance
  Unit, 66, 80, 90–92, 95
pressure maintenance unit, 91
Preston Moore drilling school,
  51
Price, Dorothy, 78
Price Waterhouse, 72, 77–78,
  92–93, 94–95, 103, 104, 132
Puff, Thomas Hill, 165–66

Rabalais, Fred, 49
Rangoon Racquet Club, 52
Raymond, "Boots," 40–41

Red Adair Well Control Specialists, 40

Richardson, Gary L., 169–70, 174, 183, 184, 185, 186–91, 192, 194, 195, 210; fee splitting agreement and, 148–49, 171–73, 183, 192–93, 219–20, 226, 244–45, 246; Billy Jarvis directly paid by, 139–40, 141, 142, 144, 188, 189, 192, 239; knowledge of Billy Jarvis's involvement with IRS and, 194, 195; reimbursed by Mike Moncrief, for Billy Jarvis's services, 145; settlement with, 210, 212–17; state bar's disciplinary case and, 225–28, 240; sworn statement of, 215–16, 219–20

Richardson and Stoops, 139–40, 141, 188. *See also* Richardson, Gary L.

rigs, drilling, 39–40

River Crest Country Club, 21, 34

Rolfe, James A., 119, 120–21, 126, 139, 141, 143, 148, 169–70, 181–82, 183, 186, 190–91; deposition of, 188; fee splitting agreement and, 128, 148–49, 171–73, 192–93, 219–20, 226, 239, 244–45, 246; sworn statement of, 171–73, 209, 226, 241

Roper, Richard, 133, 136–37, 138, 142, 146, 158–59, 164, 238, 239

Ross, Ed, 73–77, 163

Rossotti, Charles O., 208

Rostenkowski, Dan, 72, 145

Royal, Darrell, 41

Sanders, Mike, 15–16, 136, 138, 233, 236, 239

Schneider, Mary, 99–100

Scurry Area Canyon Reef Operating Committee, 39

Searcy, Marshall, 14, 71, 119, 133, 139–42, 143, 145, 146–47, 148, 152, 195, 196, 210, 211–12, 213–14, 215–16, 217, 218, 230

Secret Service, 82

Shady Oaks Country Club, 105

Shady Oaks Ranch, 29–30

Shannon Gracey, 210

Shiel, Marty, 11, 14

Shoemaker, Bob, 226

Silverman, Paul, 197, 200

Simpson, O. J., 134

Sinclair, Harry, 33–34

6666 Ranch, 69

Skadden, Arps, Slate, Meagher & Flom, 72, 73

Skipper, B. A. ("Barney"), 31–32

slant-hole driller, 74

Smith, Don, 6, 8, 11, 12–13, 15, 129–30, 181, 239

Smith, "Uncle Billy," 26

Sneed, Beal, 22

Sousa, Carla Jones, 172, 192, 219, 241; deposition of, 173

Spivey, Broadus, 236, 237

Stagner, David, 152–53, 154–57, 211

Standard Oil, 34
Steeplechase Ball, 167

Tampa Bay Buccaneers, 134
Teepee Flats, 51, 52–54
Tennison, Gloria, 52, 88
Tennison, Harry ("Bwana"), 52
Tennison, Kit. *See* Moncrief, Kit
    Tennison
Texaco, 51
Texas Electric Service Company,
    108
Texas Lawyer, 153
Texas State Bar, 174, 209, 228;
    Board of Disciplinary Appeals
    of, 227; David Broiles's letter
    to, 173–74, 225; case against
    Graber, Don Jarvis, and
    Richardson and, 225–28, 240;
    Commission for Lawyer Disci-
    pline of, 226–27; disciplinary
    committee of, 119n, 171;
    Grievance Committee hear-
    ings in Dallas and, 225–26;
    Charlie Moncrief's pursuit of
    justice from, 173–74, 225–28,
    240
Texas State Board of Public
    Accountancy, 174, 209, 225,
    240
Texas State Supreme Court, 227,
    228
Thorsen, Eric, 201–2
Titusville, Pennsylvania, 25–27
Top of the World Hotel, 53
Trapp, F. F. ("Ferrell"), 35, 57
Trapp, Jack, 35–36, 57

Trapp, Jewell Moncrief, 35–36
Trapp, Mary Daisy Wiley ("Dee").
    See Faxel, Dee
Trapp, Michael Joseph. *See* Mon-
    crief, Michael Joseph Trapp
    ("Mike")
Tyson, Mike, 96
Tyson Buick, 99

United States Senate: Tex Mon-
    crief's testimony and, 200–208,
    212; passed bill to overhaul
    IRS investigation practices,
    208

W. A. Moncrief and Sons, 37
W. T. Waggoner Building, 30, 31,
    37
Wall Street Journal, 208
Wallace, R. H., 210, 215–16
Wanick, Don, 126, 239
Watkins, George, 5, 18
Wayman, Max, 83–84, 85
Westbrook Hotel, 23
wildcatter(s): defined, 25; first,
    25–27; Monty Moncrief
    (Granddad) as, 30–34, 37, 43,
    45–47, 49, 50; Tex Moncrief
    as, 37, 40–41, 45–47, 48–49,
    50, 53–54; Tex Moncrief's
    description of, 73–74; number
    of, 25
Wiley, Mary Daisy ("Dee"). *See*
    Faxel, Dee
Wiley, Stan, 56, 176
Wiley, Wade, 60, 168, 174, 175,
    176, 184, 195; knowledge of

Billy Jarvis's involvement with IRS and, 194, 195; prior knowledge of IRS raid and, 196

Williams & Connolly, 72, 135; Billy Jarvis's lawsuit against, 235–36

Williston Basin Pipeline Co., 64–65

Woods Petroleum Corp., 91

Word, Walter, 4, 8

Wright, Kathy, 162, 219

Yont-Lee Oil Company, 34

Young, Kelly, 42–43

Zinn, David, 138